Foucault and Fict

**Continuum Literary Studies Series**

# Foucault and Fiction

## The Experience Book

Timothy O'Leary

**continuum**

**Continuum International Publishing Group**

| | |
|---|---|
| The Tower Building | 80 Maiden Lane |
| 11 York Road | Suite 704, New York |
| London SE1 7NX | NY 10038 |

www.continuumbooks.com

**British Library Cataloguing-in-Publication Data**
A catalogue record for this book is available from the British Library.

ISBN: 978-1-4411-8210-4 (Paperback)

**Library of Congress Cataloging-in-Publication Data**
A catalog record for this book is available from the Library of Congress.

Typeset by Newgen Imaging Systems Pvt Ltd, Chennai, India
Printed and bound in Great Britain by the MPG Books Group

*For Phoebe and Bene*

# Contents

# Acknowledgements

This book was a very long time being written, but that period would have been even longer and more arduous without the help and support of many individuals and institutions. First of all, I would like to thank the Department of Philosophy and the Faculty of Arts at the University of Hong Kong, both of which supported periods of study leave and sabbatical that gave an important boost to this work in its middle phase. My colleagues in the Department of Philosophy, in particular, have given practical encouragement and, at seminars, usefully probing questions. I would also like to acknowledge the School of Philosophy at the University of New South Wales, Sydney, where I spent part of a sabbatical in 2006. That School proved to be a congenial and supportive environment for my work, especially given the presence of Paul Patton and a visit by Jana Sawicki, both of whose support is greatly appreciated. Several of these chapters have also been presented at seminars in the School of English at HKU. Not only were these enjoyable events, but my thinking about literature benefited from the comments of those who attended.

I rarely publish work without subjecting it to the critical eye of Dan Robins. His intelligent and acute comments have helped to improve several chapters in this book. I have also benefited more recently from the critical input of Tim Rayner, whose own work on Foucault and experience forms a partial backdrop to this book. My colleague in Hong Kong, Bill Haines, was tireless and relentlessly critical in his reading of two of these chapters; so relentless, in fact, that he lived on for quite some time in my super-ego. Chris Falzon offered a different kind of support, combining good humour with a rare Foucauldian intelligence.

On a more personal level, this book is dedicated to my daughters, Phoebe and Bene. Almost within the time-span of this book's development, their reading of literature has graduated from Beatrix to Harry Potter, going from Dr Seuss to Mr Norrell and opening up vistas that include everyone from Galadriel to Lolita. If they ever get around to reading this particular book, I hope they might find the experience in some way enlightening.

Finally, I want to thank my wife, Lié Fhung, for her love and support throughout the process of producing this book. She is as aware as any reader of literature that novels, plays and poems can change our perception of the world and broaden our conception of our fellow humans; and, more importantly, that these effects are really only valuable when we can share them with an other.

Excerpts from *Translations* by Brian Friel. Copyright © 1981 by Brian Friel. Reprinted by permission of Faber and Faber, Inc., an affiliate of Farrar, Straus and Giroux, LLC.

Excerpts from *Plays One* by Brian Friel. Copyright © 1996 by Brian Friel. Reprinted by permission of Faber and Faber Ltd.

Excerpts from *The Spirit Level* by Seamus Heaney. Copyright © 1996 by Seamus Heaney. Reprinted by permission of Farrar, Straus and Giroux, LLC and Faber and Faber Ltd.

Earlier versions of some chapters have appeared in the following Journals: Chapter 2: 'Governing the Tongue: Heaney Among the Philosophers' in *Textual Practice*, vol. 22, no. 4, December 2008, pp.657-677. Chapter 3: 'Foucault's Turn from Literature' in *Continental Philosophy Review*, vol.41, no.1, March 2008, pp.89-110. Chapter 5: 'Foucault, Experience, Literature' in *Foucault Studies*, No.5, January 2008, p.5-25.

# Chapter 1

# Literature, Experience and Ethics

Early in Joyce's *Ulysses*, the young Stephen Dedalus reflects on the deaths of Pyrrhus and Julius Caesar and wonders if those events necessarily had to happen. It is undeniable, he admits, that they have actually occurred: 'Time has branded them and fettered they are lodged in the room of the infinite possibilities they have ousted' (Joyce, 1973: 31). But what about the chance that things could have been otherwise? Were the ousted possibilities really possible in the first place, Stephen wonders, or 'was that only possible which came to pass?' If the events of the past had such inevitability, that would seem to suggest that our present is equally closed, and that we too lie branded and fettered in a room that one imagines without windows. But there is also the other possibility: that even though history cannot be 'thought away', every present moment confronts us with a field of innumerable possibilities. The question then would be, which of these possibilities will time brand and fetter? And what role can we play in determining that choice? One of the central themes in Joyce's work is the complex interplay, in any given present, between the constraining reality of past events and the present struggle to break those bonds. For Joyce, given his experience as an Irish man of his time, these constraints are principally felt at the level of language, empire and religion. In particular, Joyce's characters, especially the pseudo-autobiographical Stephen Dedalus, are keenly aware of the weight of past discourses, which not only filter their experience of the present but also threaten to set the shape of their future. But Joyce, like the character Stephen, is intent on opening up a space of freedom within this tangle of past events and things said; a space that would allow the future to be arranged otherwise. And this is a task that he tries to achieve through works of fiction.

One of the things that allows Joyce to do this, quite simply, is the way that he writes. The sentence I quoted, with its 'branded', 'fettered', 'lodged' and 'ousted', has an effect that is as much visceral as cognitive. If it succeeds in making us aware of a certain truth about the past, it is partly because its repeated verbs seem to hammer the point home like nails being driven into a coffin. We feel the brute force of past events, their unavoidable givenness, their dead weight. Naturally, the effect this experience will have on us is unpredictable, especially when we consider that every reader of the sentence inhabits a different present, with a different set of past events, and a different set of predisposed futures. And, of course, the effect of a novel is by no means reducible to the force of its style; this is only one element in the way the narrative works on the reader. But, even if we set aside these concerns, does it make any sense to think of a novel, a poem or a play as helping us to re-shape our present and our future? Can they really force us, or encourage us, to 'think otherwise'?[1] And if they can, how do they do it? My intention in this book is to try to answer these questions by thinking about literature in relation to experience and ethics.

Michel Foucault, as we will see in more detail later, has given us a way of thinking about ethics as, at least in part, involving the open-ended set of practices through which we shape and re-shape our relations to ourselves and others. These practices include not just critical assessment of our ethical ideals and goals, but also diverse pursuits such as the study of history, science and philosophy, or even practices such as meditation, exercise and diet. Foucault shares with Joyce a heightened sense of the weight of the past, of things said and things done, on the present. But this sense in no way leads to pessimism or apathy. In fact, the key elements of the ethical attitude that emerges out of Foucault's work are, first, a recognition of the contingency and fragility of the present, and, secondly, a relentless drive to re-make the selves and the worlds we inhabit. His books, which with minor exceptions are all histories, have two unspoken objectives: to demonstrate, through the use of historical research, the lines of fragility that run through the ways of knowing and doing that we take for granted in our present; and, to provoke a consequent effort to change those forms through an experimental ethics and politics. Any book that can achieve these ends is, in Foucault's words, an 'experience book' rather than a 'truth book' or a 'demonstration book' (1980a: 246[47]). Such a book functions as a kind of 'limit experience'; that is, an experience that tears us away from ourselves and leaves us no longer the same as before (ibid.). If it is opposed to a truth book and a 'demonstration book', does this mean that there is no truth in such a book? Certainly not; but what it does mean is that the experience book has a special relation to fiction, a relation that will require some careful analysis as we proceed. For the moment, let's say that the experience book enacts a kind of *poesis*, a making and re-making both of the past and of the future.

During the 1950s and 1960s, many of the books that functioned as experience books for Foucault himself were works of literature: works such as Samuel Beckett's *Waiting for Godot*, the stories of Jorge Luis Borges, the novels of Raymond Roussel, and the poetry of Stéphane Mallarmé. At this time, his many writings on literary figures were suffused with a metaphysical, almost mystical, conception of the powers of literary language to place us in contact with a domain beyond our everyday experience. However, by the time Foucault had come to work out a more sophisticated basis for a philosophical understanding of experience and its possible transformation, his interest had shifted towards the history of political technologies and the practices of ethics. Hence, the idea that works of literature can contribute to the transformation of experience, as a part of the practice of a critical philosophy, was never developed by him.

And yet, as Foucault's own reflections on his early engagement with literature demonstrate, such works regularly produce the kinds of effect that in his later histories he sought to provoke. When, in 1983, Foucault describes the effect that seeing *Waiting for Godot* had on him in the late 1950s – it provoked the first break, he says, in his early philosophical training – we have a perfect example of an experience (seeing the play) that can begin to undermine the viewer's fundamental conceptions of the world (2004a: 176). In this book, I will investigate the extent to which works of literature are capable of having such effects. Drawing on the perspective offered in Foucault's later work, I will approach literature as something that can provoke an ethical shift through the intervention it makes in the experience of the reader. In particular, I will try to show both *how* it is capable of having such an effect, and *where* these possible changes are moving. My central questions, therefore, will be what is it about individuals and works of literature that makes the former susceptible to the latter? And, why should we value these changes, given that such unsettling experiences could be deemed to be undesirable?

I will try to answer the first of these questions by combining Foucault's later, more sophisticated understanding of experience with his idea of fiction as involving a special relation to our everyday world. My response to the second question will be guided by Foucault's understanding of ethics as a multiplicity of practices that can be oriented towards a loosening of constraints and an opening-up of greater spaces of freedom. However, the philosophical content of this exploration will not be limited to the thought of Foucault. After all, the idea that we can think of the effects of literature, and art, in terms of a transformation of experience is not unique to him. On the one hand, two thinkers who will be helpful in this book are Dewey and Gadamer. I won't be asking whether Foucault was influenced by these philosophers (I don't think he was, but I also don't think it matters); instead I will draw on them to give us a broader conception of some of the issues that are at stake in the constitution and transformation of experience. On the other hand, in Chapter 2, I will confront Plato's expulsion of the poets and his denigration of poetry, in so far as this is a stumbling block to the approach that I want to develop here. Plato's rejection of poetry, and his exile of the poets from his ideal city, has long served as a succinct statement of a particularly dismissive attitude towards literature. This is an attitude according to which literature is both frivolous, because it is a mere reflection of our world, and dangerous, because it arouses strong passions. In the case of Plato, this attitude is complicated by the fact that his own writing is more poetic than that of almost any other philosopher in the Western tradition. In the next chapter we will see how Seamus Heaney can help us to clear the ground for an anti-Platonist approach to poetry.

## Literature and Philosophy

While it is true that Foucault is not the only philosopher to engage with these questions, it is equally true that philosophers are not the only ones to have approached them either. It is hardly surprising that writers themselves have a particularly strong sense of, and strong investment in, the possible effects that their words will have. In this book I will try, as much as possible, to allow this questioning to come to the fore and, occasionally, to guide my approach. In doing this, I will endeavour to follow a course that runs between the academic disciplines of philosophy and literary studies. This will, perhaps, involve dissatisfying both camps, but that is a risk that is worth taking. The first demand that one might expect from philosophy, as least as it is practised in many parts of the world, is that I should give some formal definitions of what I am talking about, starting with 'literature' itself. What exactly do we mean when we speak of 'literature'? Isn't it reasonable to expect that a book about literature that has at least one foot in philosophy should start with a definition of what it is talking about? My approach, however, is based on the idea that the concept of literature has such a long, varied and continuing history, and that it comprises so many forms of writing (and speaking), that a precise definition would be neither possible nor useful. In this I will adopt Nietzsche's view of the incompatibility between definition and historical phenomena: '. . . all concepts in which an entire process is semiotically concentrated elude definition: only that which has no history is definable' (1989: 80).

Instead of trying to give a general definition of literature, instead of trying to approach it as a substance, then, it might be better to approach it as an event. This would involve taking into consideration the time of literature – at two levels. On the one hand, it is clear that if one is interested in the potential effects of a work, then one has to allow for the way those effects change over time. I will be suggesting later that Swift's *Gulliver's Travels* (1726), for example, is capable of having a potentially transformative effect on readers today, but one that is clearly different from the effect it may have had in the eighteenth century. It is equally clear that whatever effect a book such as Joyce's *A Portrait of the Artist as a Young Man* (1916) may have had on, say, a young Irish man in 1916 would be very different from the effect it might have, say, on a young Chinese woman in the twenty-first century. In this case, the temporality of the work involves not just changes in the social and political environment, but also changes in forms of subjectivity. In other words, one can expect that the way an eighteenth-century reader relates to a literary text may be different from the way a twenty-first-century reader will do so. It follows that I will not be trying to assign particular effects to particular works as if those effects were in some way guaranteed by the works themselves, or as if they functioned in a way that was independent of their milieu and their readers. On the other hand, however, we also have to take into consideration the temporality of the event of literature at the level of the individual reader or viewer. It is a common experience, perhaps, to read a work and find that it has a profound effect, only to re-read it later and find that its effect is minimal. This points to the fact that such transformative experiences are always conditioned, not only by the work in question, but also by the particular circumstances of the reader. Since our experience is a constantly unfolding continuum there is no reason to expect that effects produced at one time would be reproduced at a later time. It follows, once again, that I will not be defining particular works in terms of their effects; instead, I will try to give an account of the way the transformative force of particular works can act upon the experience of individuals in ways that are aleatory and unpredictable.

In one of Foucault's discussions of his understanding of critical philosophy, he explains his method as a kind of 'eventalisation' (1990: 393[47]). This is a matter of taking apparently stable universals such as 'sexuality', 'punishment' or 'mental illness', and dealing with them as historically singular events. These events are then treated as arising out of a multiplicity of causes and as connecting up with a multiplicity of possible effects. Their development is never linear or assured, but is always open to appropriation, deviation and derailment. The view of history that emerges from this eventalization is one that could be called kaleidoscopic. Patterns may emerge in history, but they are never more than the result of a contingent, fragile arrangement; they are singular events. Treating literature in this way, as something that doesn't have a single form or a timeless essence, has the advantage of freeing us from the temptation to assign unitary effects and common methods to such works.

Related to the question about definitions, we may also want to ask whether there is something distinctive about literature as an experience-transformer. Am I suggesting that it is distinctive in the *kind* of transformation it can effect? Or, is it distinctive only in the *way* it effects transformations? This book is situated within a framework of thought in which transformation can be effected through a whole range of practices – from philosophy and psychoanalysis to painting and meditation. I do not, therefore, wish to argue that literature is capable of a unique kind of transformation – a kind of which other forms of art or thought would be incapable. Instead, I would argue that literature has a distinctive way of bringing about changes which, for other individuals, or at other times, may be effected by different means. But, what is this distinctive mode of action of literature? Is it possible to give an at least minimal account of what is shared across all the varieties of literature, from poems and plays to novels and short stories?

The feature I will highlight here is the fictionality of these works. A fiction is, of course, something that is not true, and there is a fundamental sense in which the content of a work of literature is not true. However, fiction is also that which is made; it is a product of a poetic technique, one that produces something previously unseen and unheard. If we think, for a moment, of fiction as a verb rather than as a noun, we can say that works of literature are distinctive in so far as they make things through language: such works are fictional, they are fictioned and they fiction. There is a sense, therefore, in which works of literature are both true and untrue, both real and unreal. Foucault captures this duality of fiction when he identifies the fictive as the capacity of language to bring us into contact with 'that which does not exist, in so far as it is' (1963 [280]). However, for Foucault, the concept of fiction is not only applicable in the field of literature; it also has a much broader relevance. When he says that his histories are themselves 'fictions' he doesn't mean that they aren't true, he means that they try (and sometimes succeed) in producing an effect that generates a new set of attitudes and new forms of practice (1977a: 193[236]). Using fiction as a verb, he explains: 'One "fictions" history starting from a political reality which makes it true, one "fictions" a politics which doesn't yet exist starting from a historical truth' (ibid.).

The advantage of choosing fiction as the aspect of literature that will be highlighted here, is that literature can then be viewed as one instance of a practice that takes many forms. Literature is not a hermetically sealed endeavour that follows its own concerns and methods regardless of other modes of discourse and practice around it. Rather, it can be seen as one manifestation of a broader need to find ways to re-imagine and re-shape ourselves and our world. In this sense, the term fiction will apply just as well to literary forms such as lyric poetry as to forms that are more conventionally seen as fiction, such as novels and plays. For the moment we can state in general terms, therefore, that the ethical significance of literature is made possible by its fictionality: its counter-position in relation to the world and to reality. It is on this basis that it facilitates a mode of resistance to, borrowing Joyce's words, the branding and fettering of time that ousts a myriad possibilities.

## Experience

The experience book is a book that helps us to detach ourselves from ourselves, to re-orient ourselves towards the world, and to modify our ways of acting in the world. But, why is a book that does that (if such a thing is possible) called an 'experience' book? What does experience have to do with it? For Foucault, I will be arguing, experience comes in two forms: on the one hand, a kind of long-term, background experience that we share with our culture and our time, and that gives the world to us in a certain form. This is experience in the sense that Foucault discusses 'the classical experience of madness' in *History of Madness*, and the 'modern experience of sexuality' in *History of Sexuality, volume 2*. It comprises a set of beliefs, practices and forms of knowledge that are shared by a more or less coherent group during a more or less defined historical period. In the most general terms, therefore, experience in this sense can be understood as the historical mode in which being is given to us as 'something that can and must be thought' (1984a: 6–7[13]). On the other hand, however, there is an experience that is more temporally discrete, and more individual (at least initially), and that is lived as something that is in conflict with the long-term, background experience. While it might be possible to have the former kind without the latter kind, it is clear that the latter, transformative kind is only meaningful against the reality of the long-term, background form. The transformative experience, which is offered by the experience book, is one that interrupts and potentially modifies the background experience. Experience is then a limit-transcending, challenging event, but also the dominant historical structure which is to be challenged. But, what is the relation between these two senses of experience: experience as the general form in which being is given to us 'as something that can and must be thought', and experience as that which tears us away from the familiarity of our everyday lives and forces us to enter into a new relation with ourselves and the world? We will be returning to this question many times in this book, but for the moment it might help if we make two detours: first, through some of the semantic richness of the term 'experience', in both the French and the English languages; and, secondly, through the idea of 'art as experience' that was developed by John Dewey.

First of all, in French the term *expérience* can mean both experience and experiment. So, when Foucault says that he wishes to write experience books this implies books which not only convey the experience of the author, or change the experience of the reader, but which also constitute both an experiment which the author carries out on him or herself, and an experiment in which the reader too can participate – thus participating in the subjective transformation which the book makes possible. Foucault wants to write books that will lead to a transformation in his own form of subjectivity and that will also facilitate a similar transformation on the part of his readers. This connection between the notions of experience and experiment, as Raymond Williams points out (1976: 99), also existed in English at least until the end of the eighteenth century. It was only at that time that the term experience ceased to cover both the experimental test itself and the 'consciousness of what has been tested or tried, and thence a consciousness of an effect or state' (ibid.). But, in both languages, experience is a consciousness that emerges, as the Latin root of the word indicates, from an openness to the world, an openness which is inherently dangerous. In Latin, *expereri* (to try, or to test) is linked to the word for danger – *periculum*.[2] Experience, therefore, in both of its possible senses, is something that emerges from (ex-) a necessarily perilous encounter with the world – or with the strange and the foreign.

One philosopher who mobilizes this way of conceiving of experience is John Dewey; particularly in his 1932 lectures on the philosophy of art (1980). For Dewey, experience is not something that simply happens to us, it is not something in which we are merely a passive recipient. It is also a form of activity.

In its broadest sense, it is the interaction of an organism with its environment. The central idea here, is that experience is a matter of doing and undergoing. In experience, Dewey says (1980: 246), 'the self acts, as well as undergoes, and its undergoings are not impressions stamped upon an inert wax but depend upon the way the organism reacts and responds'. The organism, therefore, 'is a force, not a transparency' (ibid.). If the organism, or the individual, is a force rather than a passive recording surface, then we can say that every experience is an experiment in the sense that something new is produced, that something new emerges from the interaction between organism and world. The distinctive feature of Dewey's approach to art in general, is the idea that the aesthetic is continuous with our everyday forms of experience. In other words, art cannot be isolated and confined to a special realm in which we use special faculties such as imagination and creativity to produce and discern objects of beauty. Rather, according to Dewey, art is 'a quality of doing and of what is done' (1980: 214). In his aesthetics, as in the rest of his philosophy, Dewey was resolutely opposed to hypostatization. Any abstract term such as art, mind or imagination which took on the form and solidity of a substantial entity or faculty was subject to rejection. In all such cases he urged us to rethink the concept as an adjective or a verb, rather than as a noun. What Dewey wants us to notice is that the substantive nouns 'art', 'imagination', and even 'beauty', just like the nouns 'building', 'construction' and 'work', get their meaning from the adjectives that qualify the way we engage in certain activities. And the point that these are activities is crucial: 'without the meaning of the verb that of the noun remains blank' (1980: 51).

What we must remember is that the work of art engages the activity of both the artist and the audience. And experience, in general, has this same quality: it is not something that simply happens to us, it is not something in which we are merely a passive recipient. It is also a form of activity. In its broadest sense, experience is 'a matter of the interaction of organism with its environment' (1980: 246). Every interaction between the human organism and its environment – both natural and social – is constitutive of experience. But not all experience is equal in Dewey's view. There are experiences which are qualitatively different, and of greater value, because they constitute a unified, whole experience. In other words, it is sometimes a matter of having *an* experience, rather than just experience. And it is this type of experience that art, among other things, can provide. The living organism is continuously in the midst of a flow of experience; a flow that springs from the constant interaction between the organism and the environment. In general, this flow of experience is inchoate. In contrast with this, we have *an* experience, Dewey says, when 'the material experienced runs its course to fulfillment' (1980: 35). So, for example, the solving of a problem, the playing of a game of chess, the eating of a meal may all be experiences in this sense. There are two characteristic features of this type of experience. First, it combines the seamless flow of successive parts with an increasing distinctness of each part. In other words, it combines the unity of an experience with the diversity of a potentially great number of distinct elements. Secondly, this type of experience is distinctive in its beginnings and its endings. In fact, according to Dewey, it does not have a mere beginning, but an initiation, and not a mere ending, but a concluding or a consummation (1980: 40).

If, to use one of Dewey's examples, playing a game of chess can constitute an experience because it begins, develops and is consummated in a certain way; then we can say that reading a poem, listening to a piece of music or looking at a painting can do the same. But these experiences – the experience of an artwork – are different from the experience of a game of chess, first, because of their expressive nature (an artist has tried to express something through the work) and, secondly, because of their ability to enter into and modify the experience of their audience. If experience in the most general sense is a matter of doing and undergoing, then the experience of works of art is equally active on the part of the audience. Of course it is possible to be passive in the face of a work of art, but for Dewey any such experience is not aesthetic. To have an aesthetic experience is to re-create the work in one's own experience. 'A new poem,' he writes, 'is created by everyone who reads poetically' (1980: 108). And, in fact, a work of art is only complete, in Dewey's view, once it 'works in the experience of others than the one who created it' (1980: 106). The crucial feature to note here is this idea of the work working in the experience of others; this is crucial, not only for Dewey's philosophy of art, but also for the question I am addressing here, the question of what works of literature can do to us and in us.

When Dewey talks about this kind of experience, he points out that while the work was, most probably, spurred by some particular, datable occasion, yet what keeps the work alive is its capacity to 'enter into the experiences of others and enable them to have more intense and more fully rounded out experiences of their own' (1980: 109). A work of art makes possible 'the expansion and intensification' of experience. And, 'just because it [itself] is a full and intense experience, [it] keeps alive the power to experience the common world in its fullness' (1980: 133). It would seem, then, that according to Dewey the value of the work of art is that it expands and intensifies our experience – and not just our experience of the work, but our experience of what he calls 'the common world'. Because the viewer, or the reader, of a work of art who wishes to 'perceive esthetically' must, Dewey says, 'remake his past experiences so that they can enter integrally into a new pattern. He cannot dismiss his past experiences, nor can he dwell among them as they have been in the past' (1980: 138). In other words, engaging with a work of art not only has an effect on our future experiences, it also changes our past experiences and forces us to re-cast them in a new pattern. And, according to Dewey, the person who does this, the person for whom something is 'undergone in consequence of a doing', this person will be modified in the process (1980: 264). The work of art, therefore, can be seen as a kind of catalyst or reagent that introduces a modification into the organism on which it impinges.

This brings us back to the point I made earlier about the connection – both semantic and conceptual – between experience and experiment. And Dewey, in fact, shares with Foucault the idea that experimentation is central to aesthetic experience. Foucault, as we saw, regards his experience books as experiments that he carries out on himself – and on others. 'I am an experimenter,' he says, 'in the sense that I write in order to change myself and in order to no longer think the same thing as before' (1980a: 27[42]). For Dewey too, one of the 'essential traits' of art is that the artist is 'born an experimenter'. The artist must be an experimenter because they have to express 'an intensely individualized experience through means and materials that belong to the common and public world' (1980: 144). In other words, the task of aesthetically conveying a private experience to the public world, requires constant experimentation with the artistic media. And it is only by virtue of this experimentation that the artist is able to 'open new fields of experience and disclose new aspects and qualities in familiar scenes and objects' (ibid.). But Dewey's claim about experimentation is not confined to what happens in the artist's studio – it is not just a matter of experimenting with materials and forms. For when the artist remakes their experience through the act of expression, what happens is not, Dewey insists, an 'isolated event confined to the artist and to a person here and there who happens to enjoy the work'. Much more significantly, it is also 'a remaking of the experience of the community' (ibid.).

At this stage we can briefly raise the question of the value of such a transformation. While it is not clear how exactly this remaking extends from artist and audience to the community, it is quite clear that for Dewey it is this potential remaking that forms part of what he calls 'art's office'; and for him it is a remaking in the direction of 'greater order and unity' (1980: 81). Similarly, while discussing the role of the viewer in creating the work of art, he comments that the outcome of this interaction is 'an experience that is enjoyed because of its liberating and ordered properties' (1980: 214). But, what kind of order and unity does Dewey envisage, and how would such a view sit with the approach Foucault takes? For Dewey, art plays a twofold role. In the public, shared world it unifies by breaking down conventional distinctions that usually prevent us from seeing and expressing the common elements of the world; while, at the level of the individual, it unifies by building up the complexity and richness of the individual personality. On the one hand, it changes the way we see and experience the world by removing barriers and differences; on the other hand, it changes our self by composing differences (1980: 248). One way of stating the value of art, then, would be to say that it promotes the expansion of the community of experience. In a world which is full of divisions that limit this community, works of art are the only 'media of complete and unhindered communication' (1980: 105); they are 'communication in its pure and undefiled form' (1980: 244). And it is literature, in particular, which has the power to communicate in this way – because, unlike other art forms, its medium is language. But within literature, Dewey distinguishes between prose, which works by 'extension', and poetry, which works by 'intension' – the poetic 'reverses the process' that occurs in narrative prose. 'It [the poetic] condenses and abbreviates, thus giving words an energy of expansion that is almost explosive' (1980: 241).

According to Dewey, then, the potentially explosive intensity of the poetic is capable of liberating us from the constraints and barriers that narrow our experience of the world. And, similarly, it makes it possible for us to expand ourselves, by giving us the means to incorporate more of the conflicting and opposing elements of our being. A poem could, therefore, work in our experience by, in Dewey's terms, expanding ourselves and our experience of the world, or in Foucault's terms, by intervening in and modifying our forms of relation to self and others.

Let's return now to the question of the relation between the two forms of experience that I called 'everyday' experience and 'transformative' experience. How different are they from each other, how are they constituted, how do they act on one another? And, more importantly, what do they have to do with aesthetic experience? We won't be able to give a full answer to these questions until a later chapter (Chapter 5), but now, following Dewey's account, we at least have a way of beginning to think about this problem. In particular, we can say that the mode of experience we undergo when we engage with a work of art is not discontinuous with the mode we undergo in any other part of our lives. In itself this may not seem a very surprising or promising start. But, when we add that our everyday mode of experience is as much an active engagement as a passive recording, and that works of art have an irreducibly experimental character, then we can begin to see how these works may be able to change our everyday forms of experience. Hence, we have two forms or modes of experience, and what's crucial in Dewey's contribution is the idea that both forms, of experience, but especially the second, are closely linked to experimentation.

Naturally, these claims raise as many questions as they hope to answer; and the task of the following chapters is to answer them as well as possible. In particular, we will have to say a great deal more about this idea that our everyday experience can be transformed. What would it mean to emerge, say, from a reading of *Ulysses* with a transformed experience? At first sight this way of speaking about the effect of literature may not seem to make much sense. Of course, we can understand that a reader of Joyce may subsequently have a modified experience of the city of Dublin, just as a reader of Proust may enjoy eating madeleines even more after reading his novel. But, while this kind of example does indeed give us an important insight into the way that literature lives on in our experience, our concern here will be to ask whether, and to what extent, such works can provoke more profound shifts in our subjectivity. And, more importantly, we will want to investigate the ethical significance and value of such shifts. For the moment, however, I want to leave those questions aside and turn to another peculiarity of this book: its exclusive focus on Irish literature.

# Ireland

In a book that investigates the transformative power of literature, there wouldn't seem to be any particular reason to favour one national tradition over another. Of course, for illustration, one would try to choose works that exemplify a transformative tendency, but this choice could range over literatures of any time or place. In this book, however, all the literature that I will discuss in any detail is, in some sense, Irish. There are two reasons for this; one of which has to do with the nature of the material itself, and the other with the nature of my own engagement with it. First, in relation to the material, I would suggest that there is something exemplary, although by no means unique, about the way that much Irish literature engages with the ethical and political issues that will occupy us here. For several centuries, works of literature including poems, ballads, songs, plays and novels, have played a significant role in the processes of transformation that have moulded Ireland. This has frequently been as a result of a deliberate, occasionally crude attempt, on the part of poets and writers, to influence public debate. However, my focus here will be on a body of work that takes a less utilitarian, or less direct, approach to the ethical and political responsibilities of literature. At two turning points in recent Irish history (the late nineteenth and the late twentieth centuries), for example, there was a burgeoning of such work around two major literary movements: the Irish Literary Theatre in the 1890s and the Field Day Group in the 1980s. I will discuss the role of W. B. Yeats in the first of these movements below, while the work of Seamus Heaney and Brian Friel (who were both closely associated with Field Day) will be the focus of two later chapters. This is only a partial justification, however, since I won't be focusing exclusively on work that is associated with these movements. In later chapters I will look in some detail at works by Joyce, Swift and Beckett in a way that doesn't prioritize their Irish context. I must emphasize, therefore, that throughout these chapters it will not be the Irishness *per se* of the works that will be my focus; instead, my primary interest will always be in their more general relevance to the theoretical concerns of the project developed here. Hence, I won't be concerned, for example, with questions such as whether Swift or Beckett should be seen as specifically Irish authors.[3]

My second reason for focusing on works of Irish literature has to do with their personal significance for me. There is a certain kind of philosophy of literature that is carried on as if the works under discussion had never had any real impact on the philosopher who is writing about them. For example, one comes across discussions of emotional responses to fictional characters that leave one wondering, perhaps unkindly, if the author has really experienced such a response. On the other hand, there is a tendency on the part of theorists discussing European philosophers to limit their examples to Holderlin, Célan, Mallarmé, Kafka, and so on; in other words, to the poets or writers that the philosopher in question discussed. The problem, however, is that the commentator doesn't necessarily have the same relation to those works as the philosopher under discussion, and the danger is then that the whole endeavour becomes an academic exercise that misses the original importance of the works. My point is not that one can only respond meaningfully to one's 'own' literature; I am not arguing for some kind of ethnic or cultural exclusivity. The point is simply that when one writes about these issues it is best if one focuses on works to which one has responded in an appropriately relevant way. In my case, it just so happens that many of the works that best fit this description are written by Irish authors. Combining these two considerations, I think I have a reasonable justification for the limited range of works to be discussed here. It goes without saying – but I will say it anyway – that the general philosophical argument of this book does not essentially depend on the specifics of Irish literature.

Beyond these two reasons, we can also draw a connection between my choice of literary examples and the idea of the event of literature, with its two levels of temporality. If the work of literature itself is not a substance, but must be thought of as changing over time as a function of social and cultural transformations, then it may be useful, especially in a project such as this, to take into account the context in which the work was produced. So, for instance, in the case of Seamus Heaney it is important to consider the political context in which he is writing, at least if we want to assess the potential impact of those works. But, once a work is produced, it begins to operate in worlds that are subtly, if not radically, different from the one in which it was originally received. My stress on this context is not intended to diminish the potential for further change; it is simply to say that the work should be considered in relation to both the world in which it is produced and the world upon which it acts. Let me give a quick example: in late 2001, in response to the 9/11 attacks in New York, Seamus Heaney translated and re-wrote a poem by the Roman poet Horace. This poem, on the subject of the suddenness with which the gods can turn our world upside down is, at least in part, a statement of religious awe in the face of divine power. However, re-worked by Heaney in 2001, the poem becomes an expression of shock, sympathy and foreboding at the terrible forces that are being unleashed in our own century: 'Anything can happen, the tallest things/ Be overturned, those in high places daunted,/ Those overlooked regarded' (2004: 11).

What Heaney has done here is to bring out certain potentialities that were in the original poem, to connect them up with the concerns of our own present moment, and to create a new work that has a different, although analogous, effect on us today. But this re-working is not just something that a poet can do through re-writing and translating; it is essentially something that each reader does – as Dewey noted – in their active engagement with a work. So, if we pay attention to the context in which, for example, Heaney and Friel, produced their work, this is not to deny the fact that these works will act, differently, upon different times and places. The point is that in order to give an adequate account of the transformative effects of literature, we must bear in mind both the time of the work and the time of the reader. That is, the work follows its own course as a function of changing historical contexts, while the reader follows a different, but no less complex, path of potential changes and blockages. It is when these two paths intersect that a work generates its effect.

Let's now look in some detail at that significant moment in recent Irish history, when a literary movement emerged to promote a political and, in my sense, ethical project. In the early 1890s, writing after the death of the Irish parliamentary leader Charles Stewart Parnell, the poet W. B. Yeats described his 'supernatural insight' that 'Ireland was to be like soft wax for years to come' (1955: 199). Parnell, who was Protestant, had failed to bring about Home Rule for Ireland within the British Empire and he had been abruptly brought down as leader due, at least partly, to official Catholic hostility towards his involvement in the divorce of his lover from her husband. Both the political campaign for a limited form of independence, and the subsequent uproar, scandal, and death of the 'Chief' at the age of 46 years, had divided the country in a way that left behind both deep animosities and a powerful demand for political and cultural change. For Yeats, this represented an opportunity for people such as himself to try to guide the growth of a new sense of cultural independence.

It is not unusual for those who espouse great programmes of cultural reform to see the raw material for this art as wax in their hands. Yeats, with Lady Gregory and the other founders of the Irish Literary Theatre (1898), set out to achieve nothing less than a national cultural revival; a revival in the realm of cultural production which, in Yeats's view, was made possible by the delay, after the fall of Parnell, of the rebirth of a nation in the political domain. The temporary disappointment of many people's hopes for Home Rule had left a residue of energies which Yeats was to try to harness in the cause of cultural independence. The principal tools he was to use to harness these energies, and to mould this wax, were poetry and drama. Turning to Yeats's own autobiographical and critical writings, we see a poet who is keenly aware, not only of the external demand that he should write, in some sense, 'for' a movement, but also of the contrary demands that his art itself would make.

Yeats is a poet who was at odds with the values of the society in which he lived; he is a poet who resists the demands which are made on him, while trying to bring about the conditions in which those demands would change. The kind of literature that the revival wants to foster, he says, will not 'plead the National cause', and will neither 'insist upon the Ten Commandments, nor the "glory" of Ireland' (1976: 147). Yet this literature, Yeats insists, will influence cultural life immeasurably more than propagandist poems and stories, precisely because it will 'leave to others the defence of all that can be codified for ready understanding . . . It will measure all things by the measure not of things visible but of things invisible' (ibid.). In the epigraph that Heaney (1980) later used for his own first collection of essays, Yeats insists that the commitment to this vision 'is little different from the following of religion in the intense preoccupation it demands'. It is this kind of preoccupation that motivates the members of both the late-nineteenth-century and the late-twentieth-century literary movements in Ireland.

Seamus Heaney suggests in a 1978 lecture that Yeats can be taken to be an exemplary poet. Yeats, like Heaney's ideal poet (one could give examples such as Osip Mandelstam and Czeslaw Milosz), wanted to bring his poetry into an effective relation with the cultural context in which he was writing.[1] Heaney praises Yeats because he 'bore the implications of his romanticism into action: he propagandized, speechified, fund-raised, administered and politicked in the world of telegrams and anger, all on behalf of the world of vision' (1980: 100). In response to common charges that Yeats retreated into a disdainful, haughty arrogance (an arrogance that highlighted both his colonial mentality and his irrelevance) Heaney expresses admiration for the fact that he 'took on the world on his own terms'. 'I assume,' says Heaney, 'that this peremptoriness, this apparent arrogance, is exemplary in an artist, that it is proper and even necessary for him to insist on his own language, his own vision, his own terms of reference' (1980: 101). Presaging his own much later hope to contribute to the good of his own society, Heaney admires the way that Yeats, in his work and his life, aims 'to be of service', to 'ply the effort of the individual work into the larger work of the community as a whole' (1980: 106). Heaney admires the fact that Yeats conceived of his life 'as an experiment in living' (1980: 100), the fact that he continuously re-made himself in response to his cultural and political surroundings, the fact that he sought 'a style for resisting his environment rather than a style that would co-opt it' (1980: 106). Finally, he admires the fact that, whereas Joyce rebelled and left Ireland to create the fictional character Stephen Dedalus, Yeats rebelled and remained in Ireland to create the fictional character 'W. B. Yeats'.

Almost a century after the founding of the Irish Literary Theatre, and confronted with the social consequences of the same political disappointment that had confronted Yeats, the playwright Brian Friel and the actor Stephen Rea founded the Field Day Theatre Company in Derry, Northern Ireland, in 1980. Initially set up to produce Friel's play *Translations* (to be discussed in Chapter 3) in a series of performances around Northern Ireland, the Company quickly expanded both its board of directors – to include poets, writers and critics such as Seamus Heaney, Tom Paulin and Seamus Deane – and its agenda – to encompass nothing less than the re-imagination of the cultural and political landscape of Northern Ireland.[5] In an indication of the close parallels which, despite a century's distance, exist between these two literary movements, Seamus Deane has written of Friel: '. . . no Irish writer *since the early days of this century* has so sternly and courageously asserted the role of art in the public world'.[6] Reading between the lines we could say that not only was Field Day the successor to the

Irish Literary Theatre, but that Friel, its founder, is the inheritor of Yeats's particular attempts to make the world of art have some impact upon the world of politics. Like Yeats's original Irish Literary Theatre, this company also aimed to contribute to a cultural transformation that would assist, or alleviate, a political situation. And they, like Yeats, chose as the central tools of cultural intervention the theatre, poetry and criticism. The crucial difference between the two programmes, however, was that while Yeats – the revivalist – saw himself as contributing to the foundation of a national literature and mythology, the members of Field Day – whom we could call counter-revivalists – saw themselves as trying to deal with the social and political disaster which, in Northern Ireland, was one part of the legacy of that national myth-making.

In the chapters that follow, when I come to discuss the work of Heaney and Friel, I won't be concerned with the details of their involvement with Field Day, nor with the heated debates that surrounded many of that group's initiatives. Instead, having taken account of the contexts in which the works were created and initially received, I will focus as much as possible on the potential that the works contain within themselves to generate certain effects on readers today – whether or not those readers share or are familiar with the experiences of their authors. My objective, in other words, will be to see to what extent a work such as a poem or a play can make possible an interaction that will produce a change in the everyday experience of a reader. This is a potential that would give such works a particular ethical significance.

## Foucault's Ethics

Let's return now to the concept of ethics that emerges in Foucault's late work, and to my suggestion that this concept gives us a way of understanding literature as one possible technique for ethical self-transformation. There are two key elements in Foucault's final approach to ethics. The first is the idea that within any moral system we must distinguish between three components: morality, ethics and behaviour. On this account, morality comprises the set of rules, prohibitions and norms that the adherent to the system is expected to follow. Ethics is about the modes of relation to self that the adherent will cultivate. It comprises the ways in which individuals bring themselves to obey the prescriptions and, importantly, the range of techniques that are made available to them to assist in this task. Behaviour, unsurprisingly, comprises what the adherents of the system will actually do in terms of moral and immoral practices. The second key element is Foucault's observation that while the field of morality, at least in the Western tradition, undergoes little historical change (fundamental prohibitions, for example, are highly resistant to change), enormous changes occur in the field of ethics. Hence, both echoing and contrasting with Nietzsche, he proposes to undertake a 'genealogy of ethics' (1983a).

Ethics understood in this way, as what we could call the self-regarding component of morality, has four aspects: ethical substance; mode of subjection; ethical
techniques; and telos.[7] Foucault worked out this schema in his history of classical Greek sexual ethics, but it is clearly not limited in applicability to the ethics
of any particular culture or era. The first aspect, ethical substance, comprises
the part of oneself that will be the object of intervention. In classical Greek
sexual ethics, this was 'the pleasures' (*aphrodisia*); in Christian sexual ethics it
was 'desire' or 'the flesh'. The second aspect, the mode of subjection, is the way
one understands the authority of the code, or the model of behaviour, to be followed. For example, does it arise from a free personal choice, or is it a matter
of obeying a divine command? The third aspect, the ethical techniques, comprises the techniques that one uses to bring oneself to follow a given model of
behaviour. In the field of sexual ethics, these techniques may include enforced
abstinence, careful scrutiny of one's thoughts and desires, and confession of
one's weaknesses to a spiritual advisor. The fourth aspect, the telos, indicates
the goal towards which a particular ethics leads. This may be conceived as a
state of freedom in relation to one's own passions, a relation of mastery to oneself and others, or a state of conformity to a divine will that promises salvation.

If we broaden our scope from sexual ethics to ethics in general, however, it
becomes more difficult to neatly define each of these aspects. For the average,
not particularly reflective member of a modern Western society for example, it
would be hard to say what comprises the ethical substance, or mode of subjection, of their ethical practice in general. One possible reason for this is the fact
that, first of all, not all moral systems put a great deal of emphasis on ethics (in
Foucault's sense). We can distinguish, in fact, between those systems in which
obedience to a time-honoured code is all that is demanded, and those systems
in which a great deal of ethical work is required. This difference even appears
within moral systems: consider, for example, the different demands, in terms of
ethical self-elaboration, that are placed on a medieval Christian monk and a
medieval Christian labourer. Another reason may be the fact that, at least in
modern Western societies, there are a range of moral systems all operating side
by side, even for the same individuals. Hence, one may be broadly utilitarian in
one's attitude to food (vegetarian, opposed to environmentally destructive
farming practices, and so on), but broadly Kantian in one's respect for persons
and one's commitment to principles of justice. While it would be impossible to
generalize about such a person's ethical substance or mode of subjection, that
need not be a problem for the approach I am adopting here.

All I wish to suggest is that an individual who is at least minimally open to
reflection about their own practices and their relation to the world is capable
of changing themselves, and of being changed, through an engagement with
certain works of literature. And this engagement and this change are, at least
sometimes, best thought of in terms of ethics; that is, the change which
is effected is one that may alter the way the person relates to themselves and

others. According to this model, we will then view the reading of works of literature as being, potentially, an ethical technique or a practice of the self – analogous to, for example, the Stoic practice of keeping a private diary, or the Buddhist
practice of meditation. Keeping in mind the earlier discussion of the event of
literature, with its two different time frames, we can easily concede that this ethical potential of literature has not necessarily always been a part of the reading of
poems and stories. And, similarly, it is not necessarily a feature of all engagement with literature, in all places, today. My suggestion, however, is that today
literature does have this potential; and this is something that writers have been
aware of for some time.

At this stage, two questions need to be addressed: first, how important is the
initial attitude of the reader in realizing the ethical potential of a given work?
And, second, does this emphasis on the ethical imply that any change which
emerges from an engagement with a work of literature will be a change for the
good? And if so, how does the approach developed here understand this good?
My response to these questions will develop over the following chapters, but for
the moment I will discuss them in a preliminary way. First, the idea that reading
literature is potentially a technique of transformation raises the question of the
will of the reader. All the other examples I have given of ethical techniques
clearly require that the individual consciously engage in them with a certain
ethical aim in view. The Stoic who regularly abstains from luxurious foods, for
example, does so deliberately in order to become less dependent on the unreli-
able things of the world. But, do readers approach literature with the aim of
transforming themselves in this way? Well, perhaps some do, but my argument
here in no way assumes that they *must* approach it like this. In fact, at a very fundamental level, none of the potential effects I discuss could come to fruition
unless the reader were largely motivated by the pursuit of pleasure: a work that
gives no pleasure is a work that will have little effect. However, I still do assume
a certain openness on the part of the reader to the transformative power of the
work. The reader doesn't have to know in advance, or be able to predict, what
these changes would be. In fact, it is impossible to know in advance how a
poem, for example, will affect any given reader. But any possible effect will be
stronger, the more open the reader is to the transformative potential of the
work. It is clear, then, that there has to be both a certain kind of work and a
reader who is open to a possible transformation. As Dewey observed, the recipient of the artwork must be active in the doing and the undergoing.

However, the relative contribution of each side will vary depending on the
specifics of work and reader. For example, reading Joyce's *Ulysses* already
requires a certain commitment from the reader to reading a difficult text; any
effect the novel can have is, therefore, dependent on a significant labour on the
part of the reader. In contrast, reading Harper Lee's *To Kill a Mocking Bird* is
arguably less demanding, but no less (or perhaps more) potentially transformative; hence its popularity as a set text in secondary schools. For the moment,

therefore, we can say that a certain openness to re-evaluation must be present on the part of the reader, but that whatever effect takes place will emerge from a complex interplay between the work, the reader and the reader's world.

Let's turn now to the second question to which I wanted to give a preliminary response; the question of the value of ethical transformation. For Foucault, ethics is essentially conceptualized as a matter of self-fashioning. The Greek male aristocrats who reflected on the number, type and timing of their sexual acts did so as part of an effort to transform themselves into a certain type of person: in effect, masters of both themselves and others. However, when Foucault speaks of the ethical task that faces us today as one of searching for an 'aesthetics of existence' (1984d: 49[732]), he doesn't have mastery in his sights as the goal of this search. The use of the word 'aesthetics' here might suggest that his aim is to create an effect of beauty, but even this would be to misunderstand the nature of his project.[8] I would suggest that in this case, as with 'fiction', we should understand 'aesthetics' as a verb rather than as a noun; in which case, an 'aesthetics of existence' will be a practice of creating a mode of life. And this act of creation will, like the creation of a work of art, be experimental and non-reducible to a set of rules and norms. However, we must also acknowledge that this creation will not be *ex nihilo*; whether in art or in life, it is impossible to begin with a blank canvas.[9] In the case of self-transformation, we always begin from the modes of subjectivity and the social, political and epistemological structures in which we live. And it is these structures that a great deal of Foucault's effort goes towards examining; his histories are, essentially, dedicated to understanding how it is that we came to be as we are in the present. But Foucault's project is not just to understand the way we are; it is also to change the way we are. The kind of critical philosophy that he wishes to practise is one which would not just discover what we are, but would help us to refuse what we are. 'We have to promote,' he insists, 'new forms of subjectivity through the refusal of this kind of individuality which has been imposed on us for several centuries' (1982: 336).

The ethical significance of this kind of critical philosophy is that it can play a role as a technique that helps us to distance ourselves from those forms and structures of our world that seem to have a rigid inevitability. Thinking in terms of Foucault's four-fold analysis of ethics, we can say that this critical philosophy takes as its ethical substance those historically changing forms of subjectivity that are most rigidly imposed and, in some sense, are most intolerable.[10] Its mode of subjection would be a decision to engage in an experimental, non-foundationalist practice of modification. Its techniques would include both the kind of work that Foucault carried out in his books, and the kind of work he undertook in a range of political activities during the 1970s and 1980s. Finally, its aim would be quite simply to help us to untie the knots of our identity so that we can re-constitute them in new and less constraining ways.[11] This is what Foucault (1984c: 319) calls 'a patient labour giving form to our impatience for liberty'. On the basis of this account, we can say that the value of the hoped-for transformation arises from its freeing-up of our modes of thought and action, in particular those regarding our relations to self and others. It would focus on those aspects of our experience from which we suffer most, and would help us to find new ways of living.

It is important, however, to remember that this process is experimental. There is no guarantee that any new mode of thought and action will be, on any criteria, better than what preceded it. But, from the point of view of the ethical attitude that emerges in Foucault's work, it is the opening-up of the possibility for continued, sustained experiment that is itself valuable. This is the possibility that the process by which time brands and fetters certain possibilities, to the exclusion of others, is open to our intervention and tenuous modification. In the following chapters, I will be arguing that this is the kind of experiment that certain works of literature make available for their readers. With this idea of experiment we have now returned to our central concern with experience, and its possible transformation. Foucault's late concept of experience will give us a way of understanding, in some detail, the mechanism by which an ethical technique is capable of changing our mode of relation to the world. If our ethical work on ourselves includes, for example, trying to understand the history of our current forms of sexual identity, then we will be able to show how this change in our self-understanding modifies our overall orientation within the world, and thus changes our experience. In a similar way, the following chapters will show how particular works of literature have the potential to modify this orientation, even if these changes are often very difficult to detect, even for the person who undergoes them.

In the next chapter, I will begin to give an account of this potential through a reading of the work of Seamus Heaney. Heaney is noteworthy from our point of view because of his engagement with philosophical questions about the capacity of poetry to be an effective force within society. In particular, Heaney, like many poets in the Western tradition, feels the need to answer the attack on poetry that was mounted by Plato in the *Republic*. Since the working out of an anti-Platonist account of poetry is a preliminary task to the project of this book, we will begin by seeing what help Heaney can give us in trying both to understand and to overcome the Platonist conception.

Chapter 2

# The Ungoverned Tongue:
# Seamus Heaney

In 1979, Seamus Heaney was travelling by train from Dublin to Belfast when an old school friend, who had just been released from Long Kesh prison, and who therefore was presumably a member of the IRA, entered the carriage. In the poem in which he describes the event, Heaney says the man 'enters and sits down/ Opposite and goes for me head on./ "When for fuck's sake, are you going to write/ Something for us?"' he demands.[1] Even bearing in mind that IRA strategy was soon to become 'The Armalite in one hand and the ballot box in the other', one might wonder what this man could possibly do with a poem.[2] An entire critical and philosophical tradition stretching back to Plato will tell us that a poem has no place in political struggles, and that such demands must not be made on poets. Yet, as Heaney and his old school friend well knew, it is rarely possible to maintain such a division between these two spheres – that Heaney at one point calls 'Art' and 'Life'. This is an impossibility which has been especially felt in twentieth-century Ireland – at least since Yeats worried that one of his plays may have 'sent out certain men the English shot'.[3] Heaney, whose work spans a period of both intense political violence and political change in Northern Ireland, is a poet who is keenly aware of the conflicting forces that strive to govern the poet's tongue. It would seem that everybody, from philosophers and literary critics to the self-appointed defenders of the tribe, would tell the poet what to write. And, on the other hand, there are many poets who, at least through some of their works, would try to influence the political life of their contemporaries.[4] This situation gives rise to pressing questions about the role of the poet in his or her society, and about the effects (positive, negative or non-existent) which poetry might have on its readers.

In order to address this question of the relation between poetry and the social world, I will read Heaney's poetry and prose as detailed responses to Plato's contradictory attack, in which poetry is apparently condemned for both its insignificance *and* its dangerous power. Rather than setting up philosophy in opposition to poetry, however, I want to draw on Heaney's writing as both a challenge and a resource for philosophy, in particular for the attempt to develop non-Platonist ways of understanding literature. Focusing, in particular, on

Heaney's prose writings and lectures and on one of his later collections of poetry (*The Spirit Level*, 1996), I will follow Heaney in his struggle with Plato in order to see how his work might help us to formulate a non-Platonist account of literature. In a 1970 essay on the work of Gilles Deleuze, Michel Foucault suggests that we should see philosophy, and practice it, as an essentially anti-Platonist endeavour: 'Overturn Platonism: what philosophy has not tried? If we defined philosophy at the limit as any attempt, regardless of its source, to over-turn Platonism, then philosophy begins with Aristotle; or, better yet, it begins with Plato himself . . .' (1970: 343).[5] If philosophy can indeed be seen as any attempt, 'regardless of its source', to overturn Platonism, then it would have to include not only the works of thinkers like Deleuze and Nietzsche, but also the works of the major artists and writers of the twentieth century. Indeed, in one of his last lectures at the Collège de France in 1984, Foucault comments on the anti-Platonism of modern art, which stretches from Manet to Francis Bacon, and from Baudelaire to Beckett.[6] In this chapter, however, what interests me is the fact that a contemporary Irish poet, rather than a Foucault or a Deleuze, feels the need to challenge and ultimately overturn the Platonist conception of art and literature. While Heaney's grappling with these issues, especially in his prose writings, is instructive, I will suggest that, ultimately, his poetry is already operating according to an understanding of art and its relation to the world which is profoundly anti-Platonist. A close reading of some of Heaney's work will help us to see how much the philosophy of literature and art stands to learn from this practice of poetry.

## Wrestling with Plato

According to Heaney, the modern poet, and more generally the modern artist, is faced with an apparently impossible choice between the contrary demands of life and of art. On the side of art, there is a demand that the artist should follow the internal, formal requirements of artistic production and remain, we might say, true to the muse; while on the side of life there is a demand, and often a desire, on the part of the artist to address and engage in the social and political concerns of the times in which they live. These contrary demands give rise to an anxiety which Heaney sees manifested in the work of many modern and contemporary writers. In Chekhov, for example, who spent five years living in a penal colony to observe the conditions under which the inmates lived, Heaney sees a writer who displays a 'characteristic modesty and prophetically modern guilt about the act of creative writing itself' (1989: xvi); while, in the case of Wallace Stevens, who defends poetry as an 'imagined response to conditions in the world' (1996b: 2),[7] Heaney identifies a tell-tale anxiety in the face of an imagined heckler. This heck-ler would echo Thomas Mann's judgement that'In our time the destiny of man presents its meaning in political terms', and thus would undercut the poet's claim to social relevance.[8] And Heaney himself admits to feeling the same anxiety: an 'anxiety that in arrogating to oneself the right to take refuge in form, one is somehow denying the claims of the beggar at the gate' (1989: xxii).

If the modern poet is caught in this double bind, between the demands of art and life, and is beset by an anxiety that poetry itself can do very little, then the modern Irish poet is perhaps in a marginally better predicament. Taking Heaney as an example, it is significant that his problem is not so much 'how do I use my poetry to intervene?', but 'how do I respond to the demand that poetry must engage in a political situation?' In other words, for Heaney the problem is not to convince the world of the efficacy of poetry, since that seems to be already accepted (even by the IRA activist), but to balance this demand with the equally weighty demands of the art of poetry itself. How, in other words, does the poet respond to the demand 'when for fuck's sake are you going to write something for us?', without renouncing the autonomy of the poet's tongue? For Heaney then, in a society which suffers from extreme social and religious divisions, the question of the relation between poetry and politics also becomes a question about the relation between the poet's work and life.

As an outsider, it is easy to be opposed to imperialism and colonialism, whether British or not, but closer to home it is more difficult for the poet, at least the poet in Northern Ireland, to situate him or herself in the context of a highly complex political situation. Here, in the twentieth century, there were no clear lines between justice and oppression, between good and evil. There were legitimate demands for justice on all sides, there were atrocities carried out by all sides, and there was a severe polarization of views which tended to drown out voices of moderation and balance. Given this situation, it is not surprising that Heaney was forced to think about the effect which his words would have. What would happen, for instance, if he, as unofficial laureate of the Catholic community, were to write a poem denouncing loyalist atrocities, or calling for a British withdrawal? Did he, apparently like Yeats, want to send men out to be shot? Certainly not, and neither in fact did Yeats; and yet he wanted to do something, something that would help the situation.

But what can poetry do? This is the question that drives Heaney back to Plato in many of his prose writings: because Plato is the thinker who stands at the beginning of a long line of critics who seem to say that poetry should not try to *do* anything, at least in the realm of politics. Before looking at Heaney's response to Plato, however, I want to outline Plato's denunciation of poetry – and all the so-called mimetic arts – in the *Republic*.[9] At the beginning of Book X, Plato has Socrates declare himself to be particularly satisfied with the decision to expel the poets and artists from the ideal city-state which is being planned. This rejection is now, in Book X, justified in three interlinked charges against the representational artists. Plato's first charge is that these artists merely make copies of copies. Their works are like the images in a mirror which is held up and 'turned round in all directions' (*Republic*, 596d). The artist may appear to be creating this world of animals and plants, stars and planets; but really all they are doing is reflecting the appearance of objects which, in Plato's epistemology, are themselves merely copies of a Form that exists in another realm. The representational artist (tragedian, poet, painter) stands, therefore, at a third remove from reality, or from 'the throne of truth' (*Republic*, 597e).

Plato's second charge is that, even though poets and painters are capable of representing every craft and skill, they are capable of practising none of them: Homer, for example, founded no cities, wrote no constitutions, and led no military campaigns. His only skill was a certain knack at representing the appearance of the skill of others; but these were skills of which he himself was completely ignorant. It could be said, therefore, that the poet can indeed *do* nothing. Up to this point, Plato seems to be suggesting that poets and painters must be excluded from the *polis* simply because of their ineffectiveness and irrelevance; why, he seems to suggest, would a well-ordered city use its resources to support such a worthless class of people? The question that this raises, however, is why, if poetry is so hopelessly ineffective, is it conceived as such a threat to the *polis*? In other words, why does philosophy, in the figure of Plato and an endless line of epigones, go to such lengths to disqualify – or, in Arthur Danto's phrase, to 'disenfranchise' (1986) – art from the serious business of living a life and pursuing a truth?

In Plato's third charge against the poets and painters we get something like an answer to this question. The first charge, as we saw, was based on the epistemological distinction between the inferior world of sense-experience and the superior world of Forms. His third charge is based on the analogous and related distinction between the lower, affective function of the soul and its higher, rational function. The flaw in poetry, and the source of its dangerous power, is that it appeals only to this lower function of the soul: it operates through sense-experience and speaks only to that part of the soul for which the stick in water really is bent and doesn't just appear to be bent. Representational art is, therefore, 'an inferior child born of inferior parents' (*Republic*, 603b). The danger of such art is that these spurious representations are conveyed to the weaker part of the soul in the most powerful and effective form possible. Employing all the 'natural magic of poetry' (*Republic*, 601b), the poet is capable not only of corrupting the soul of his listeners but, by extension, of undermining the very laws of the state (*Republic*, 607a). Dramatic poetry, in particular, is guilty of encouraging the 'womanish' expression of powerful feelings, as opposed to the manly self-control and moderation that Plato valorizes (*Republic*, 605e). Socrates finally suggests that in the absence of the ideal city, which would exclude such powerful magic, whenever we listen to poetry we should 'recite this argument of ours to ourselves as a charm to prevent us falling under the spell of a childish and vulgar passion' (*Republic*, 608a).

Essentially, what Plato presents us with, therefore, is a schema of the relation between reality and images. It is a schema in which the artist produces images that are pale reflections of an already corrupt reality. These images are, however, all the more effective, and dangerous, for being so far removed from true reality. In fact, so dangerous are they that they must be subjected to the strict control of the philosopher-kings. Underlying this official version of the schema, however, and undermining it, is the apparent acknowledgement that philosophy – the discourse of truth – is also in the business of producing myths and lies which will deceive the citizens. And not only that, but Plato recommends that the philosopher – at least the trainee philosopher – should recite Socrates' arguments as if they were a charm to protect him from the witchcraft which the poet wields; he, in other words, will fight magic with magic.

It is important at this stage to be clear about the kind of disenfranchisement Plato is enforcing here. He is not saying that poetry is powerless and ineffective, and therefore worthless. He is, in fact, saying the opposite. For Plato, poetry is enormously powerful – so powerful that even philosophers (especially Plato himself) must borrow its forms and methods. The problem, however, is that poetry, as a form of mimesis, is epistemologically suspect – it has no access to truth, it is on the side of passion rather than reason. This fact, when combined with its highly seductive and charming magic, makes it a dangerous and potent tool; one which must be limited and controlled. Or, as Heaney might say, one which must be governed.

The second point to bear in mind is that Plato – through the essentially *fictional* character Socrates – acknowledges his own love and admiration for poetry. Adapting the classic, paternalistic school-teacher mode, he seems to be saying 'this banishing of the poets hurts me more than it hurts you'. And so, at the end of the discussion, he makes a kind of peace offering. He says that if the poets can defend their art they will be allowed to remain in the city. But what kind of defence does he want? Well, one on his own terms, of course; one in which the poets would show that poetry is 'not only pleasurable but also a good thing – for political regimes and individual human lives' (*Republic*, 607d). Ultimately, therefore, Plato's condemnation of poetry is of a moral-political nature. Poetry is a charming and powerful, but nefarious, influence which must be severely controlled if the city is to be well-ordered.

Now, what exactly is wrong with this approach to literature? Why would we wish to overturn Platonism? If we adopt the perspective of the poet rather than the philosopher, we can say that there are in effect two major problems. First, as we will see in the following discussion, the mimetic view of poetry, based on Plato's ontology and epistemology, is an inadequate way of understanding what poetry and art do in the world; in other words, the metaphor of the mirror is a misleading image of this relation. Secondly, Plato's ethical condemnation of poetry, and the claim that it must be subjected to the government of reason, could only ever limit and hinder the capacities which poetry possesses. It might help here if we think about the options that Plato leaves open for poetry. If the poets choose to stay within the city, they will have to submit to the government of the philosopher-kings, which is to say that they will be allowed to write only 'hymns to the gods and verses in praise of good men' (*Republic*, 607a). Their only other option, in effect, would be to re-create themselves as ineffective purveyors of pretty, worthless images; that is, to present themselves as being so politically insignificant as to escape the attention of those who govern. Since neither of these options would be a satisfactory choice for a poet such as Heaney, Plato looms as a figure who must, in some way, be dealt with.

Every defence of poetry – from Sir Philip Sidney to Wallace Stevens – is, as Heaney points out, an argument with Plato, and a protest at his removal of the 'special prerogatives or useful influences' that poetry would claim for itself within the city (1996b: 1). There is a significant worry, however, associated with responding to Plato's call for a defence of poetry. Because any defence of poetry which Plato would accept would have to be made in the very terms that Plato uses to disenfranchise poetry in the first place. In his prose writings, Heaney seems to recognize the trap which Plato is setting here, but there are also grounds for suggesting that he is in danger of falling into that trap himself. In a discussion of the Polish poet Zbigniew Herbert, Heaney speculates about what kind of poetry Socrates would have written in the final hours before his death, and goes on to say that Herbert's oeuvre itself 'resemble[s] what a twentieth-century poetic version of the examined life might be' (1989: 54). These poems are by no means simply 'hymns to the gods and verses in praise of good men', and yet Heaney thinks that Plato may have been impressed enough to have allowed him into the Republic as poet laureate. It is as if he imagines that Herbert's genuine concern for the well-being of the city will melt Plato's heart and make him reconsider the poets' exile. Heaney, however, recognizes that Herbert himself would never have trusted such an offer (1989: 69), and he therefore seems to recognize the trap.

Nonetheless, there are times when we might suspect that Heaney himself walks right into it. On one occasion, for example, he goes so far as to suggest that poetry relates to the world of social and political conditions *through* Plato's ideal forms; and that it is these forms which provide the 'court of appeal' through which poetry tries to redress a wrong or correct an imbalance (1996b: 1). While this suggestion is passed over in one sentence, and may simply function as Heaney's own olive branch extended to Plato (in response to Plato's final peace offering to the poets), it does give rise to a worry about the difficulty of actually escaping from Platonism. However, Heaney's confrontation with Platonism cannot be so easily pinned down to one such formula. Rather than accepting the terms of Plato's schema, in fact, we could say that his thought mirrors the ambiguities and complexities of Plato, not in the form of a representation or an imitation of them, but as an *agon*, a struggle, a kind of wrestling match which counters the moves that Plato makes. So, if Plato is saying that poetry can only be allowed a minor role within the city, the problem for Heaney is how to counter this assertion without abandoning the idea that poetry must remain its own, independent reality. In other words, he must construct his own defence of poetry in terms that both relate to the anxieties of the modern poet and respond to the judgements of the ancient philosopher.

## The Weight of Imagination

Heaney is a writer who lives in the tension between opposing claims on the poet's tongue, and opposing evaluations of its capacity to act in the world. The two contrary truths that drive Heaney, and that he tries to hold in a productive balance, are that, on the one hand, 'the efficacy of poetry is nil – no lyric has ever stopped a tank', and on the other hand, its efficacy is 'unlimited' (1989: 107). This is particularly clear, for example, in his collection *The Spirit Level*,[10] in which he explores the relation between poetry and the world and attempts to find a balance between them that would allow each their own weight. This collection was published in 1996, at a time when it began to seem possible that the Northern Ireland 'Troubles' would be resolved by political means. Perhaps more so than in his earlier collections, therefore, Heaney's poetry is here imbued with a certain optimism that a balance can be achieved, not only in the political sphere, but also between the spheres of poetry and the world. Heaney's contribution to this task is to engage in a subtle and complex investigation of the very nature of weight, counter-weight and balance. In 'Weighing In', for example, Heaney shows us how a '56lb. weight', 'the immovable/ Stamp and squat and square root of dead weight' can, if it is balanced against an equal weight, be transformed into a thing which trembles and flows 'with give and take'. But weighing in is also what one does before a fight, and Heaney is not afraid to say that sometimes balance can only be restored if we 'refuse the other cheek'; sometimes 'only foul play cleans the slate'. To achieve balance, to clean the slate, is a difficult task however, one that Heaney associates in this poem with a world that is higher than this one in which we live. The old morality of 'Peace on earth, men of good will, all that' can only be maintained, he suggests:

> . . . as long as the balance holds,
> The scales ride steady and the angels' strain
> Prolongs itself at an unearthly pitch.

However, Heaney is not the sort of poet who will call on some *deus ex machina* to restore human harmony, and he knows that we cannot depend on the angels to assure our peace. In fact, in Heaney's world, even the very idea of the pursuit of balance itself can be dismissed as a fool's errand. In the poem 'The Errand', the poet as child recognizes the absurdity of the errand and stands his ground against the adult's joke:

'On you go now! Run, son, like the devil
And tell your mother to try
To find me a bubble for the spirit level
And a new knot for this tie.'

But still he was glad, I know, when I stood my ground,
Putting it up to him
With a smile that trumped his smile and his fool's errand,
Waiting for the next move in the game.

To find a bubble for a spirit level is indeed an absurdity and yet, in a sense,
that is exactly what Heaney as a poet is looking for. The bubble is itself, literally,
nothing and yet it indicates when a balance, an evenness, has been achieved. In
its infinite lightness it hovers between opposing forces, knowing when they are
in equilibrium. So, Heaney the child may have trumped the man's joke with his
knowing smile, but he also knows there will be more moves in the game, moves
which will come as he takes on the mantle of poet and public figure.

Heaney is well aware that for him, as a poet, balance is always precarious. The
lyric poet, in particular, enjoys the unconstrained exercise of the tongue, but
he or she must balance this against the demands of 'the beggar at the gate'. If
the poet is traditionally the member of the community who accedes to a higher
level of reality, then Heaney, as a poet who stands his ground, has the difficult
task of bridging these two worlds. The poem 'Poet's Chair' directly addresses
the complexities of these demands as the poet tries to negotiate between flights
of imagination and the contrary pull of gravity and earth. Ultimately, however,
what Heaney will assert is the weight of the imagination itself; a weight which
counter-balances and compensates for the weight of the world. The chair in
'Poet's Chair' is, in fact, a sculpture[11] which Heaney describes as follows:

On the *qui vive* all the time, its four legs land
On their feet – catsfoot, goatfoot, big soft splay-foot too;
Its straight back sprouts two bronze and leafy saplings.
Every flibbertigibbet in the town,
Old birds and boozers, late night pissers, kissers,
All have a go at sitting on it some time.
It's the way the air behind them's winged and full,
The way a graft has seized their shoulder-blades
That makes them happy. Once out of nature,
They're going to come back in leaf and bloom
And angel step. Or something like that. *Leaves*
*On a bloody chair! Would you believe it?*

The chair seems, like poetry itself, to be a mediator between sky and earth,
firmly planted on its feet, but sprouting saplings too. And, on the *qui vive*, it

watches out for the late-night passers-by who, like the poet, enjoy 'the way the air behind them's winged and full'. But the poet is obliged, not only to share this chair with the 'old birds and boozers', but also to share his tongue with the voice which says 'Leaves/ On a bloody chair! Would you believe it?'. For Heaney, the Keatsian and Yeatsian dream of leaving nature for the immortality of art is a closed possibility.[12] What, then, can the lyric poet do? At the end of the poem we find the poet, again as a child, sitting in the middle of a field watching his father plough. Already, however, he is full of a particular knowledge relating to his craft:

> . . . I am all foreknowledge.
> Of the poem as a ploughshare that turns time
> Up and over. Of the chair in leaf
> The fairy thorn is entering for the future.
> Of being here for good in every sense.

The poet insists on remaining, 'for good', in the middle of a newly ploughed field, firmly grounded on the earth. We can see this groundedness as a self-imposed condition for his sitting in the poet's chair, as his way of balancing the contrary pull of earth and sky. And once again the flight of imagination, the growth of the fairy thorn, will only be allowed if the poet's words can also be a force 'for good in every sense'. Only in this way, for Heaney, can the characteristic anxiety of the modern lyric poet be assuaged.

At the end of another poem, 'The Swing', a similar balance is indicated. The swing is just a rope strung up in the shed with 'an old lopsided sack in the loop of it' and yet, like poetry, it is a 'lure let down to tempt the soul to rise'. In spite of how the children 'favoured the earthbound', represented here by their mother, and in spite of the exertion required to get the swing going 'sky high', it is still chosen:

> So who were we to want to hang back there
> In spite of all?
>                    In spite of all, we sailed
> Beyond ourselves and over and above
> The rafters aching in our shoulderblades,
> The give and take of branches in our arms.

What is this aching that is associated with flight? We have already seen, in 'Poet's Chair', that the passers-by are captivated by 'the way a graft has seized their shoulder-blades'.[13] This graft, which is no doubt painful, is also echoed in the poem 'St Kevin and the Blackbird'. Here Heaney draws on a traditional story about Saint Kevin which tells that his monk's cell was too small to allow him to pray with outstretched arms, so he used to put one arm out the window.

However, one day, as he is praying, a blackbird nests in his palm and Kevin has to stay kneeling silently 'Until the young are hatched and fledged and flown'. One of the things Heaney focuses on in this story is the way that Kevin's arm, which is initially 'stiff/ As a crossbeam', must become living and fluid, 'Like a branch', in order to provide a home for the bird. And Heaney also asks about Kevin's pain in this transformation: 'Which is he?/ Self-forgetful or in agony all the time/ From the neck on out down through his hurting fore-arms?' This is a pain which the children in 'The Swing' also feel, this aching of 'The give and take of branches' in their arms. It would seem, then, that both the power of flight and the power to maintain a 'give and take' bring with them a character-istic pain.

If we return to 'Poet's Chair', we will see yet another instance of this ache. Between the stanza describing the chair, and that describing the young poet watching his father plough, there is a section which introduces a new figure of mediation, and perhaps balance: the philosopher as poet. Now, Heaney imag-ines Socrates sitting in the same poet's chair, discoursing 'in bright sunlight' with his friends, while awaiting his own execution:[14]

> . . . Socrates
> At the centre of the city and the day
> Has proved the soul immortal. The bronze leaves
> Cannot believe their ears, it is so silent.
> Soon Crito will have to close his eyes and mouth,
> But for the moment everything's an ache
> Deferred, foreknown, imagined and most real.

The first question to ask here is, why does Socrates sit in the poet's chair? In what sense do he, Plato and Heaney share the same seat? Perhaps Heaney is here referring to the story Plato tells: that between his death sentence and his execution, Socrates began to write poetry just in case that was what the god had wanted of him all along.[15] No doubt he is also alluding to the fact that Plato, who gives us this account of the event, was himself a writer of great poetic power. But more importantly, Heaney is making a link between philosophy and poetry, between the proof of the soul's immortality and the craft of the poet, and also between poetry and the life of the city. Socrates, sitting in bright sunlight, at the heart of the city, has proven something that even the bronze leaves on the chair find astonishing. And this proof is, we might say, poetic both because Socrates speaks from the poet's chair, and also because of its association with that which is 'Deferred, foreknown, imagined and most real'. This kind of knowledge, or certainty, is not of the same order as our other certainties, and one of its char-acteristic features is precisely this 'ache' which accompanies it. In this case, the ache is partly the pain felt by Socrates as the hemlock does its work, but it is also the ache of a deferred flight and the knowledge of an imagined future.

Later in the poem, when the child is sitting in the ploughed field, he too will be full of this kind of foreknowledge; knowledge of the power of poetry, in this case, to turn time up and over. The idea that a poem can effect a kind of excavation had already appeared in the very first poem in Heaney's first published collection, 'Digging' (Heaney, 1991). In that poem, the young Heaney reflects on how both his father and grandfather were expert diggers (of potatoes and turf, respectively). He, however, has 'no spade to follow men like them' and so he will dig with his poems instead: 'Between my finger and my thumb/ The squat pen rests./ I'll dig with it.' At this early stage, there is little indication of what kind of digging the pen can effect, apart from uncovering the personal development of the poet. The later poem suggests, however, that the excavation of the past is now to be carried out in the service of a collective future; a future which may be imagined but is, nonetheless, most real. And it is this capacity to imagine a future which is one of the things that gives poetry its importance in political life.[16] Against the voices which would say 'Leaves on a bloody chair! Would you believe it?', and against the poet's own anxiety, therefore, Heaney now wants to affirm both the independent value and the socio-political importance of poetry. And so, in this poem, the philosopher-poet sits at the centre of the city, in bright sunlight, engaging in discourse with any passers-by, and almost casually proves the immortality of the soul, before going quietly to his own death. In the same way, the young poet watches his father ploughing, secure in his foreknowledge that his own ploughshare (poetry) can make just as important a contribution to the future good.

The kind of balance which can be achieved in a poem, however, is not quite enough to satisfy Heaney and to allay his anxiety. So, at the same time as he has been working through these tensions poetically, he has used his prose writings of the last three decades to develop a detailed defence of poetry that responds to and counters Plato's schema.[17] Summarizing, we can say that his position comprises the following three elements. First, poetry is a special form of language which must not be governed by any extraneous demands, no matter how politically or morally justified. 'The fact is that poetry is its own reality and no matter how much a poet may concede to the corrective measures of social, moral, political and historical reality, the ultimate fidelity must be to the demands and promise of the artistic event' (1989: 101).

However, it is the nature of this event – a form of 'release' (1989: xxii) – that allows us to say, secondly, that such autonomously created poetry is paradoxically the most capable of having an effect on society. The achievement of a poem is, initially for the poet, an experience of release: in a poem, 'a plane is – fleetingly – established where the poet is intensified in his being and freed from his predicaments. The tongue, governed for so long in the social sphere by considerations of tact and fidelity, by nice obeisances to one's origin within the minority or the majority, this tongue is suddenly ungoverned' (1989: xxii). This idea, that a poem opens up a plane on which an increased intensity and freedom are possible, is one that we will find later is echoed in some of Deleuze's ideas about the power of literary language. The potential of this experience of release is not confined to the poet, however; now the poem, having gained access to a 'condition that is unconstrained', is free to act in its own 'not necessarily inefficacious' way in the world (1989: xxii).

But how is the poem to do this? The third element of Heaney's defence is to argue that poetry gives body and weight to the imagination, a weight which can counter-balance and push back against the weight of the everyday world in which we live. Heaney develops the idea of the 'redress of poetry' to capture this capacity of a redressed poetry to assist in redressing the imbalances of the social world. He appeals to Wallace Stevens' assessment of poetry as 'the imagination pressing back against the pressure of reality' (1996b: 1), and combines this with Simone Weil's principle that it is our moral and political duty to 'add weight to the lighter scale' (1996b: 3). He concludes that the particular power of the poet is to use the imagination in order to redress the imbalances in social and individual reality. The imagined reality will itself have weight, 'because it is imagined within the gravitational pull of the actual and can therefore hold its own and balance out against the historical situation' (1996b: 3–4). Overall, therefore, it is only when poetry is redressed, or restored, in its autonomy within our everyday use of language, that it can be of service to 'programmes of cultural and political realignment' (1996b: 15).

What finally emerges is an account in which poetry, and art in general, are seen as presenting a sketch of a possible world. Contrary to Plato, Heaney insists that art is not 'an inferior reflection of some ordained heavenly system', it is not a pale distorting imitation of the world of Forms (1989: 94). In what he calls, perhaps misleadingly, a 'revision of the Platonic schema', Heaney characterizes poetry instead as 'a rehearsal' of that heavenly system 'in earthly terms' (ibid.). And this is precisely what gives poetry its power – its 'governing power': the fact that it can 'hold in a single thought reality and justice' and yet do so in a way which is neither 'supplicatory nor transitive' (1989: 108). Poetry, on this account, brings our everyday world together with an imagined world; an imagined world which, if it has been given sufficient weight and solidity by the poet, is capable of acting as a corrective pressure on the world in which we live. Poetry would now constitute, not an image or a reflection of the world, but a 'threshold', one which reader and writer constantly approach and constantly depart from (ibid.). The approaching of this threshold is the event that poetry makes possible; because a poem, as Heaney points out, is indeed 'an event . . . not the record of an event' (1989: 129).[18]

We can, therefore, consider Heaney's entire oeuvre, both poetry and prose, as an anti-Platonist defence of poetry. Heaney rejects the ontological and epistemological basis of Plato's assessment of poetry – the claim that poetry is a fundamentally unreal reflection that knows nothing about the world. Likewise, he rejects Plato's moral/political condemnation of poetry as a dangerous influence on society. So, when Plato says that poetry is an imitation of a copy of a model (the Idea), Heaney responds that poetry is neither a copy nor a model – it is 'its own reality' (1989: 101). And, when Plato says that poetry must either obey or be exiled from the city (and therefore be excluded from political life), Heaney responds that poetry should accept neither obeisance nor exile. The poet's tongue must be free to speak and intervene in the political life of the city in its own way. But Heaney, as we would expect, wishes to carry out this defence in a balanced way. Hence, against the Plato who would deny the political and social prerogatives of poetry, he insists on the capacity of poetry to contribute to the political life of a community. But, on the other hand, against the simple-minded propagandists, he insists on the inherent autonomy of poetry – as an event which cannot be subjected to the needs of a political programme.

Similarly, on the question, raised by Plato, of the separation between poetry and reality, he seems to want to answer both 'yes' and 'no' – that the poetic illusion is both its own separate reality, and also a part of the concrete world in which it is produced. On the one hand, we might suspect that he has preserved the dualisms of the Platonist schema, while reversing the value judgement that Plato makes about poetry. On the other hand, however, there are themes in Heaney's exploration of poetry which provide a basis for undermining that schema: themes such as the counter-balancing weight of the imagination, and the idea that poetry is capable of an excavation which can have an effect at the level of a culture. While Heaney is undeniably admirable in wrestling with this Platonic schema, therefore, his struggle also shows the dangers and difficulties that face any such strategy.

In spite of any such worries, however, we can say that in his poetry itself Heaney has already put into practice an effective overturning of Platonism. Once the model-copy distinction is rejected, then the very basis of the idea of art as imitation has disappeared. The mimetic model for understanding art is, as we saw in Plato, most conveniently encapsulated in the metaphor of the mirror. By maintaining a fundamental distinction between models and copies, the primary effect of this mirror is to establish a barrier between the work of literature and the world. Its aim, in fact, is to block literature from having an impact on the world – in order to preserve that privilege for philosophy. Philosophy, according to Plato, will govern the world – not the poet. And, of course, philosophy will govern the poet too. Hence, to overturn Platonism in this field would mean neither moving to the other side of the mirror, nor allowing the poet to govern, but in fact destroying the mirror. And this, in effect, is what Heaney manages to do in his work. By rejecting the Platonist schema, he can insist that literature is neither a distorted image of the world, nor a nefarious influence on the life of the city. He shows us how we can conceptualize literature as a form of language which is on a par with the world in which we live, and is therefore capable of a direct engagement with that world. However, not only is it capable of such action, but contrary to Plato's fears we can say that its interventions are of positive value. Plato wishes to govern the poet's tongue in the interests of his vision of social order, but such government can only ever stifle and distort. As Clytemnestra's watchman, in Heaney's poem 'Mycenae Lookout', says:

> And then the ox would lurch against the gong
> And deaden it and I would feel my tongue
> Like the dropped gangplank of a cattle truck,
> Trampled and rattled, running piss and muck . . .

Dare we say that the governed tongue is constrained to talk bullshit? And what of the ungoverned tongue? Its value is not that it reflects, either accurately or distortedly, the world in which we live. Rather, it creates a world, or an order of reality, which exists alongside our everyday world and maintains a complex set of relations with it. Some of these relations are those that Heaney describes as pressing back against reality, adding to the lighter side, and so on. But, there is no need to give an ontological priority to our everyday reality; we can simply say that the imagined world created by poetry, thanks to its ungoverned nature, is capable of having an effect in another order of reality. And this effect is something that we can think of as an effective intervention, one which is capable of leaving our everyday world changed – even if only in infinitesimally small ways.

## Turning Time Up and Over

Now, in order to demonstrate this potential, I want to give a detailed reading of one final poem from *The Spirit Level* – 'Damson'.[19] This is a poem in which Heaney attempts to 'turn time up and over', by representing the conflict in Northern Ireland partly in terms of Greek mythology. And, as we will see, this turning over may also be seen as an overturning of, amongst other things, Platonism.

### Damson
Gules and cement dust. A matte tacky blood
On the bricklayer's knuckles, like the damson stain
That seeped through his packed lunch.
                                        A full hod stood
Against the mortared wall, his big bright trowel
In his left hand (for once) was pointing down
As he marvelled at his right, held high and raw;
King of the castle, scaffold-stepper, shown
Bleeding to the world.
                                        Wound that I saw
In glutinous colour fifty years ago –
Damson as omen, weird, a dream to read –

Is weeping with the held-at-arm's-length dead
From everywhere and nowhere, here and now.

*

Over and over, the slur, the scrape and mix
As he trowelled and retrowelled and laid down
Courses of glum mortar. Then the bricks
Jiggled and settled, tocked and tapped in line.
I loved especially the trowel's shine,
Its edge and apex always coming clean
And brightening itself by mucking in.
It looked light but felt heavy like a weapon,
Yet when he lifted it there was no strain.
It was all point and skim and float and glisten
Until he washed and lapped it tight in sacking
Like a cult blade that had to be kept hidden.

*

Ghosts with their tongues out for a lick of blood
Are crowding up the ladder, all unhealed,
And some of them still rigged in bloody gear.
Drive them back to the doorstep or the road
Where they lay in their own blood once, in the hot
Nausea and last gasp of dear life.
Trowel-wielder, woundie, drive them off
Like Odysseus in Hades lashing out
With his sword that dug the trench and cut the throat
Of the sacrificial lamb.
                              But not like him –
Builder, not sacker, your shield the mortar board –
Drive them back to the wine-dark taste of home,
The smell of damsons simmering in a pot,
Jam ladled thick and steaming down the sunlight.

This poem was written in the context of the apparently endless cycle of sectarian violence which plagued Northern Ireland from the late 1960s to the late 1990s. It is a product of Heaney's sense that in such a society a poet must *do* something: but the question is what, and how? What can a poet do in the face of the curse of violence which runs through society like the red stain of a damson? The path Heaney chooses is to address that red stain directly and to try to modify our experience of it. In this poem, the damson is at once symbol of blood, in all its murderous implications, and carrier of domestic comfort – the bricklayer's packed lunch, and the hot jam simmering in a pot. The first word of the poem, 'gules', casts forward to the ghouls who appear later in the poem, but is also the ancient term for the colour red on heraldic devices. It is at the same time the red mouth (from the French *gueule*) of the ghosts, the cut throat of the sacrificial lamb, and the red hand of Ulster.[20] Blood, however, is not only a symbol of death, it also represents life. As with many other poems in this collection, Heaney here mobilizes a set of opposites which he attempts to balance in their apparent contradictoriness. The trowel is made clean by 'mucking in', it looks light but feels heavy, it glistens and yet must be hidden like a 'cult blade'. The bricklayer, whose wound is 'shown/ Bleeding to the world', hovers between builder and sacker of cities; he is both 'King of the castle' and 'woundie'. What all this imagery of blood leads to, is the figure of the bricklayer, pursued by ghosts hungry for a 'lick of blood', in which Heaney dramatizes the perennial problem of how the living should respond to the claims which are made on them by the dead. Like vampires risen from the grave, these ghosts, victims of sectarian violence, rise up from the doorways and streets where they had lain in their own blood, and demand the blood of others. The question posed by the poem is, how should we respond to this demand? And, more particularly, how should we break this cycle?

On the one hand we are presented with the example of Odysseus in Hades, lashing out at the dead with his sword. In Homer's *Odyssey*, Odysseus visits Hades and makes a sacrifice of a lamb to attract the dead with the smell of blood. Any that are allowed to drink the blood can speak to him, but the others he drives away with his sword. Heaney takes this story and re-works it for his own ends. The wandering warrior, sacker of Troy, destroyer of civilizations, is transformed into the wounded bricklayer, protected by the 'mortar board' of his trade (and also, perhaps, of learning). The opposition between that terrible, mythic vision of the dead pursuing the living, and the domestic vision of the jam, is mediated here by the Homeric adjective 'wine-dark'. But in this case Homer's wine-dark sea (on which Odysseus is lost and tossed), becomes the 'wine-dark taste of home'.

This transformation, which is striking in its sensuality, is central to the effect the poem makes possible. Throughout the poem our senses are directly engaged by the world the poet presents to us. We feel the 'matte, tacky blood' that is mixed with cement dust; we see the wound from fifty years ago in 'glutinous colour'; we hear 'the slur, the scrape and mix' of the mortar being laid on; we taste and smell the rich red damson jam. Clearly the poem doesn't attempt to convince us of anything through a rational argument. Rather, it plays with a sequence of images which, in their sensual richness, strive to effect a transformation in our relation to the stain of violence. It gives us the image of the wounded bricklayer, his blood mixed with cement dust, battling not only with the ghosts of the dead, but also with the ghost of Odysseus, who had seemed to offer a solution. The path the poet suggests for this wounded champion is to lead the dead home; to break the cycle of violence by, literally, laying them to rest, giving them their due – thick damson jam instead of matte, tacky blood. In the end, however, we have to say that it isn't the brick-layer who is driving the dead back: rather, it is the poet. He is the one who gives us the image of the wine-dark taste of home; he is the one who ladles the thick jam 'steaming down the sunlight'; and he is the one who makes it possible for us to modify our relation to this stain.

But, a sceptic may ask, isn't it true that all of this can be said about the poem without mentioning Heaney's attempt to overturn Platonism? After all, one could hardly claim that the philosophy of literature is one of Heaney's central concerns. So, what value is there in this approach? What does it add to any reading of this poem? Let me start by saying that in this poem – as in many of the poems in this collection – Heaney is wrestling with a set of apparently irreconcilable oppositions within himself. He is doing this, we might say, in order to carry out a test on himself; but also to allow others to carry out this same test on themselves through their reading. The test, or the challenge, of the poem is to see if it is possible to think otherwise; that is, to experience the world, the world of blood, violence and jam, otherwise. The poem should not be seen primarily as an expression of a personal experience, or a personal world-view – rather, it is an attempt to re-make experience at an individual level which aspires to make something possible at the collective level. It comprises, for example, a re-making of the classical heritage which is a part of the Western experience; and an attempt to re-make the experience of the poet's own community in Northern Ireland. It cannot be understood in Platonist terms, therefore, because, despite all of Heaney's anxiety about the place of poetry in the world, he has already effected an overturning of Platonism. From the perspective of the reader, I would say that what this poem makes possible, or makes more likely, is a re-thinking of the given realities of inter-communal conflict. This re-thinking is not just a matter of thought as it is narrowly understood. It is a product of the reader's active involvement in the total, sensual experience of the poem; an engagement which exposes the reader to an imagined, but most real, world. And out of this encounter may come a modification of some of the elements that make up the reader's experience – elements which, in this case, might include: the reader's ideas of justice and retribution; their sense of themselves as belonging to a political community; or, to be mundane, the way they see and taste damson jam.

However, there is one final worry. Isn't it true that all we have done is to construct another defence of poetry; one which like all the others accepts Plato's challenge and answers it, ultimately, on his terms? In other words, isn't it true that we have simply argued, on non-Platonist grounds, for the conclusion that poetry is indeed 'not only pleasurable but also a good thing – for political regimes and individual human lives' (*Republic*, 607d)? If this is all we have done, then I can't suggest that the attempt to overturn Platonism is any more effective than the choice to simply embrace Plato's schema. In reply to this worry, however, I would say first of all that we have by no means shown that the value of poetry is positive for 'political regimes'. In fact, it is more than likely that the power of poetry to intervene in the everyday world would bring it into conflict with any political regime; or at the very least we can insist that political regimes can have no guarantee that poetry will benefit them. Secondly, at a more funda-mental level, I think we can say that this approach makes an effective break with Platonism because of the view of art and literature which it makes possible. Because now, if we want to cling to Plato's metaphor of the mirror, we would have to say that the mirror itself is capable of modifying – in their own reality – the things it reflects. Plato senses this, and would like to subject the poet to the government of the philosopher. But Heaney knows, and this is what we can learn from him, that the attempt to govern the poet's tongue will jeopardize any hope that poetry has, not of reaching an illusory world of images, but of making an effective difference in this world in which we live. And ultimately that is a power which is recognized not only by Heaney, but also by his old school friend and even by Plato – who was, after all, philosophy's first anti-Platonist.

# Chapter 3

# Foucault's Turn from Literature

Our examination of Heaney's poetry and thought has led us to the idea that what is important about literature is not that it offers us reflections of our world, but that in some sense it shapes our world; and this idea is one that inevitably moves us beyond a Platonist conception of aesthetics. In 1964, in an article linking the early-twentieth-century writer Raymond Roussel with avant-garde writers of the 1950s, Foucault formulates a similar anti-Platonist conception of the relation between language and the world. The value of descriptive language, he says, doesn't lie in its fidelity to the object, or in its ability to accurately reflect the world. Instead of following and translating perceptions, language in fact opens up a path for our subsequent perceptions. In other words, it lays down a track for our experience of the world. And it is only then, when language has intervened, that 'things begin to shimmer for themselves, forgetting that they had first been "spoken"' (1964a: [422]). This article is one among very many from the time, in which Foucault explored the intricacies (linguistic, philosophical and aesthetic) of contemporary French avant-garde literature. And readers who are familiar with this body of work might naturally assume that a book on the subject of 'Foucault and fiction' would focus primarily on these literary essays. In this book, however, my focus is on Foucault's later work, because I think it is there that we will find the conceptual tools necessary to understanding the transformative potential of literature. Nevertheless, it is also necessary, now, to investigate Foucault's engagement with literature in his work from the 1960s. My interest here is twofold: first, to see what resources that work gives us for understanding literature *per se*; and, second, to consider the implications, for my project, of the fact that at the end of the 1960s Foucault turned away from literature in a way that suggests he began to see it as having little political or ethical significance. Ultimately, what I want to do here is to begin to formulate an approach to literature that pushes Foucault's thought in directions which he perhaps envisaged, but never pursued; but I also want to draw upon earlier strands in his work which he himself abandoned.[1]

During the 1960s, at a time when he was writing his major studies of madness, medicine and the forms of modern reason, Foucault was also continuously engaged in an attempt to think through a series of fundamental questions about literature. What powers does it possess? What threat does it pose to our world? And what, precisely, is its relation to language, fiction and transgression? During that time he published many essays in French literary journals, on writers including Rousseau, Flaubert, Bataille, Blanchot and Robbe-Grillet; and he published a full-length study of the novelist Raymond Roussel. In addition, his books of the 1960s include significant discussions of, for example, Cervantes' *Don Quixote* and Diderot's *Rameau's Nephew* – not to mention numerous references, throughout the 1960s, to the works of Sade, Nerval, Holderlin, Borges and Beckett.[2] However, for any student of Foucault today, it would be easy to imagine that Foucault's early fascination with literature and avant-garde writing was a youthful excess which later gave way to his more serious engagement with questions about power, subjectivity and ethics. The standard accounts of Foucault's work, for example, even those written by himself, tell us that in the 1960s his concern was with forms of knowledge in the human sciences, not with the nature of literary language (1984e: 460[632]). Why, then, does literature apparently disappear from Foucault's writings after 1969? And why does Foucault's own re-writing of his theoretical biography elide this earlier interest in literature? In order to answer these questions we will have to find out what role literature played in his early thought. We will have to both identify the form that his interest and attraction initially took, and pinpoint the role these works were made to play in his major histories of that period. What is at stake here, is not just a better understanding of Foucault's thought but, more importantly, the possibility of reviving one of the potential lines of development which that thought cut short as a result of its own endless turning. The question which will emerge, then, is: what is still effective in that early formulation of the powers of literature? First of all, however, we need an overview of the shift we are investigating.

## Re-writing Writing

It should come as no surprise that Foucault, whose entire trajectory involved thinking historically, approaches literature not as a homogenous field which is open to a once-and-for-all definition, but as a form of language which is subject to discontinuities and transformations. Even though his essays on literature are littered with apparent generalizations about all of literature, it is almost always the case that these assertions apply – usually explicitly, but sometimes implicitly – only to a particular strand of modern literature. It is not by chance that, in fact, Foucault's interest in literature in the 1960s focused on those writers who were his contemporaries, or his near-contemporaries, or on writers who were seen by him as being in some way precursors of those contemporaries.[3] Because it was these writers who explored and gave voice to a certain experience that was central to Foucault's thought at this time. Due to its complexity, it is very difficult to capture this experience in a single formulation, but as we will see, it comprised elements including: the dissolution of the subject as guarantor of discourse; the experience of transgression; the relation of language to death; the possibility of coming into contact with an 'outside' of thought; and a heightened sense of the importance of the fictive in language.

In the course of the 1960s, on the basis of this sense of the philosophical and historical importance of a certain kind of writing, Foucault produced a large number of essays which contribute to what he once called an 'ontology' of literature: an account of the powers, the methods and the conditions which give literature its unique potential (1963b: 92[253]). We will look at this ontology in detail below, but for the moment I will outline two of the overriding themes that emerge in these critical writings. The first theme is the shift in the relation between language and the subject: the idea that language takes on a life and a being of its own which is not only independent of the individual who writes, but which actually leads, in some sense, to the dissolution or death of that individual. Throughout this period Foucault is attracted to, and writes about, the many forms of discourse that undermine the conscious, rational subject which he associates with humanism; and one of the key forms which this undermining takes, for him, is modern European literature. This experience of the dissolution of the subject is not, however, confined to works of literature, but also makes itself felt in the philosophical themes of anti-psychologism and the undermining of the autonomous subject – themes which can be found in such disparate thinkers as Nietzsche, Heidegger and the proponents of structuralism. If, at this time, Foucault gives a certain priority to literature as an expression of this dissolution (and, perhaps, a contributing factor), it is because works of literature are closest to what he begins to call the 'being of language' which, he says, is only revealed through the 'disappearance of the subject' (1966b: 149[521]).

The second of the overriding themes that I want to highlight, which superficially appears to be in conflict with the first, is the idea that there is something in the very act of writing itself which gives works of literature their particular effectiveness. Foucault, at this time, was very much a part of the intense theorizing of writing [*écriture*] that took place in the 1960s. He too, like Blanchot, Barthes and many others, had a tendency to focus on the moment of writing, the actual moment when the writer puts marks on a blank page, as the precise source of the act of literature. What this means for his approach to literature is that it might be said to undervalue the processes of involvement between readers and texts, preferring to focus on the relationship between a writer and language – via the page and the traces of ink. While these two themes (de-subjectivized language and the importance of the *writer*) may seem to be in conflict, they come together in the idea that it is the act of writing that puts the writer, as individual, in contact with an experience of the anonymous, subjectless and endless pouring out of language. We will see later that Foucault approaches this experience, as an experience of the outside, in terms of a

disconcerting rushing of language that tears the subject away from him or herself. This experience is important philosophically because of its relation to the
event of the disappearance of the subject; and it is important historically because
it gives access to an outside of thought which, in modernity, tends to be denied
by the dominant forms of reason. We could say that the highpoint of this
engagement with, and valorization of, literature came in 1966 when Foucault
published both *The Order of Things* (1966a, which gave a prominent role to
works of literature and art) and his essay 'The Thought of the Outside' (1966b,
his exploration of the significance of Blanchot's writing for contemporary
thought).

Ten years later, however, Foucault announced in an interview that the 'relentless theorization of writing' in the 1960s was no more than a 'swan song' (1977b:
127[155]). This theorization was, he seems to say, the final death rattle of a particular conception and practice of the writer; the conception according to
which 'great writers' had central political significance by virtue of their connection to universal human values. In the second half of the twentieth century this
figure ceded ground to the 'specific intellectual', the figure whom Foucault
now champions, and indeed embodies. But in the meantime, a last flowering of
the older conception occurred in the work of (unspecified) writers of the 1960s.
However, for Foucault, it is now clear from the fact of their endless search for
theoretical underpinnings (whether in linguistics, semiology or psychoanalysis), and from the fact that they produced such 'mediocre' literary works, that
these writers were struggling against their own disappearance. It is no exaggera-
tion to say that this is an extraordinary *volte-face*. Foucault, who had written so
many essays in praise of the avant-garde writers of the 1950s and 1960s, now
pronounces that their age has finished and that their works were, in any case,
only 'mediocre'. And not only does he make this judgement, but he does so
without any acknowledgement that he himself had played a part in that relentless theorization.

This is not an isolated incident. In another interview from the same period,
he is asked to comment on the place of literary texts in his research. He replies:
'For me literature was something I observed, not something I analyzed or
reduced, or integrated into the very field of analysis. It was a rest, a thought on
the way, a badge, a flag' (1988: 307).[4] Now, while it is true that works of fiction
are not completely integrated into his major histories, it is hard to accept that
they did not play a major role in his early thought – a role which is radically
elided here. In fact, whatever the nature of that early interest might have been,
it is here overlain with a new way of approaching literature – as a product of
institutional sacralization which raises questions, in particular, about the relation between the university and the writer. The approach he would now take to
literature, he says, is not to 'study its internal structures', but to focus on the way
in which, as a field of discourse, it is ordered and limited. When the interviewer
points out that, after all, Foucault had written many essays on literature which

never took this approach, he replies with some difficulty: 'Yes, but . . . [pause] . . . It would be fairly difficult to talk about them' (1988: 311). He goes on to say that really Blanchot, Klossowski and Bataille were important for him not because they produced works of literature *per se*, but because they gave him a way of escaping from a certain form of philosophy. Once again, he is claiming that it was not their 'internal structures' as works of literature that interested him, but their function as 'outside' in relation to his own academic discourse of philosophy: when combined with Nietzsche, they made philosophy permeable for him.

Two questions immediately arise: how and why did this shift in approach to literature come about? And, to what extent can we accept Foucault's re-writing of his own intellectual history? In one of the more thoughtful attempts to understand this turn, Rajchman suggests that towards the end of the 1960s Foucault came to recognize the limitations of focusing on literature and language if one wished to make a thorough investigation of the 'larger politics of subjectivity' (1985: 36).[5] He thus turned away from literature, towards other practices of individualization, such as confession and discipline. While this is undeniable, I would like to avoid any progressivist reading of this shift[6] by focusing instead on the possibility that the force of the earlier engagement with literature can be re-animated, rather than just surpassed.

## The Ontology of Literature

What was the nature and the source of Foucault's earlier interest in literature? We have already seen that this interest focused on certain general themes such as the dissolution of the subject, the unmasterable powers of language, and the transgressive moment of writing. And it emerged principally from his engagement with the writings of Nietzsche, Bataille, Klossowski and Blanchot. In his first important essay on literature (1963a), Foucault explores the modern experience of transgression and the attempt, in the work of Bataille, to give it expression. The significance of this work, for Foucault, is that it connects the event of the death of God, and therefore the death of a certain kind of experience, with the 'breakdown [*effondrement*]' of what he calls the 'philosophical subject' (1963a: 79[242]). This second event, which is 'probably one of the fundamental structures of contemporary thought', has led to an alteration of the relation between the subject and language. As individuals who speak and who write, we are no longer masters of our own words; language has become for us, in an important sense, a non-human phenomenon. This shift in relation leads to the dispersion and multiplication of the subject within language – while, in the realm of philosophy, it leads to the end of the philosopher as 'sovereign and primary form of philosophical language' (1963a: 79[242]). To all those who would try to maintain the integrity of this philosophical subject, Foucault opposes the exemplary case of Bataille (but we, of course, could pose the exemplary case of Foucault) – who continues to 'rupture, in himself, with perseverance, the sovereignty of the philosophising subject' (1963a: 79[243]).[7] What is announced here – in Foucault's writing, but also of course in that of Bataille – is an experience of language as something that exists outside, and independently of, the human subject. And this is an experience which, it must be said, is a liberating one for Foucault; as he says in another context, we have made a 'breakthrough [*une percée*] to a language from which the subject is excluded' (1966b: 149[520]).

But, what is the significance of transgression in this experience, and why is it important for Foucault? The first point to make is that, for Bataille, the modern experience of transgression emerges in the wake of the death of God. After this event we are denied the experience of the Limitless (in the form of God) and so are thrown back upon the limitless reign of the Limit itself. What this means, is that our world is exposed to the constant play of excess which crosses and recrosses this limit in an endless play of transgression. In other words, if it is true that the death of God means that anything is allowed, this means that transgression itself becomes impossible – and yet it cannot, for all that, disappear as an experience which is sought. Bataille, in his linking of spirituality, sexuality and excess, tries to develop a language for this experience – in effect his work constitutes, as Foucault says, a preface to transgression. The second point to make is that for Foucault (and Bataille), contrary to what one might expect, transgression is not essentially a matter of breaking limits. Of course it involves a movement which is hostile to limits, but it cannot be defined simply in terms of a negative or violent assault on limits; it doesn't aim for its own completion in an annihilation of the limit. Rather, the limit and transgression rely on each other in a mutual relation which is positive in nature. In fact transgression, according to Foucault, is a kind of affirmation; an affirmation which has no other content than the existence of difference itself. It is a contentless affirmation, a non-positive affirmation of 'division' (*partage*), which constitutes a 'testing of the limit [*épreuve de la limite*]' (1963a: 74[238]). Foucault links this idea of transgression with Blanchot's idea of *contestation* – which is 'an affirmation that affirms nothing, a radical break of transitivity' (1963a: 75[238]). With the introduction of this idea of contestation, we can see that for Foucault transgression, even at this early stage, can be connected with the much later concept of resistance – a phenomenon which is an inherent part of all power relations. In this thought there is no dream of transgressing limits, and thereby arriving at some norm-less outside; rather there is a practice of testing, resisting and contesting those limits through a continuous cultivation of excess. And for the Foucault of the 1960s, literature is one of the fields in which this excess is most apparent – and important.

In a 1964 discussion with a group of writers from the literary journal *Tel quel* on the question of a 'new' literature,[8] Foucault links his own work with theirs through these ideas of contestation and transgression. In *History of Madness*, for example, he says he had been speaking of 'an experience which was at the same time transgression and contestation', and he notes that this same experience is at the core of the 'poetic experience' (*'son expérience de poète'*) of a writer such as Marcelin Pleynet (1964b: [396]). Expanding on this theme, Foucault points out that just as every culture imposes limits of exclusion and interdiction on itself, so there will always be forces of contestation and transgression: 'So, there is this division and, ceaselessly, the contestation of this division by those who are precisely elements of transgression' (1964b: [398]). In the classical age,[9] the most violently contested division was that between reason and unreason; but now, he says, 'it is in the domain of language that the play of the limit, of contestation, of transgression appears with the most liveliness' (ibid.). Now, it is in the field of poetry and prose that 'the possibility of contestation for our culture' is most at stake (ibid.).

Having established this idea that literature embodies (or, to be more exact, can embody) a certain kind of transgressive contestation, let us now turn back to Foucault's suggestion that he might be able to offer us the elements for sketching its formal ontology. The first point to note about the essay in which he makes this suggestion (1963b), is that the tone is extremely hesitant, suggestive and exploratory: at key moments, it is full of expressions such as 'I wonder', 'It is possible', and 'Perhaps'. We could speculate that this hesitancy is perhaps a function of the mere mention of the idea of an ontology – which is not the kind of task that we expect Foucault to undertake. In any case, Foucault's tentatively proposed hypothesis is that literature is born from a certain use of language as a means of keeping death at bay. The two privileged examples of this are Homer, in whose works the great deeds of heroes live on past their bodily death; and Scheherazade, who uses narrative to endlessly postpone the moment of her own death. Language, in the image Foucault uses, sets up a vertical mirror in the face of death; and in the virtual space between this mirror and death an infinite mirroring and doubling is made possible: 'a murmuring that repeats, recounts, and redoubles itself endlessly' and in which 'our language today is lodged and hidden' (1963b: 91[252]). The existence of this structure is revealed, according to Foucault, at those moments when literary language represents itself in an impossible self-reference. For example, the moment in *The Thousand and One Nights* when, in one of her nightly tales, Scheherazade recounts the story of the thousand and one nights (1963b: 93[254]). It is the study of these moments which, Foucault suggests, may give us the elements of a 'formal ontology of literature' (ibid.). For Foucault, therefore, literary language can be defined in terms of the virtual space that is created when a vertical mirror is set up in the face of death, thus creating the possibility of an infinite murmuring of language; while the non-literary or more straightforwardly communicative use of language is defined as a horizontal conveyance of meaning.

This is a conception of language and its relation to the literary which is most fully explored in Foucault's book on Raymond Roussel (2004a). This book, Foucault says, was his most personal, most pleasurable and most secret work (2004a: 186–7). In it, he took the works of this relatively obscure novelist, poet and playwright from the early twentieth century and subjected them to a reading which attempted to draw out their significance for our understanding of the nature of language. At the core of Roussel's fiction is a fascination with two related aspects of language: that it is an anonymous, inhuman (or supra-human) labyrinth which generates meaning independently of any speaking subject; and that it entertains a far from straightforward relation with the world of things – and with death. In Foucault's words, Roussel's work is unified by a particular anxiety about language and continually returns to, and turns around, a particular vision of its power. On the one hand, Roussel sees language as something that is 'moving toward infinity in the labyrinth of things, but whose marvelous and essential poverty forces it back upon itself by giving it the power of metamorphosis; to say other things with the same words, to give to the same words another meaning' (2004a: 98). This poverty of language is, quite simply, a product of the fact that there are more things in the world than there are words to name them. There is, therefore, a fundamental lack at the heart of language: it 'speaks only from something essential that is lacking' (2004a: 167).

On the other hand it is this lack, this lack of fit between words and things, which makes possible the phenomenon of linguistic play – the fact that 'the same word can designate two different things and the same sentence repeated can have another meaning' (ibid.). And from this lack, also, follows the corresponding power of language to bring the world to light: 'without names to identify them, things would remain in darkness' (ibid.). It is this power, the power to name and bring to light – almost to bring into being – which links language, at a fundamental level, with death. The unbelievably complex 'machines' which Roussel invented, not just the machines which appear in the novels,[10] but the linguistic machines he used to generate sentences, all point in one direction: to the profound relationship that language maintains with death (2004a: 56). It is this relation between language and death, and the corresponding function of literature to keep open and constantly explore this relation, which Foucault characterized as the 'verticality' of literary language.[11]

However, while our use of literary language today may indeed be lodged and hidden within this vertical structure, in Foucault's view there has also been a radical shift in the form of literary language – one that occurred specifically around the end of the eighteenth century. In fact, Foucault's whole approach to literature is based on the premise that a major shift in Western literature – or, to be precise, the birth of what we call literature – occurred some time between the end of the eighteenth and the beginning of the nineteenth century. His various accounts of this shift are not always consistent, but its outlines are clear.[12] Up until this time, he argues, writing was practised as a transparent, communicative instrument that reflected the world; and language and discourse were taken as forming a part of the world. However, in the nineteenth century, with the emergence of writers such as Mallarmé (who is almost always prioritized by Foucault in this regard), there comes an idea of writing as not so much a part of the world, but something outside it, something which could 'constitute the antimatter of the world and counterbalance [*compenser*] the whole universe . . . [something which could] offset it . . . utterly destroy it and scintillate outside it' (1966c: 173[556]). An important part of this process is that a shift occurs in the ethic of writing. Now, according to Foucault, the value of what one writes no longer comes from the ideas one expresses (we could take Dickens or Hugo as nineteenth-century examples of this ethic), but from the very act of writing itself. Now, Foucault says, it is 'in that raw and naked act', the act of writing, that the 'writer's freedom is fully committed at the same time as the counteruniverse of words takes form' (1966c: 173[556]). It follows that now, writing begins to assert itself, he says, 'outside everything which could be said through it' (ibid, modified).

It is debatable, however, whether this means that literature simply falls back on a reflexive, self-referential play of language, a form of language which would be defined by its intransitivity, its fundamental lack of effect. While it is true, for Foucault, that modern literature appears since Mallarmé to be caught within a 'radical intransitivity' (1966a: 327[313]), this may just be a misleading surface impression. It may be more true to say, as Foucault suggests in his essay on Blanchot, that 'In fact, the event that gave rise to what we call "literature" in the strict sense is only superficially an interiorisation; it is far more a question of a passage to the "outside".' Because in literature, that is in modern literature, language escapes the demands of what Foucault here calls 'discourse' – by which he means the demands of a straightforward, mimetic speech, or 'the dynasty of representation' (1966b: 148). Language then, becomes free to get 'as far away from itself as possible', to get 'outside of itself'. In this way, writing becomes – as it was for André Breton – 'a means of pushing man beyond his limits, of forcing him to face the insuperable, of placing him near to what is furthest away from him' (1966c: 172 [555]).

With this idea of the outside we have arrived at one of the core elements in Foucault's approach to literature. In his exploration of this concept Foucault owes an enormous debt to the work of Blanchot; indeed, reading Foucault's major essay on Blanchot and the outside (1966b), it is difficult to tell to what extent it expresses Foucault's own views, and to what extent it is a work of homage (and imitation) of a writer by whom he had been greatly influenced. In particular, it is difficult to say if the many passages and formulations which echo Blanchot's Heideggerian language are a result of this imitation or the expression of a more profound resonance between Heidegger's work and Foucault's own thought at this time.[13] However, putting that question aside, and taking the essay seriously as, nonetheless, an expression of Foucault's thought, what does it tell us about his encounter with literature? Once again, in this essay, we see literature conceived as a form of language that puts the subject (the writing subject and the reading subject) in contact with an 'outside'. This outside, which is set in opposition to the interiority of 'our philosophical reflection and the positivity of our knowledge' (1966b: 150[521]), is an experience that is made possible by the 'breakdown' of subjectivity which we discussed earlier. This breakdown has profoundly altered the relation between the subject and language. We now stand, according to Foucault, 'on the edge of an abyss that had long been invisible'; an abyss which has opened up through the experience of 'a language from which the subject is excluded' (1966b: 149[521]).[14]

Foucault speculates that the first manifestation of this experience may have been with the Christian mystics, who 'prowled the limits [*confins*] of Christianity' for a millennium or more. However, he rejects this suggestion (perhaps unjustly, on the grounds that the mystics ultimately sought a form of interiority), in favour of the idea that it was a different group of outsiders who represent for us 'the first tear through which the thought of the outside came to light' (1966b: 150[521]). This group, unsurprisingly, comprises the very writers who have been at the centre of Foucault's reflection on literature: Sade, Holderlin, Mallarmé, Nietzsche, Bataille, Klossowski, and of course Blanchot. And indeed, Blanchot features here, not just as one member of the list, but as the writer who, more than anybody else, has sought to give a form to the thought of the outside. In the same way that Bataille, as we saw, gives us a 'preface' to transgression, so Blanchot now is the one who, for Foucault, has actually become the thought of the outside itself. In words that only a disciple could write, Foucault describes Blanchot as 'the real presence, absolutely distant, shimmering, invisible, the necessary destiny, the inevitable law, the calm, infinite, measured strength of this very thought' (1966b: 151[523], modified).

Foucault, however, willingly admits that the outside constitutes a problem for our thinking – and, in fact, the whole task he sets himself in this essay is to elucidate, or rather to point towards, a form of language which would be faithful to this thought. Any such language would have to avoid the pitfalls of both a reflexive discourse, which would turn this experience back towards an interiority, and a fictional discourse that would 'stitch the old fabric of interiority back together in the form of an imagined outside' (1966b: 152[523]). How, then, are we to speak adequately of this experience? Foucault suggests that Blanchot – in his critical-theoretical writings – moves towards such a faithful speech by converting reflexive language; by, literally, turning it around towards the dispersal and fragmentation of the outside. This language must be directed, according to Foucault, 'not toward any inner confirmation – not toward a kind of central, unshakeable certitude – but toward an outer extremity where it must continually be in contestation with itself' (1966b: 152[523]).[15] One might complain that this formulation still remains too much on the side of obscurity, and yet a certain clarity has emerged. We once again find the themes of dispersal, extremity and contestation, all associated with the idea that language – for 'us' – escapes the mastery of the speaking subject, in fact never was subject to that mastery in the first place. What Blanchot's writing uncovers, for Foucault, is this alien being of language, its constant 'streaming' (*ruisellement*), its pure precedence in relation to any speech or silence. This, in short, is 'a language spoken by no one', a language without a subject ('any subject it may have is no more than a grammatical fold' (1966b: 166[537])),[16] a language which comes to us from the outside and which is, occasionally, made known to us by way of literary works.

To think, or to give expression to the outside, is therefore to be open to an experience of that which is alien to the centred, rational subject. In Blanchot's writing, this outside makes itself felt in a certain experience of language: an experience of language as that which escapes the control, or even the comprehension, of the speaking and writing subject, language which de-centres and undermines the subject of knowledge, the subject which says 'I'. While for Blanchot this experience comes from and through a literary use of language, we must remember that for Foucault, even during the 1960s, the category of the outside has a much broader significance. In his work on the history of madness, for example, he traces the constitution of unreason as that which is outside Western rationality; while in *The Order of Things*, he speaks of the force by which thought will 'contrive to escape itself' through an encounter with that which functions as its outside (1966a: 56[64]). The outside is, therefore, not an absolute outside, but is always relative to the limits which a particular culture imposes. While for Blanchot we are opened up to this outside through works of literary fiction, for Foucault it is fiction, in a much broader sense, that offers a mode of access to this strange and foreign element.

In his later career Foucault began to explicitly refer to fiction as much more than a category of literary production. Indeed in the 1970s, perhaps in response to the attacks of professional historians, he came to describe his major books – *History of Madness, Discipline and Punish, The History of Sexuality* – precisely as fictions; that is, as works which both create and transform an experience and a reality. 'I am well aware,' Foucault says, 'that I have never written anything but fictions' (1977a: 193[236]). But fiction, in this sense, is as much a verb as a noun: 'One "fictions" history,' he says, 'on the basis of a political reality that makes it true, one "fictions" a politics not yet in existence on the basis of a historical truth' (ibid.). In the 1960s, however, most of these books were still to be written and Foucault's use of the idea of fiction was still largely focused on works of literature. In the essays from this period, we see the term being used primarily as a shorthand to indicate literature – or, more specifically, to indicate prose as opposed to poetry. However, there are two essays in particular where he engages in a more sustained reflection on the nature of fiction and the fictive. The first of these is a discussion of the relation between Alain Robbe-Grillet and a group of writers from the *Tel quel* group, such as Sollers and

Pleynet; while the second is an essay on the work of Jules Verne.[17] The striking thing about these two essays is that the term fiction is, at first sight, being used in a very different way in each of them. Let's look at the later essay first.

In this essay on Jules Verne, from 1966, Foucault uses the term 'fiction' to designate the narrative system, as opposed to the narrated events (the 'fable'), of any tale. Fiction is here defined as that which lies behind the events recounted (*'l'arrière-fable'*), and as that which structures them as narrative: comprising, for example, 'the narrator's stance toward what he is relating . . . the presence or absence of a neutral gaze that surveys things and people . . . an involvement of the whole narrative in the perspective of one character or several in succession or none in particular' (1966d: 137[506]). There are many possible ways in which fiction, in this sense, can operate, and Foucault points out that at any given time only a few of these modes are likely to be in use. It would be true to say, for instance, that the fictional mode which mobilizes an omniscient and judgemental narrator, which was dominant in the eighteenth century and survived into the nineteenth, has since been displaced; while today, the emergence of new modes of fiction (which mobilize a whole range of discursive modes, including a subject-less neutral language) has made it possible to read, 'according to their own architecture', a range of texts that had been excluded from literature. It is not clear if Foucault considers the work of Jules Verne to be in this category of excluded literature, but he singles him out as a writer whose narratives are 'wonderfully full of these discontinuities in the fictional mode' (1966d: 138[507]), and his essay explores key aspects of this plurality.[18]

In the earlier essay, from 1963, on the *Tel quel* group, Foucault approaches the notion of fiction in a very different and, I would say, more profound way. He also approaches it with trepidation and, he says, 'not without a little fear'. He distrusts this term, which is at the same time 'so heavy and so slim', because it carries with it associations of psychology ('imagination, fantasm, dream, invention'), and also because it can be so easily reduced to an opposition between the real and the unreal, reality and the imaginary (1963c: 279). He urges us instead to think of the fictive as arising from a certain kind of distance – not the distance between language and things, but a distance within language itself. This is the distance which makes possible the coming into presence of things through the 'simulacrum' of language. Most forms of language, of course, are inclined to forget this distance; but any form which maintains itself in this distance, and explores it, whether it is prose or poetry, a novel or 'reflection', is a language of fiction. Fiction, on this account, would be the verbal presence of 'that which doesn't exist, in so far as it is' (1963c: 280). And its relation with language – in general – would be a complex one of reliance and contestation, in which it 'spreads out, disperses, breaks down and opens up' language (ibid.). Fiction, we could say, is therefore the experience of a non-existent outside, in so far as it enters into or impinges upon our everyday reality. We must remember, however, that despite this broadening of fiction to embrace any of a whole range of possible modes of writing (from poetry to philosophy), it is still the case that Foucault prioritizes, and gives an essential originality to, the actual moment of writing itself – to the act of placing marks on a blank page. It is the simple experience which consists of 'taking up a pen and writing', that itself brings to light the distance that characterizes fiction (1963c: 280). Indeed, writing itself (*écriture*) is the pure moment of origin of this language of fiction – 'the moment of the words themselves, of barely dry ink, the moment when something is sketched which by definition and in its most material being can only be a trace' (1963c: 281).

On the basis of this overview, we can now summarize the key elements of a Foucauldian ontology of literature, circa 1966. For Foucault, literature is a specialized and distinctively valorized form of language which is freed from the demands of representation and enters into a privileged relation with that which cannot be spoken – whether that is death, the dissolution of the speaking subject, or the very being of language. It is a practice which, at least since the time of Homer, has fulfilled a function in mediating the human relation to death. However, it is also a practice which underwent a radical transformation at the beginning of the modern era, developing a relation to language which set it outside any other linguistic activity. From this time it has been, potentially, a discursive practice which, by virtue of its often imposed marginal status, is capable of stepping outside the limits of its own era or, at the very least, of casting its era in an unexpected and unpredictable light. Indeed, since Mallarmé it has become one of the primary sites of contestation within modern culture. Given that, in the 1960s, Foucault had something like this idea of literature, the next question I want to ask is: what use did he make of it in his histories at this time? If we take *History of Madness* and *The Order of Things* as our examples, what will we find when we examine the way he uses literature and art as a part of his archeological project? Are creative works treated as just one more element of the archive, or are they given a privileged status in relation to their own episteme?

In *History of Madness*, Foucault credits certain works of literature and art as, at least, *preserving* a certain experience of unreason, in the face of both the eighteenth-century practice of internment and the modern objectification of madness. He singles out works such as Diderot's *Rameau's Nephew* (written c.1761–1772) as giving expression to an experience which had been all but silenced (2006a: 351[440]).[19] These, along with other works by Sade, and later Nietzsche and Artaud, have the value of forcing the world to question itself, to justify itself in the face of its excluded other – madness. In fact, it was through works such as Sade's writings that 'the Western world', says Foucault, gained the possibility of reclaiming the 'tragic experience' of madness which had been lost at the end of the Renaissance (2006a: 660).[20] These works, in effect, were the means of the preservation and transmission of an almost totally silenced experience – that of unreason.

In *The Order of Things*, on the other hand, we have a book which, while it gives a prominent role to works of literature (and art), yet seems undecided as to what role they are to be assigned in the world. While the book opens with an extended discussion of the painting 'Las Meninas' (1656) by Velasquez, for example, it is not clear that the painting functions as anything other than an illustration of a thesis that Foucault has worked out elsewhere. Turning to Foucault's use of literature in this book, however, I think we find a slightly different situation. There is, for example, an important discussion of Cervantes' *Don Quixote*, which presents that novel as being emblematic of both the inauguration of the classical experience of language and as an exemplary work of modern literature. This novel is an important illustration of the shift from the Renaissance to the classical experience of language. The adventures of Don Quixote, indeed, mark 'the limit' of the Renaissance world (1966a: 51[60]). Now, at the end of the Renaissance, writing has ceased to be the prose of the world, and so Don Quixote must wander the world proving that the old writings – the tales of chivalry – are true, by enacting their adventures. But language, as it turns out, is not completely powerless; because, in the second part of the book (published ten years after the first), the original stories have become 'real'. Now Don Quixote meets people who have read of his past adventures, and who recognize him as the hero of that first book. So, between the first and second book, Don Quixote has achieved a form of reality; but it is a 'reality he owes to language alone' (1966a: 54[62]). The truth of Don Quixote is not, therefore, 'in the relation of the words to the world but in that slender and constant relation woven between themselves by verbal signs' (ibid.). *Don Quixote* is the first work of modern literature, Foucault concludes, because in it 'language breaks off its old kinship with things and enters into that lonely sovereignty from which it will reappear, in its separated state, only as literature' (ibid.). What is equally significant from the point of view of our investigation here is that it is at this point – at the beginning of the classical age – that the two figures of the madman and the poet emerge; two border figures who break the rules of difference and identity. These figures exist at the 'outer edge' of our culture, 'at the point nearest to its essential divisions', and from this position 'at the limit' (1966a: 55[63]) their words 'unceasingly renew the power of their strangeness and the strength of their contestation' (1966a: 55[64]).

How then does Foucault use literature in these two books? On the one hand, we can say that he uses creative works to illustrate and gain knowledge of the structures of experience of a particular time: for example, his use of *Rameau's Nephew* in *History of Madness*; and of *Don Quixote* in *The Order of Things*. What is more interesting, however, is the idea that some of these works can work within, and against, their own culture by preserving and transmitting something that Foucault would later call subjugated knowledges. We could say that the value of these works would then be that they both express something which is silenced and excluded, and also challenge, throw down the gauntlet to, the culture in which they are produced, by introducing an element of difference. Indeed one commentator, Frédéric Gros, has suggested that the very question posed by *The Order of Things* – the question of our experience of order – could only be posed *after* the experience of the collapse of the common ground between words and things which comes to us through works of art and literature – for example, the paintings of Magritte (Gros 2004: 21–3). In fact, Foucault himself seems to acknowledge this when he states at the beginning of the book that it was born from a reading of Borges' fictional Chinese encyclopedia. We could conclude, then, that for Foucault, works of literature have the capacity to introduce an element of the strange and the foreign into the experience of a particular culture at a particular time. And this capacity would be the basis of their philosophical and social significance. Yet within a few years, literature has fallen from view and writing has been 'severely denounced' (1972: 313). How did this come about?

## The Turn

In his inaugural lecture at the Collège de France in 1970,[21] Foucault inaugurates more than just his tenure as 'Professor of the History of Systems of Thought'. We could say that he also embarks on a new phase in his research, a phase in which, among other changes, literature was to lose its interest for him. At the heart of the opening passages of the lecture, in all their lyrical allusiveness, is an anxiety which is manifested in several forms: an anxiety, first of all, about inauguration and about taking the floor, in the sense of beginning to speak; but an anxiety also about discourse itself, about the very dangers of speaking and the fact that our speech proliferates indefinitely. Significantly, this theme is introduced not just in a play of language which is as literary as anything Foucault ever wrote, but also through direct reference to the writings of Beckett. And yet, this lecture can be read as marking the turning point after which, for Foucault, literature loses its special status. If it is true to say that during the 1960s literature was given a privileged status and role in Foucault's work, then from this lecture on it loses that role and becomes just one more possible object of analysis – and, in fact, an object of analysis which Foucault chose not to pursue.

The lecture, whose published title is *The Order of Discourse*, opens with a reference to the discourse which Foucault is giving, and to the ones which he will have to give, in the Collège: 'In the discourse which today I must give, and in those which I will have to give here, for years perhaps, I would have liked to be able to slide surreptitiously' (1981: 51[7]). This inaugural lecture will outline a series of research projects that investigate and analyse the modes of ordering that shape discourse, but it will do so both in recognizing its own status as discourse and also, to a large extent, in giving itself its own rules and principles.

The order of discourse is therefore both the object of analysis of this lecture and also, in so far as it is itself a discourse (the first of many), it is the aim of the lecture. In other words, the 'order of discourse' is also the function of the lecture: to establish certain methodological principles that will order Foucault's own discourse in the years to come. The second theme announced in this sentence is the idea that to speak, to engage in discourse, is a duty, but a duty which one would like to avoid. Foucault refers to this obligation twice and then says that he would have preferred to be able to slide into speech surreptitiously. Why, he asks, do so many people have an anxiety about beginning to speak? Quoting Beckett, although without naming him, he expresses this sense of obligation and impossibility: 'You must go on, I can't go on, you must go on, I'll go on, you must say words, as long as there are any' (1981: 51[8]).[22] What is the source of this anxiety in the face of discourse? Foucault suggests, first of all, that it comes from an unwillingness to consider discourse from the outside. The moment of beginning, as a moment of entry, is an occasion when we assess an object or a practice from the outside. In the case of discourse, we would prefer to be already safely within its confines, rather than having to view its 'singular . . . formidable . . . [and] perhaps maleficent' exterior (1981: 51[8]). To this unwillingness and anxiety, Foucault imagines that the institution responds with calming words, assuring the individual that discourse is subject to laws, laws which the institution itself enforces, ensuring that discourse is honoured – but disarmed. For Foucault, however, these two contrary perspectives are expressions of the same anxiety. This is the anxiety in the face of, and the fundamental unwillingness to acknowledge, discourse in all its material, unpredictable, violent reality. And this is the reality that Foucault's lecture, and his research project for the coming years, hopes to expose and analyse.

Any account of Foucault's turn from literature must give central importance to this new awareness of the materiality and violence of discourse. If multiple systems of constraint operate in the field of discourse, systems which limit what can be said and who can say it, then the issue of power becomes unavoidable. In the outline Foucault sketches in this lecture we see many of the features of his work of the 1970s taking shape – even the prediction that when we study the modern forms of sexuality we will find that prohibitions didn't have quite the role that we used to imagine (1981: 63). But more importantly, beyond this sketching of future research, Foucault gives himself a new set of methodological principles. And these principles, we might say, made it much more difficult for literature to continue to function in his thought the way it had in the 1960s. The principles arise in response to a problem and a question: 'But what is there, then, that is so perilous in the fact that people speak, and that their discourse proliferates indefinitely? Where is the danger in that?' (1981: 52[10]). In order to understand this fear, according to Foucault, we need to do three things: bring into question our will to truth; reconsider discourse in its character as event; and reject the sovereignty of the signifier. From this need, there follows a set of methodological principles, which will order his own discourse in the years to come, and two of which I will look at here.

First, the principle of reversal. Whereas traditionally, one looked for the productive source of discourse in authors, disciplines and the will to truth, Foucault will see these as producing the negative effect of rarefaction. In other words, these functions have the effect of limiting what is said, and of what it is possible to say. As Foucault had argued earlier, the author-function is, despite appearances, 'the principle of thrift [*économie*] in the proliferation of meaning' (1969: 221[811]). Hence the difficulty now, in any study of literature, of giving a fundamental significance to the act of writing. Secondly, the principle of exteriority. Foucault will approach discourse not as something which needs to be penetrated in order to discover its hidden meaning, but as a phenomenon which must be considered in all its external relations. These will be treated as the conditions of possibility which give rise to an unpredictable series of events; events which have their material, perilous and violent effects. In opposition to the traditional categories of creation, unity, originality and signification, then, he will oppose event, series, regularity and condition of possibility. What does this mean for Foucault's approach to literature? In the first place, it has to be said that these traditional categories are not those which animated his own work in the 1960s. That engagement with literature neither pursued hidden meanings, nor focused on the creative originality of the author. But what is different now, is the decision to focus – apparently exclusively – on the *external* relations which literature maintains with, for example, institutions such as publishing and the university.[23]

This shift didn't happen all at once, however, and it is helpful to look at a slightly earlier expression of its development, in 'What is an author?', a lecture from 1969 which is in many ways a preliminary sketch of the inaugural lecture. The earlier lecture seems to hover between the new approach, the 'historical analysis of discourse' which unfolds according to the new principles of genealogy, and the older interest in the power of 'fiction' to threaten our world. Foucault introduces his theme by saying that all around us, in contemporary culture, we can see the disappearance of the author, and this disappearance gives us the opportunity to analyse what remains of the 'author-function'. This function is important, not just because it tends to persist and reassert itself in categories such as the 'œuvre' and 'writing', but also because it is related to the theme of the disappearance – or at least the critical philosophical questioning – of the subject.[24] What is distinctive about the perspective Foucault takes in this lecture is that, having given a very schematic account of the 'author-function', he then imagines a time, after its demise (which is already happening now), when 'fiction and its polysemous texts' will be able to function according to another mode, with different, as yet untested, forms of constraint (1969: 222[811]). It is hard not to see this as an, admittedly muted, appeal to the possibility that the powers of fiction may soon escape from the forms of control and rarefaction to which they have been subject in the modern era. The following year, however, in the inaugural lecture, even this small hint of messianism is silenced.

Now, literature appears only in one of the sketched projects, and even then in a tangential way. One could envisage, Foucault says, an investigation of the way that literary criticism and literary history in the eighteenth and nineteenth centuries constituted the figure of the author and the œuvre on the basis of the techniques of biblical exegesis and hagiography (1981: 71[63–4]). Not only is this a project that Foucault never undertook, it is clearly a very long way from envisaging an ontology of literature. This same, new approach is voiced in an interview conducted in 1975 which I want to look at in some detail (Foucault, 1988). This interview, from a time between the publication of *Discipline and Punish* in 1975 and *The History of Sexuality, volume I* in 1976, reflects Foucault's attempts to integrate his literary and his post-literary phases, and on this occasion he gives more serious attention to a consideration of the 1960s theorization of writing. The story he now tells is that there was an admirable attempt on the part of writers such as Blanchot and Barthes to desacralize and demythologize literature by, firstly, insisting on its intransitivity. That is, literature cannot embody 'the great decisions of a culture' (1988: 310), because it is about nothing but itself – not even an expression of the author's mind. The danger with this claim, however, was that it led to a renewed sacralization of literature and *writing*, and ironically to a mythologization of it as inherently subversive and revolutionary. It is tempting to consider the possibility that Foucault has himself in mind when he speaks of this new 'exaltation' and the unfortunate fact that 'political implications' were totally absent from it (ibid.).

In any case, he now presents a new picture of Blanchot and Barthes as really tending towards a more thorough desacralization of literature than their followers had effected. Their approach, he says, implied the further questioning of how, at a given moment, some modes of discourse are given this 'very special, very strange' position as works of literature. The curious fact, however, is that during his many writings on Blanchot and others in the 1960s, Foucault had never identified this as the question that their works raised. But now, it is the question that he raises; and, in fact, it is a question which he says has never really been raised before: 'No one has ever really analysed how, out of the mass of things said, out of the totality of actual discourse, a number of these discourses (literary discourse, philosophical discourse) are given a particular sacralization and function' (1988: 308). What Foucault now calls for is an investigation of the procedures by which literature is made to function as literature; procedures of selection, sacralization and institutional validation. This investigation is the one he had begun in 'What is an author?' and had envisaged in an expanded form in *The Order of Discourse*, but had never really brought to fruition. It is the putting into practice of the principle of exteriority which we saw earlier. However, when the interviewer asks him if any of these criteria of selection are 'internal' to the texts, Foucault simply replies, 'I don't know' (1988: 309). The whole issue of the internal forms of literature, the issue which had animated his interest in writing and language for much of the 1960s, is now closed off to him. 'In order to know what literature is,' he says, in order in other words to know its ontology, 'I would not study its internal structures' (1988: 311). What would he study instead? The process by which a non-literary discourse enters the literary field. His questions now are: 'What happens? What is triggered off? How is this discourse modified in its efforts by the fact that it is recognised as literary?' (1988: 311).

To illustrate this questioning he mentions two examples – his books on Raymond Roussel and on Pierre Rivière.[25] The same question, he claims, runs through these two books: 'what is the threshold beyond which a discourse . . . begins to function in the field known as literature'? (1988: 311). Taking the book on Roussel first, however, it is hard to accept Foucault's claim that the central question here was the threshold between the literary and the non-literary. Or at least, it is hard to accept that its focus was on the *external* conditions of this institutional validation. After all, Roussel's books were, in his own lifetime, published as works of literature. And while it is true that they have often been seen from a point of view which highlights his mental illness and psychiatric treatment, Foucault aims to circumvent this psychologizing of the works. Indeed, his book sees them, Pierre Macherey has observed, as 'the site for the emergence of a truth . . . not a psychological truth . . . but a truly literary truth which belongs to literature as such, and which may perhaps define literature' (1995: 213).

In the case of the publication of the memoir written by Pierre Rivière, on the other hand, there is undoubtedly an interest in the uncertain status of this text. But two points must be made here. Firstly, it was Foucault's own effort in publishing this memoir which gave it any status, literary or otherwise, which it may have today. And while he does raise the question of its ambiguous position, he is also clearly fascinated by some, dare we say, literary power which it possesses. Indeed, in the Foreword he admits that it wasn't so much the importance of the text as a site of conflict of discursive appropriations which motivated his interest, but quite simply the 'beauty' of the memoir. Speaking for the other editors, he says 'the utter astonishment it produced in us was the starting point' (1978: x).[26] Secondly, arising from this point, we must wonder whether it is at all possible to give a complete account of this validation without taking into consideration the internal conditions of the text itself. In other words, why is *this* text capable of being treated as literature? What potential does it contain within itself to act in the way that we expect works of literature to act? This, it seems to me, is a question that is forgotten when Foucault's thought turns exclusively towards the external conditions of the production of literary discourse. But it is a question to which, in the 1960s, as we have seen, he had provided some of the conceptual elements necessary for an answer.

At this point, two warnings must be sounded. Firstly, I am not suggesting that the modern institutions of literature (universities, publishing, etc.) have a special skill in spotting true literary value, which they would then validate and sacralize. It would be more reasonable to suppose that these institutions engage in procedures which operate simultaneously along both the axes which we, and Foucault, have been calling internal and external (bearing in mind that this 'external' is not the same as the 'outside' of thought). That is, neither the internal nor the external axis is sufficient to explain the validation of certain texts as literature. If a text such as Rivière's memoir is now a viable candidate for this status it is *both* because of some quality in the text itself, *and* because of an institutional procedure – which, ironically, is in this case largely mobilized by Foucault himself. The shift I have been identifying in Foucault's work is one in which he turns from an intense consideration of these internal criteria to an appeal to the importance of the external criteria, before apparently dropping his interest in the entire field. And along with this shift he re-tells, or re-fictions, his own engagement with the field in a way which appears to elide, or even deny, his earlier interest. And this brings us to the second warning. My point is not to berate Foucault either for his change of focus or for his re-telling of his intellectual biography. What Foucault says about the demise of the author, and about the irrelevance of a psychologizing reading, must be taken seriously. In another book from the 1960s, Foucault makes the famous appeal to leave such questions of the author's identity to the police and bureaucrats (2002: 19[28]);[27] while, throughout his work, he continuously emphasizes the importance of allowing the work of thought to force us to wander from ourselves, to make us no longer think the same thing as before. So, it is not a question here of complaining about his shifting opinions or his developing methodology.


## A Renewed Potential?

In one of his final books, Foucault comments on the irony that, having imagined that we have travelled far from our earlier modes of thought, we find that we are merely a little higher up, looking down on ourselves. This metaphor, that we travel in a spiral rather than a straight, or even crooked, line, suggests that Foucault now finds himself not distanced from his earlier thought, but 'at the vertical' to his earlier thought (1984a: 11[17]). But travelling in such a spiral can also cause one to abandon the thread of earlier positions. So, rather than trying to pin Foucault to one stage of this spiral, my aim here has been twofold. First of all, to understand the nature of this turn in his thought, this turn away from literature. This was a turn which, I would say, prematurely cut off an intense investigation of the powers that certain forms of language – which we call literature – possess. There is no doubt that the addition of the dimension of power relations to any consideration of such works is valuable. But such an approach can neither replace nor supersede an analysis that focuses on and gives at least equal significance to the powers of literary language itself.

Arising from this, my second aim has been to hold out the possibility that the potential which the earlier stage made possible can be re-animated in the context of certain elements of Foucault's later thought. What, therefore, can be reclaimed from Foucault's abandoned engagement with literature? The core insight from this period is, I would say, the idea that literature is capable of functioning within modern culture as a fundamentally transgressive and contestatory form of language. It can do this, not so much by virtue of its content, but primarily by virtue of the unique relation which it sets up between language and the world. This is a relation which we can variously describe as fictive, anti-representational, or oppositional. In so far as it introduces a foreign element into our thought and our experience, literature can then be conceived as a practice which, in terms of Foucault's later work, is capable of playing a role in the constitution, and re-constitution, of the subject of ethics. It would then become necessary to approach literature not just from the point of view of its relations with, for example, the university and publishing, but also to consider its potential as a force which intervenes in and modifies forms of subjectivity. That will be the project of the following chapters. For the moment however, we can conclude that the challenge in following Foucault in his sometimes dizzying turns and convolutions, is to maintain an openness towards the possibilities inherent in elements of his thought that he himself may appear to have surpassed. For us, there is no reason why these abandoned paths cannot be pursued and renewed.

# Chapter 4

# Language, Culture and Confusion:
# Brian Friel

Combining the insights we have gained from Heaney's wrestling with Plato, and from Foucault's engagement with twentieth-century avant-garde writing, we can now characterize works of literature not as simple, or distorting, reflections of human nature and the world, but as potentially transgressive interventions that contest the social and political forms of the worlds in which they are received. At the core of this potential is the special relation that works of literature establish between language and the world; a relation that Foucault identifies with the nature of fiction in general. In literature, language is freed from the demands of representation and is capable of creating fictional worlds that can sustain complex and effective relations with our everyday world. And they do this, at least in part, by disturbing the relation that we generally assume to obtain between words and things. Certain works of literature suggest to us that this relation is not a simple one of reflection or representation; instead, it is one in which our language lays down the channels by which we will subsequently perceive and experience the world. This gives us a basis on which to investigate the possibility that these works are also capable of modifying those channels and thus of changing our perception and experience.

To disturb the channels through which we experience our world is, inevitably, to create confusion. But these disturbances don't always come neatly packaged in works of literature; for many cultures in the modern era they have arrived in the form of colonization. Perhaps the most profound effect of colonization, brought about through the imposition of a new language, is the shift it effects in the way a linguistic community relates to its world. In the case of Ireland, this shift happened primarily in the nineteenth century, but its consequences, in politics and in literature, can be seen right up to the present. Brian Friel is a playwright whose work has frequently focused on questions about language, identity, history, and the effects of colonization. In particular, his play *Translations* (1980) explores the multiple effects of the displacement of the

Irish language, but does so in the context of the fraught politics of its own time in Northern Ireland. For Friel, confusion is one of the inevitable effects of this displacement, and of its aftermath, but it is an effect which, as we will see, is not necessarily to be regretted.

In their book on Kafka, Deleuze and Guattari suggest a way of understanding works of literature that emerge in this kind of linguistically confused context. Their concept of a minor literature will be helpful in understanding aspects of Friel's situation and his literary practice. Kafka was a member of a community (the Jews of Prague) which had lost its former language (Czech), and was now speaking and writing a form of German. This gave Kafka the opportunity to set up what Deleuze and Guattari call a 'minor' use of the German language, thus making possible a 'minor literature' (Deleuze and Guattari, 1986: 16). The first characteristic of a minor literature is that it is written in a major language, but using a variant of the language that both profits from, and further extends, a loosening up and confusion of its linguistic structures. This constitutes a 'deterritorialization' of language (ibid.), in which its rigid and established forms are diverted from their dominant usage and re-channelled in new and disturbing ways. Its second characteristic is that in a minor literature everything is immediately political; all personal relations, intrigues, love affairs, and so on, connect up directly with the political context. In the work of minor literature, these connections are incessantly exposed and emphasized. The third characteristic of this type of literature is that it takes on a collective value; it is given, or adopts for itself, the task of expressing the experience of a particular community. At a certain level, this may appear to be the actual minority community of which the writer is a member, but it is also and more importantly another, possible, community, one that embodies 'another consciousness and another sensibility' (Deleuze and Guattari 1986: 17). Approaching Friel's play with this schema in mind, we can say that not only does his play illustrate Deleuze and Guattari's thesis, not only is it an example of a work of minor literature, but it is also an exploration of the conditions that make possible any such work. By focusing on the moment, in the first half of the nineteenth century, when the Irish language began to be displaced, and by situating this in the complex cultural politics of the late twentieth century, Friel gives us a way of understanding both the cost and the advantages of the condition of minority.

At the centre of the play is an insight about the ubiquity of confusion, especially in our relation to language and in our experience of the way it reflects and forms our world. This is something which may be particularly striking in the context of colonization, but it is also more general than that. With regard to minor literature, for example, Deleuze and Guattari concede that their account of it can be taken as an account of something much broader than the writing of minorities. The minor, they say, can be taken to designate 'the revolutionary conditions for every literature within the heart of what is called great (or established) literature' (Deleuze and Guattari 1986: 18). In other words, all

innovative literature creates a minor use of a major language.[1] In the situation
of colonization and its aftermath, however, the implications of this minoriza-
tion are pushed to the fore and are easier to examine. One of the implications
of Friel's play, which is important in his own context in Northern Ireland in
1980, is that the confusion which is an essential part of the experience of the
minor brings with it its own range of potentials. 'Confusion', as one of the play's
characters says, 'is not an ignoble condition'.[2]

But what kind of confusion are we talking about here? It is a striking fact that
much Irish literature, at least for several centuries, has had a strong sense of the
capacity of literary or fictional writing to effect political and cultural transformation. From Swift and Yeats to Sebastian Barry, Colm Toibin and Seamus
Heaney, many Irish writers have taken it upon themselves to use their pens to
provoke their readers to experiment with their relations to themselves and
their culture. One way of explaining this propensity would be in terms of the
fundamental linguistic confusion which has prevailed in Ireland since the start
of colonization. The linguistic and cultural confusion that comes from being
between-two-tongues and between-two-cultures would, on this view, account for
the ease with which fiction is allowed to play a role within the stubborn realities
of social and political life. And it is this kind of confusion – both linguistic and
cultural – on which Friel explicitly focuses. But, while the play consists of a dramatic presentation of this type of confusion, it also quietly enacts another kind
of confusion: that is, the confusion between politics and literature. Deleuze and
Guattari note, with respect to Kafka, that his writing is by no means an escape
from life: 'living and writing, art and life, are opposed only from the point of
view of a major literature' (Deleuze and Guattari 1986: 41). In the case of Friel,
as much as for Heaney, it is also true that writing must be brought into some
kind of effective relation with life, or politics. And this is the point at which
I want to begin my discussion of the play and the cultural context in which it
was produced.

## Having a Field Day

Critics who take the view that art and politics are better not mixed, generally
take one of two options: either they argue that art just happens to be incapable
of affecting politics; or they suggest that while art may influence politics, and
politics may influence art, the effect is almost always deleterious – in both
spheres. In a poem written on the death of W. B. Yeats in 1939, W. H. Auden
chose the former course, suggesting that poetry can have no effect on society.
He praises Yeats' poetry, but doubts its political efficacy: 'Now Ireland has her
madness and her weather still/ For poetry makes nothing happen.'[3] In Auden's
judgement, despite Yeats' persistent artistic attempts to mould the public life of
his time, he had left Ireland the way he had found it: an island of foul weather

and mad politics. Almost fifty years later, writing in the context of this continuing madness, one of Northern Ireland's leading poetry critics, Edna Longley, made a plea for the separation of poetry and politics that appealed to the second option, according to which the confusion between poetry and politics is possible, but always has a negative effect. 'Poetry and politics . . . should be separated', she argued, for the same reason that church and state should be: because 'mysteries distort the rational processes which ideally prevail in social relations; while ideologies confiscate the poet's special passport to terra incognita' (1986: 185). The 'unhealthy intersection' between these two spheres, in Longley's view, breeds both bad poetry and bad politics.

These critical responses, which either reject an art/politics intersection as impossible, or condemn it as unhealthy, irrational or unenlightened, have not however been shared by all Irish writers. And if Auden was referring primarily to Yeats' work in the Irish Literary Theatre, which became the Abbey Theatre at the beginning of the twentieth century, then Longley is referring primarily to the work of the Field Day Theatre Company which began in 1980 with the production of Friel's play *Translations*. Both the Irish Literary Theatre and Field Day were based on the premise that art neither could nor should be insulated from the political contexts in which it was produced and received. Further, both were based on the conviction that since many of the features of those contexts were determined by the political imagination, then the arts of poetry and drama were ideally suited to the task of political transformation. Motivated by this belief in the possibility of political change, both also exhibited a strong capacity to inspire committed followers. An actor in the early days of the Abbey Theatre, for example, recalled that 'we talked in terms of the movement . . . and walked home with shining eyes and heightened colour to dream dreams of great plays'.[4] In a similar vein, Seamus Deane employed an almost military metaphor when he introduced a collection of Field Day 'pamphlets' with an account of the threefold enterprise of the company which would shortly complete 'the first phase of its operations' (1990: 14). Despite the many differences between these two movements, then, they share a common conviction that a significant part of the task of politics can be carried out through the medium of drama, poetry and criticism. But what exactly is the task of politics, or, to be more precise, how did these two movements conceive of this task?

In the most general terms, we can say that both movements placed the colonial relation between Ireland and Britain at the core of their political analysis. For Yeats, Lady Gregory, and the other founders of the Irish Literary Theatre, the task to be accomplished was the re-assertion of Ireland's cultural independence from the imperial centre, as a prelude to its political independence. For Friel and Field Day, the task was to come to terms with the bitter sectarian aftermath of colonization in Northern Ireland. For them, the political task was neither independence nor union, but the working out of new ways of accommodating the Catholic nationalist and Protestant unionist traditions. If the period from the 1890s to the War of Independence in 1922 can be seen as a period of intense anti-colonial struggle, then the period from 1980 to the present can be seen as a period of intense post-colonial labour. That is, the objective more recently has no longer been to achieve independence from colonial rule, but to achieve some sort of freedom from the pernicious and multiple effects of its legacy. For Auden and Longley, and for a whole tradition in Western philosophy, while such an objective may be laudatory, it is by no means a suitable task for literature. Surely, they would say, drama cannot act in this way; and surely any drama that tries to bring political change risks becoming mere propaganda, a contemporary version of Soviet agitprop perhaps. What we will see in Friel's play *Translations*, however, is that dramatic speech can indeed act: not only has Friel not sacrificed his passport to 'terra incognita', but his play actually provides us with some elements of a theory of culture which shows precisely how dramatic speech is capable of acting even in the most stubborn of political landscapes.

## Translations

Friel's *Translations* is a play that draws its dramatic force from the clash between two cultures, a clash in which one culture seems doomed to lose its distinctive world-view in the face of a violent aggressor. Even though the play evokes the tragedy of the erasure of one culture by another, however, it refuses to fall back on the simple oppositions which, in Ireland, have mediated this tragedy. If the legacy of colonization in Northern Ireland has been a mutually opposed entrenchment behind mutually opposed cultural essentialisms, then Friel's play attempts to open up a space for cultural re-imagination which might lead to a less divided post-nationalist condition. And it does so in large part by dramatically presenting a theory of culture-as-translation that Friel finds in George Steiner's *After Babel* (1975).

Set in 1833 in Baile Beag (or Ballybeg), the fictitious Donegal town which is the scene of many of Friel's plays, *Translations* dramatizes the moment when traditional rural Irish culture finally succumbs to the twin forces of imperialism and modernity. These forces are represented, firstly, by the presence in the community of a detachment of Royal Engineers who are making the first Ordnance Survey map of the area, and who, in the process, are standardizing and anglicizing all the local place-names; and, secondly, by the news that a new national school system is to be introduced in which the language of instruction will be English rather than Irish. The setting for most of the play is the hay-barn in which Hugh O'Donnell holds his hedge-school, helped by his eldest son Manus. The students in the school are all adults and range from Sarah, who suffers from a chronic speech impediment, to Jimmy the sixty-year-old 'Infant Prodigy' who sits in a corner reading Homer in Greek and falling in love with Pallas Athene, 'the flashing-eyed goddess'. The students pay Hugh and Manus partly in milk and turf and Hugh enjoys the high status of village scribe, since even the priest seems to be illiterate. However, when Hugh's younger son Owen returns from Dublin in the role of translator to the Ordnance Survey team, whatever stability this community initially had is quickly lost.

Owen is cast in the role of an outsider who is thoughtlessly betraying the community from which he has come. He consistently refuses to recognize the significance of the map-making exercise – even when his brother in exasperation calls it 'a bloody military operation' (T, 408) – and he delays telling his employers that his name is not in fact Roland (as they have mistakenly interpreted Owen), saying to his brother 'Owen-Roland-what the hell. It's only a name. It's the same me, isn't it?' (T, 408). As Owen blindly insists that names don't matter, however, it is his English colleague Lieutenant Yolland who slowly becomes convinced that there is something sinister in the Ordnance Survey project. As the two work, methodically translating place-names for the new maps – Lis na Muc becomes Swinefort, Druim Dubh becomes Dromduff, Machaire Ban becomes Whiteplains – Yolland the Englishman begins to realize that this is 'an eviction of sorts', and that 'something is being eroded' (T, 420). He also begins to follow the well-worn path of the accidental colonizer, falling in love with the landscape, the people and the language of the colony. He begins to imagine that if he can learn the language he will be able to unlock the secrets of the natives, but then realizes that even his pronunciation of the word 'poteen' – of which he drinks a great deal – immediately marks him as outside the tribe. And, ultimately, it is the importance of these tribal boundaries that unleashes the tragic consequence of the play. Yolland falls in love with Máire, who had been the rather unwilling 'intended' of Manus, and the two have a brief love-scene which is observed by the almost mute Sarah. The next morning Yolland has mysteriously disappeared, presumed dead at the hands of the shadowy Donnelly twins. The commanding officer, Lancey, orders mass evictions and the destruction of livestock if information is not forthcoming. Finally, Manus flees under suspicion; Owen changes sides and leaves to join the nationalist resistance; Hugh learns that he is not to be given the job of master at the new National School; and Máire, who has lost both Yolland and Manus, prepares to emigrate to America.

While it would be easy to tell this story as one of Paradise lost, with perfidious Albion in its usual role, Friel is careful to avoid the over-simplifying categories of Irish nationalism. In addressing, in a complex and nuanced way, the question of the loss of the Irish language, he undermines the assumption which is so often made that an authentic nation requires a unique linguistic character. Cultural and political nationalism in Ireland has always been closely related to efforts to preserve the native tongue. The fact that these efforts, at least at the level of the living language, have all but failed has not broken the pious belief that something essential has been lost, that Irish people today are still speaking an alien language. However, even in 1843 one of the great champions of the

Irish language, Thomas Davis, could not himself speak it – coming as he did from an Anglo-Irish family. So when he used the English language to promote his own version of non-sectarian nationalism he was already, as he says, 'adrift among the accidents of translation'.[5] More than 60 years later, one of the managers of the Abbey Theatre, Frank Fay, argued that 'an Irish Theatre must, of course, express itself solely in the Irish language: otherwise it would have no *raison d'être*'.[6] Voilà – a curiously hybrid appeal to Irish linguistic purity expressed in English using a French idiom! And when Northern Irish Republicans in the 1970s spray-painted Tiocfaidh ár Lá (Our Day Will Come) on neighbourhood walls, they too had more than likely learnt their maternal language at night classes in the local Catholic school. Writing in a context in which the language question is politically charged and riven with paradoxes, then, one of Friel's central objectives is to re-pose that question in the light of a more adequate appreciation of the complex connections between language, culture and identity.

This effort, however, has not always been appreciated by the play's critics, and many have read it as a simple re-peddling of the old myths of Irish nationalism.[7] In the juxtaposition, for example, of classically educated peasants and philistine soldiers (the latter are curiously unable to tell the difference between Irish and Latin), and in historically inaccurate details such as the arming of the surveyors with bayonets, Friel has been accused of uncritically reproducing nationalist prejudices of the past. One of the key assumptions of this charge – and it is an assumption that is frequently made – is that the opening scenes of the play present a pre-colonization Eden which is quickly and deliberately destroyed by the English invaders. The debate about the supposedly Edenic quality of these opening scenes of the play is significant from the point of view of the impact of the play on the cultural politics of Ireland in the 1980s. If a simple opposition is made between idyllic, classically educated peasants and their philistine oppressors, then it becomes easy to conclude that the political task in the present is to evict the oppressor and reinstate the pre-lapsarian community. While such a politics may (and even this is questionable) have been an adequate response to the conditions of the early twentieth century, for Friel and Field Day it is not an adequate response in the 1980s. It is, therefore, essential to Friel's project that he complicate the simple oppositions of Irish nationalism, and one of the ways he does this is by addressing the myth of the rural idyll. In Friel's play there is no Edenic past from which the hapless peasants are expelled; there is rather, as we will see, an ironic toying with the mutual prejudices of the colonial relation.

In addition, it is crucial that the attack on traditional culture in Friel's play does not come exclusively from the English. The play carries allusions to impending events such as the Irish Famine (1846–49), which was to play a significant role in reducing the use of the Irish language, and to indigenous champions of modernization such as Daniel O'Connell (the 'Liberator') who is reported in the play as saying 'the old language is a barrier to modern progress' (T, 400). Again, through the character of Máire, who wants to learn English in order to prepare for her emigration to America, the play foreshadows economic migration as one of the central causes of rural decline in nineteenth- and twentieth-century Ireland.

But more generally, there are in fact two very good reasons why the community of Baile Beag in 1833 is not a pre-colonization Eden. The first and most obvious one, which is curiously overlooked by many critics, is that 1833 did not see the beginning of the colonization of Ireland. In fact the process had already been taking place for several centuries, and indeed by 1833 the ancestors of today's Unionist population of Northern Ireland had already been living there for up to 200 years. Anyone who imagines that Friel's presentation of the rural hedge-school is Edenic should also recall that such schools were only present in eighteenth- and nineteenth-century Ireland as a result of the colonial destruction of traditional social structures and the concerted attempts to suppress Catholicism. So, while it is possible to take a romanticizing view of the hedge-schools, in so far as they are an indication of a culture's will to survive, there is no basis for seeing them as part of a pre-colonization paradise.

The second and much more significant reason why Baile Beag should not be read as an Eden is because, in Friel's vision, humanity has always already fallen. If, before Babel, humanity was one and spoke the same language, then Friel's play is concerned with the implications of the post-Babel confusion of tongues. In *Genesis*, when God says, 'let us go down and there confound their language, that they may not understand one another's speech' (*Genesis* 11:7), the groundwork for the ubiquity of translation is laid: and it is this ubiquity which preoccupies Friel. At the centre of the play's concerns, then, is a question about language. How, the play asks, can a culture survive the imposition of an alien tongue – even if many of its members rush to embrace it? What happens to a community which loses not only its traditional way of life, but also its traditional way of being in the world through language? These questions are asked, however, in the full recognition that the relations between language, culture and identity are always fraught with difficulties: this is not just a result of colonization, it is a part of the human condition. It is in recognition of this fact that, for example, Friel's *Programme Notes* for the original production quote Heidegger's statement that 'Man acts as if he were the master of language, while it is language which remains master of man.'[8] And it is also for this reason that the play is littered with allusions to, and sometimes even direct quotes from, George Steiner's book *After Babel* (1975).

The theme of language and identity is introduced from the very opening lines of the play, when we see the master's son Manus trying to teach Sarah how to say her own name. According to the stage directions, Sarah has a speech defect which is so bad that she has always been thought, both by herself and others, to be mute (T, 383). In coaxing her into speech, to say the simple phrase

'My name is Sarah', it is significant that Manus reassures her with the words 'This is our secret . . . Nobody hears you' (T, 384). The communicative power of the apparently simple speech act of naming oneself is from the beginning brought into question: Sarah can only give herself a name on the condition that nobody is listening. This anxiety about naming is again underlined when Bridget announces to the class that the unmarried Nellie Ruadh's baby is to be christened that day – and that she is threatening to give it its father's name. Of course nobody knows who the father is – yet. So, as Bridget says, 'there's a lot of uneasy bucks about Baile Beag this day' (T, 391).

At a more fundamental level the audience is made to focus on language by the realization – about five minutes into the play – that the characters have actually been speaking Irish, not English, all along. In the course of a discussion of the relative merits of learning Latin, Greek and English (and Hugh's school teaches only Latin and Greek), we learn that Máire actually speaks no English when she proudly recites her only English phrase: 'In Norfolk we besport ourselves around the maypoll' (T, 388). Throughout the play, then, the actors speak only English (with occasional Greek and Latin phrases) while Irish, the native tongue, is only heard in place-names – even though we are to understand that they are speaking Irish all the time. Apart from the obvious fact that had it been written in Irish the play would not have reached a significant audience, even in Ireland, this device allows Friel to play with the idea that below the English words of the Irish characters on stage lies a hidden other language which remains largely silent. The device also suggests that this community is very far from resembling the one people/one language which, according to the Book of Genesis, existed before Babel: in fact, this people speak three languages and are represented on stage using a fourth.

For those who cherish cultural and linguistic purity this condition is no doubt to be regretted. However, Friel's play avoids such easy conclusions by staging multiple responses to the dilemma of colonization. Manus, for example, refuses to speak the language of the colonizer, even though he is one of the few people in the community who can; and rather than compete against his father for the position of master of the new National School, he accepts a position as hedge-school teacher on a remote western island – thus underlining his own retreat in the face of change. Owen, on the other hand, initially argues the case for a commonsense, rational approach to the problems of cultural translation. He assures Yolland, the English officer, that entry to the tribe is possible, and becomes impatient with his doubts about the cultural impact of their work. When Yolland insists on the retention of the name Tobair Vree for an obscure cross-road, for example, Owen explodes:

> . . . why do we call it Tobair Vree? I'll tell you why. Tobair means a well. But what does Vree mean? It's a corruption of Brian – (Gaelic pronunciation) Brian – Tobair Bhriain. Because a hundred-and-fifty years ago there used to

be a well there, not at the crossroads, mind you – that would be too simple –
but in a field close to the crossroads. And the old man called Brian, whose
face was disfigured by an enormous growth, got it into his head that the water
in the well was blessed; and every day for seven months he went there and
bathed his face in it. But the growth didn't go away; and one morning Brian
was found drowned in that well. And ever since that crossroads is known as
Tobair Vree – even though that well has long since dried up. I know the story
because my grandfather told it to me. But ask Doalty – or Máire – or Bridget
– even my father – even Manus – why it's called Tobair Vree; and do you think
they'll know? I know they don't know. So the question I put to you Lieutenant, is this: what do we do with a name like that? Do we scrap Tobair Vree
altogether and call it – what? – The Cross? Crossroads? Or do we keep piety
with a man long dead, long forgotten, his name 'eroded' beyond recognition, whose trivial little story nobody in the parish remembers? (T, 420)

Owen's initial position is to reject such piety as confused and irrational, and
to replace the cultural richness of Tobair Vree with the totally unevocative
Crossroads. However, by the end of the play, having witnessed the effects of his
own work, he finally answers his question in the affirmative and sets out on the
path of national piety and anti-colonial resistance. Meanwhile Yolland, the
unwilling colonizer, is one of the few characters who, from the beginning, seems
to fully appreciate the cultural significance of the act of mapping and re-nam-
ing the country, eventually defending the Irish names against Owen's sometimes arbitrary imposition of English: Bun na hAbhann, for example, which
literally means 'mouth of the river', inexplicably becomes Burnfoot (T, 410).

At the centre of the play, both dramatically and conceptually, is the brief love-
scene which takes place between Yolland and Máire. A familiar response to the
trauma of colonization is to believe in the power of individuals to overcome the
pernicious effects of cultural misunderstanding and hostility. Yolland wants to
believe that cross-cultural understanding and communication is possible. He
wants to gain access to the secrets of the tribe, and this drive is intensified by his
growing interest in Máire. Máire, too, tends to underplay the differences
between the two cultures. Early on she reports that the sappers have offered to
help with the hay-making, and even though she doesn't know a word they're
saying, she says 'that doesn't matter, does it?' (T, 389). However, this belief in
the capacity of the private realm to provide an alternative and a remedy to the
public realm is one which, according to Seamus Deane, has always been opposed
by Field Day.[9] Once again, in so far as the play is a work of minor literature, it
demonstrates how all personal relations are immediately political. There can be
no escape for the protagonists from their political and historical context,
because this context is continuously 'vibrating within' their individual concerns
(Deleuze and Guattari 1986: 17). As for Friel's portrayal of Yolland and
Máire's attempt to take refuge in a private space, it certainly allows them no

sanctuary from the forces of history. Finally, after several failed attempts, the
two manage to be alone together after a dance at Tobair Vree, but their efforts
to communicate range from the comic to the poetic. Yolland speaks to her in
English, which she cannot understand, while Máire first tries Latin ('tu es cen-
turio in exercitu Britannico . . .' T, 427), but of course Yolland speaks no Latin.
She then tries her one English phrase, 'In Norfolk we besport ourselves around
the maypoll' (T, 428), to which Yolland replies, like an eager puppy: 'Good
God, do you? That's where my mother comes from – Norfolk. Norwich actually.
Not exactly Norwich town but a small village called Little Walsingham close
beside it. But in our own village of Winfarthing we have a maypole too and every
year on the first of May . . .' (T, 428) – and then he realizes that she doesn't
understand a word he's saying. The lovers are not, however, dismayed by this
difficulty and they eventually communicate using their shared knowledge of the
local place-names. Tentatively at first, Yolland begins to recite the Irish names
that his survey has been erasing: 'Bun na hAbhann . . . Druim Dubh . . . Poll na
gCaorach . . . Lis Maol'. Máire responds: 'Lis na nGradh . . . Carraig an Phoill'.
And finally the two exchange place-names in a poetic enactment of their love:

**Yolland:** Carraig na Rí. Loch na nEan.
**Máire:** Loch an Iubhair. Machaire Buidhe.
**Yolland:** Machaire Mor. Cnoc na Mona.
**Máire:** Cnoc na nGabhar.
**Yolland:** Mullach.
**Máire:** Port.
**Yolland:** Tor.
**Máire:** Lag. (T, 429)

This exchange can be understood in terms of what Deleuze and Guattari call
the deterritorialization of language that is a feature of minor literature. For
Deleuze and Guattari, all language is initially a deterritorialization of the mouth,
the tongue and the teeth; that is, a diversion of these organs from their more
primitive function of eating. However, the production of sound is then reterri-
torialized in sense or meaning; articulated sound, produced according to the
correct or established patterns, takes on a representative function as it designates things in the world. It is here that the phenomenon of the minor use of
language intervenes in order to once again deterritorialize articulated sound;
this time, by diverting it from its representative function towards a more visceral
production of affects. In Kafka we see this, for example, in the sounds Gregor
makes after his metamorphosis, and more generally we could say that we see it
in any poetic language that prioritizes sound over meaning. In the case of this
passage, there is a paring back of meaning to expose the sounds themselves,
which can now function with more intensity for the characters than if sense had
been prioritized. This represents what Deleuze and Guattari call a 'line of

escape' along which language moves in ways that evade and undermine the established patterns of the major (Deleuze and Guattari 1986: 22).

However, Friel's dramatization of the powerful effect of language at a pre-semantic level is quickly undermined by the chance arrival of Sarah – the one-time mute. Sarah now uses her newly found powers of speech to tell Manus what she has seen, and by the next morning any chance of mutual understanding through newly invented languages is washed away. Yolland has disappeared, presumed murdered, and the English captain is threatening reprisals against the local people. In this post-Babel concatenation of voices it is Hugh – the old master – who has the task of formulating his community's response to the loss that colonization brings with it. Hugh's attitude to the language question can best be summed up in the title of the book which he claims to be writing: 'The Pentaglot Preceptor or Elementary Institute of the English, Greek, Hebrew, Latin and Irish Languages; Particularly calculated for the Instruction of Such Ladies and Gentlemen as may Wish to Learn without the Help of a Master' (T, 419). This title conveys not only Hugh's predilection for pomposity, but also the fact that he seems to move easily between Irish, Greek, Latin and English (although he admits to having no knowledge of Hebrew). Both characteristics are displayed, for example, when Hugh first arrives home from the pub having spent all day celebrating the baby's christening. Doalty, one of the less bright students, had just said 'The bugger's not coming at all. Sure the bugger's hardly fit to walk' (T, 397), when in he walks:

> **Hugh:** Adsum, Doalty, adsum. Perhaps not in sobrietate perfecta but adequately sobrius to overhear your quip. Vesperal salutations to you all . . .
> Apologies for my late arrival: we were celebrating the baptism of Nellie Ruadh's baby . . .
> And after the caerimonia nominationis – Máire?
> **Máire:** The ritual of naming.
> **Hugh:** Indeed – we then had a few libations to mark the occasion. Altogether very pleasant. The derivation of the word 'baptize'? – where are my Greek scholars? Doalty?
> **Doalty:** Would it be-ah-ah-
> **Hugh:** Too slow. James?
> **Jimmy:** 'Baptizein' – to dip or immerse.
> **Hugh:** Indeed – our friend Pliny Minor speaks of the 'baptisterium' – the cold bath.
> **Doalty:** Master.
> **Hugh:** Doalty?
> **Doalty:** I suppose you could talk then about baptizing a sheep at sheep-dipping, could you? (T, 397)

Despite Hugh's apparently antiquated pomposity, however, he is the one character who insists that in order to survive, the community needs to adapt to the changes that the English are enforcing. Even though he enjoys having fun at the expense of the English surveyors by appealing to the cultural stereotypes of the colonial relation – English, he says, is suited only to commerce (T, 399), while Irish is a rich, spiritual language (T, 418) – he is also well aware of the constant mutability of language and culture. In other words, he never actually believes in these myths of cultural identity. In echoing George Steiner's view that, to quote Hugh, 'a civilization can be imprisoned in a linguistic contour which no longer matches the landscape of fact' (T, 419), he seems to appreciate that 'fact' – which is the fact of modernity as well as of colonization – dictates a radical change in the traditional life of Baile Beag. This assessment is underlined again at the close of the play when, having reluctantly agreed to teach Máire English, Hugh recites one of the opening passages of Virgil's Aeneid, in which the destruction of Carthage – the city Juno 'loved above all the lands' – is predicted (T, 446). If the goddess Juno could not prevent the annihilation of Carthage at the hands of Rome, the words seem to suggest, then what hope do the mere mortals of Baile Beag have to defend their language and traditions? Nellie Ruadh's baby, whose christening opened the play, is now dead, Sarah has been returned to mute silence by the threats of Captain Lancey, and the whole community is facing eviction; and yet Hugh picks up the name-book that Owen has discarded and says: 'We must learn those new names We must learn where we live . . . We must make them our new home' (T, 444).

The play closes with a reading from Virgil's *Aeneid*, just as it had opened with a reading from Homer's *Odyssey*. The opening passages, which Jimmy had read aloud in Greek, tell how Athene transformed Odysseus into a beggar on his return home, so that he could pass unnoticed into his own house; the closing passages tell how a son of the defeated Troy was destined to become the founder of a great empire – an empire which would one day defeat the Greeks as well as the Carthaginians. On the surface, this juxtaposition seems to suggest a cyclical view of the impersonal forces of history: just as Troy fell to the Greeks and Carthage fell to the Romans, so Ireland must fall to the English and there is nothing that any individual can do to prevent it. However, tying the play together between these two *texts*, these two works of poetry – Homer's and Virgil's – is not just about giving us a history lesson; it is also a way of showing that translation is a fundamental feature of culture. Just as Aeneas' journey of exile across the Mediterranean is a translation of Odysseus' journey of homecoming across the Aegean, so Virgil's text is a translation of Homer's. Virgil transfers Odysseus from Greece to Rome, just as Joyce was to transfer him from Troy to Dublin, and Heaney transfers him from Hades to Northern Ireland. When Hugh, paraphrasing Steiner, suggests that 'it is not the literal past, the facts of history, that shape us, but images of the past embodied in language' (T, 445), he opens up the possibility that if these images are re-made, if these translations are re-worked, then we might be re-shaped.

## Translation and Metaphor

The central thesis of George Steiner's book *After Babel*, a thesis which informs Friel's whole approach to the politics of naming, is that translation is not just something which happens between languages: it is also, at a more fundamental level, the central feature of human communication and culture. At the level of individuals, language translates – or tries to translate – between privacies. At the level of culture and tradition, it is the human capacity to 'translate out of time' which, in Steiner's view, makes 'civilization' possible; culture, he suggests, is the 'translation and rewording of previous meaning'.[10] For a language, a culture or a tradition to survive, then, this process of translation and 'rewording' must never cease. This process of translation is, however, also a process of transformation; the thing which is carried over, translated, is always a renewed version of the original. There is, however, no possibility of a return to an original pre-Babel unified language. Indeed, for Friel and Steiner the whole problematic of the translation's relation to the original is undermined by the assumption that since the process is unending there is, strictly speaking, no original with which one could have a relation.

Steiner's argument, that the driving force behind human culture is endless translation, is strikingly analogous to Nietzsche's idea that the 'fundamental human drive' is 'the drive toward the formation of metaphors' (1979: 88). And indeed Nietzsche, like Friel, appeals to the experience of confusion to convey this idea. It is this continuous drive to form new metaphors which, for Nietzsche, ensures that the conceptual freezing of old metaphors is always under attack. This drive 'continually confuses the conceptual categories . . . by bringing forward new transferences, metaphors and metonymies' (1979: 89). If we follow the etymological connection between 'translation' (Latin: carry over/across) and 'metaphor' (Greek: carry over/across) then it would seem that both Steiner and Nietzsche are identifying the same drive as being fundamental to human reality. And both also identify it as the drive towards the transformation of the world we live in – a drive which is fundamentally creative. Nietzsche expresses this idea in words that Yeats might have written when he says that this impulse 'continuously manifests an ardent desire to refashion the world which presents itself to waking man . . . in the colours of the world of dreams' (1979: 89) while for Steiner, similarly, this drive towards 'fiction' and 'counterfactuality' indicates that the relation between human consciousness and reality is a creative one (1975: 473). And if an Auden, or a Longley, were to object that these fictions, these metaphors, cannot do anything, then both Steiner and Nietzsche could reply that they can indeed do something, since the 'original' reality with which they are dealing is itself a metaphor, a translation, a fiction. And what better way is there of modifying a metaphor, of shifting a translation, than replacing it with a new one? In *Translations*, Friel attempts to bring the audience to an acknowledgement that such a transference is possible, by demonstrating on stage the endlessly translated nature of cultural reality. Contra Auden, then, Friel shows how it might be possible, through drama, for Ireland to escape both its own madness and that of its neighbouring island.

According to Deleuze and Guattari, the third feature of a minor literature is the way it takes on a collective value; that is, it accepts the task of expressing and giving a certain shape to a particular community. This community may be the actual minority community, or it may be an imagined community that does not yet exist. At the end of Friel's play, we see that the dilemma facing Hugh and his community is how to continue living in a culture and a place which is being translated out of all recognition. If the translation of mere place-names from Irish into English is so destructive, if even the translation of exogamy is so impossible, then how can a culture survive the ordinary, everyday ubiquity of translation? Whether the force of this change comes through colonization or modernization, or both, its paradox is that it represents both the life-blood and the death-knell of a culture. The Donegal of Carraig na Rí, Machaire Buidhe and Cnoc na Mona, doesn't exist today any more than the Norfolk of Winfarthing, Barton Bendish and Saxingham Nethergate. When Máire recites these names in memory of her lover she grants them the same power and significance as the names of her own place. And when Hugh recommends learning the new place names, he seems to be encouraging his community to re-form itself in the light of a new political reality.

For Friel, writing in the context of Northern Ireland politics in the 1970s, there is also an attempt to formulate a new community, one that could move beyond the cultural atavisms of the past. His task is to make possible the formation of a community that would embody 'another consciousness and another sensibility' (Deleuze and Guattari 1986: 17). A community with another sensibility is a community that has undergone a transformed experience. In particular, Friel seems to be suggesting that it is the recognition of the parity of loss that might provide part of the basis for future transformation. If the task of a postcolonial politics is to overcome the legacy of colonization, and if that legacy – at least in Northern Ireland – manifests in an entrenched cultural essentialism that focuses on language (and frequently the language of place-names: e.g. Londonderry vs. Derry), then an enterprise such as Friel's and Field Day's can be effectively political to the extent that, to use Nietzsche's phrase, it 'confuses these conceptual categories'. What the play shows, therefore, contrary to the views of Thomas Davis, is that we are all already 'adrift among the accidents of translation'. And it is only by accepting this confusion that we can hope to create new linguistic, cultural and political formations.

I want to step back from the details of this particular play now and return to the viewpoint from which I started. Since my interest is in the general conditions that make it possible for works of fiction to have transformative effects, one part of my task is to identify what it is about these works that gives them this capacity. So far as Friel is concerned, the question would be how is it possible for this play to work in the way I say it does. If we were to just read Steiner's book, some Nietzsche, and some Deleuze and Guattari, wouldn't that be just as good, just as effective? Why do we need Friel, or any other writer, to transform the way we think about, or experience, culture, language and identity? At this stage, we can say that this potential has something to do with the enactment of a certain kind of confusion. Works of fiction, whether poetry, plays or novels, introduce an element of confusion into our experience of the world in so far as they disrupt the familiar channels of our perception and thought. While it is certainly true that works of, for example, philosophy can have the same impact, literature does so uniquely in that its use of language is more fully free to expose, as Foucault says, 'that which does not exist, in so far as it is' (1963c: 280). It is this capacity, which can be seen as its power to escape established linguistic practice on improvised lines of flight, that distinguishes the literary form of language from language that pretends to straightforwardly name a pre-given world. While many of the striking examples of this effect may come from contexts, such as those of Kafka and Friel, in which the conditions for a minor literature exist, it is by no means confined to these cases. My suggestion, therefore, is that it is this confusion, which we can understand as a confusion between that which is and that which is not, that gives fiction its capacity to intervene in that which is (our given forms of experience and thought) in order to bring about that which is not (a transformed experience). The great value of Friel's play is that at the same time as it explores the linguistic and cultural confusions of the Irish experience, it enacts and puts into practice this more fundamental confusion, the confusion which is the source of the power of literature to change the world we live in.

# Chapter 5

# Foucault's Concept of Experience

In his *History of Madness* Foucault refers to a book, any book, as something that is merely a 'minuscule event, a small manageable object' (2006: xxxviii[9]). In a similar vein Italo Calvino observes, in a discussion of the possible political effects of a novel, that 'a book is a grain of sand' (1987: 87). But if a book is a minuscule event, a small object, a mere grain of sand, how can literature have any of the effects that we have been attributing to it? In one of several interviews in which he discusses his dissatisfaction with the philosophical milieu of his student days, which was dominated by Marxism, phenomenology and existentialism, Foucault makes the following startling claim: 'for me the break was first Beckett's *Waiting for Godot*, a breathtaking performance' (2004: 176). It might be best to take this statement as an example of nostalgia tinged with hyperbole, for how could a play really be part of what provokes a thinker to re-orient their thought? Yet, apart from any question of Foucault's own intellectual biography, we have already begun to see some of the ways that literature might be able to have this kind of effect. We have begun to piece together the peculiar characteristics of works of literature, the characteristics that give them the capacity to effect this kind of change. Continuing now from the recognition that the work of literature can only be fully understood as occurring in the interaction between a reader and a text, we have to address both sides of this dyad. In other words, we must now begin to find a way to think about the features of the human subject that make it susceptible to transformation through an engagement with fiction. Our question now becomes: what is it about our forms of subjectivity that makes this kind of transformation possible? In what ways can a human being be changed, or change themselves, through reading a poem or seeing a play? In order to answer these questions, I will draw on the concept of experience that emerges in Foucault's late work. This is not a concept that emerges fully formed in that work, however, and in order to adequately understand it we will need to carry out a detailed excavation of its development in the course of his thought, from the earliest to the latest.

# The Formation of Experience

Among the central terms of Foucault's thought – power, knowledge, truth, critique – the one which has perhaps received the least attention is experience.[1] And yet 'experience' runs through Foucault's works from the earliest to the latest in a way that rarely draws attention to itself, but occasionally bursts out in such resonant phrases as 'limit experience' and 'experience book'. In an interview given in 1978, for example, Foucault gives an account of his entire philosophical development in terms of this concept (1980a). There were certain works, he says, by Bataille, Blanchot and Nietzsche, which opened up for him the possibility of philosophy as a 'limit experience' – an experience which tears us away from ourselves and leaves us no longer the same as before (1980a: 241[43]). Such books, which he also wishes to write himself, he calls 'experience books' rather than 'truth books'; and they are experimental (remembering, as we have seen, that *expérience* also means experiment) in the sense that they put the author and the reader to the test of their own limits (1980a: 246[47]). Hence his books on madness, the prison and sexuality not only examine our forms of knowledge and our practices, they also try to transform them. But running alongside this dazzling use of the concept is a more mundane sense in which experience seems to mean the general, dominant background structures of thought, action and feeling that prevail in a given culture at a given time. We could say that, from *History of Madness* to the final volumes of *The History of Sexuality*, Foucault offers historical studies of particular modes of experience; from the experience of madness in the eighteenth century to the experience of sexuality in ancient Greece. In fact, even in his very last lecture at the Collège de France, he can still speak in terms of a contrast between a general Christian experience and a modern European experience of philosophy.[2] These are two quite different uses of the term experience, therefore, and we will have to trace both of them through Foucault's work.

Let us begin our exploration of this theme with Foucault's first major work, the *History of Madness*. In the Preface to the first edition Foucault quotes, without attribution, a passage that comes from one of René Char's prose poems, ending with the sentence '*Développez votre étrangeté légitime*' ('develop your legitimate strangeness/foreignness').[3] This imperative could stand as an epigraph to Foucault's entire work, a series of books that in their effort to 'think otherwise' [*penser autrement*] (1984a: 9[15]) constantly explore whatever is foreign to our ways of thinking and acting. The work on madness, in particular, sets out to explore the original gesture by which madness and unreason were expelled from the rational experience of the modern West – the division in which they became what is most strange, foreign and excluded for reason.[4]

When the book was republished in 1972, however, Foucault removed the original preface and wrote a new one. In the new Preface, he steps back from

the role of authorial voice, resisting what he sees as the temptation to impose a
law of interpretation on the work. After all a book, he says, may indeed be
'a minuscule event' (2006a: xxxvii[9]), but it is an event which is followed by a
proliferating series of simulacra – interpretations, quotations, commentaries –
which an author cannot and should not try to limit. Making a curious distinction, Foucault says he would not want a book to claim for itself the status of
'text', to which criticism would like to reduce it. He would like it to present
itself, instead, as 'discourse': by which he means 'at the same time battle and
weapon, strategy and blow . . . irregular encounter and repeatable scene'
(2006a: xxxviii[10]). What then is the series of events in which this book on
madness is inscribed? To what battle and struggle does it contribute? One way
to answer these questions is to begin with the centrality of the notion of experience that structures and animates Foucault's approach to madness.

At the centre of this book, as the original Preface shows, there are two notions
of experience. On the one hand there is the idea of a 'limit-experience', a foundational gesture by which a culture excludes that which will function as its outside (2006b: xxix[161] ); in this case, the exclusion of madness and unreason
by reason. Hence, it is a question in this book of going back to the 'zero degree'
(2006b: xxvii[159]) of the history of madness, where reason and unreason are
still undifferentiated and not yet divided, to a time before this exclusion.[5]
Foucault suggests that one could do a series of histories of these limit-experiences, which might include the construction of the Orient as other to the West,
the fundamental division between reason and dream, and the institution of
sexual prohibitions. To this list we could add the division, represented for us by
Plato, between the discourse of reason and the language of poetry. It is worth
noting that this 1961-vintage 'limit-experience' is not exactly the same as the
one Foucault appeals to in the 1978 interview which I quoted in relation to the
'experience book' (1980a). In that interview, a 'limit-experience' is an extreme
experience which transgresses the limits of a culture – an experience, that is, of
the sort that Bataille both describes and conjures – while here it is the experience in which a culture actually creates those limits. Once again, we see that the
tension between the senses of experience has reproduced itself, but this time
*within* one of its forms. However, let us remain for the moment within the context of *History of Madness*. In order to understand the limit-experience that
divides reason from madness, it is necessary to turn to what Foucault calls 'the
classical experience of madness'.[6] In this phrase, which recurs throughout the
book, 'experience' is taken as arising from the whole set of the dominant ways
of seeing, thinking about, and acting towards madness – ways which include systems of thought, institutions and the legal apparatus ['notions, institutions,
judicial and police measures, scientific concepts'] (2006b: xxxiii[164]).

The first point to note about this use of the term is that Foucault
never gives an explicit definition of experience: he never tells us exactly what
the term covers. Early in the book we read phrases such as 'all the major

experiences of the Renaissance' (2006a: 8[21]),[7] 'the Western experience of madness' (2006a: 16[34]), 'the experience of madness in the fifteenth century' (2006a: 24[43]), and of course the ubiquitous 'classical experience of madness' (2006a: 15[32]), but experience itself is never defined. Nevertheless, it is possible to piece together a Foucauldian concept of experience. In the first place, it involves the way in which a given object is *seen* and *conceptualized* for a given culture. For example, at the beginning of the Renaissance, Foucault tells us, there was a confrontation between two possible forms of the experience of madness – a 'tragic' and a 'critical' experience (2006a: 26[45]). And these two forms, we are told, are the basis of 'everything which could be felt (*éprouvé*) and formulated (*formulé*) about madness at the beginning of the Renaissance' (2006a: 27[46]). Later, speaking of the great enclosure of unreason, he says that it is this 'mode of perception' which must be interrogated in order to understand the classical age's 'form of sensibility to madness' (2006a: 54[80]). The practice of internment, he suggests, partly explains 'the mode in which madness was perceived, and lived, by the classical age' (2006a: 55[80]). Out of this practice, a 'new sensibility' (*sensibilité*) towards madness is born (2006a: 62[89]), a new object is created, and the many ways of engaging with unreason are organized around a form of 'perception' (2006a: 101[140]). A final example: 'Classicism felt (*éprouvé*) a delicacy in front of the inhuman which the Renaissance had never felt (*ressentie*)' (2006a: 143[192]). The first aspect of any experience, then, will be the forms of perception or sensibility which it makes possible – or even necessary. A given structure of experience makes possible, and gives rise to, certain ways of sensing, seeing and feeling an object.

But these forms of perception are not the only components of a structure of experience. Despite Foucault's apparent focus on phenomena of perception and (individual) consciousness, it must be emphasized that for him the experience of madness is not just a form of sensibility. It also comprises both the institutional practices of internment and the forms of knowledge which develop within and bolster those institutions. In an interview given shortly after the original publication, Foucault makes the following claim, which could serve as a summary of the book: 'Madness only exists in a society, it does not exist outside the forms of sensibility which isolate it and the forms of repulsion which exclude or capture it' (1961: 169). These forms of repulsion, which both exclude and capture, may be taken to comprise what Foucault would later call the power/knowledge aspects of the relation to madness. There is, for instance, a certain 'practice and concrete awareness (*conscience*) in classicism' which is part of its distinctive experience of madness (2006a: 158[211]). Indeed, this experience is 'expressed' in the 'practice of internment' (2006a: 137[185]). In the classical age, then, the forms of repulsion comprised the great hospitals (such as Bicêtre in Paris and Bethlehem in London), combined with the modes of knowledge which tried to explain madness, for example, in terms of a purely negative absence of reason.

To speak of 'the classical experience of madness' is, then, to speak of the forms of consciousness, sensibility, practical engagement and scientific knowledge which take 'madness' as their object. And even though Foucault was later to admit that his use of the term experience was 'very inconstant' [*très flottant*] in *History of Madness* (1984f: 336[581]), it is nevertheless a concept that recurs with a certain regularity throughout the rest of his work. So, for example, in *The Order of Things* we are told that his aim is to show what becomes of the 'experience of order' between the sixteenth and nineteenth centuries. His question here is: how did the 'experience of language' – a 'global, cultural experience' – of the late Renaissance give way to a new experience in the classical age (1966a: 45–6[56])? It would be wrong to suggest, however, that the history of Foucault's use of the concept is entirely seamless. It is clear, for example, that after the late 1960s, and up until the late 1970s, he was less and less willing to characterize his work in terms of an investigation of experience. We can surmise that this was a result of his increasing dissatisfaction with the fluidity of the concept, but also of the fact that the concept, with its connotations of individual psychology, clashed with his new focus on bodies, resistance and power. We can note, for example, his comment in *The Archaeology of Knowledge* that *History of Madness* had given too great a role to an inchoate notion of experience – one which was in danger of reintroducing 'an anonymous and general subject of history' (2002: 18[27]).[8]

Nevertheless by the late 1970s, accompanying the final twist in Foucault's trajectory, the concept of experience had returned. Now it was no longer quite as inconstant as it had been before, and this is largely due to the increased complexity of his methodology as a whole. Summarizing briefly, we could say that Foucault's approach to any question will now contain three moments, each representing a particular phase his work has gone through. So, in a field such as sexuality, firstly he will consider the forms of knowledge (*savoir*) and discourse which are generated around sexual behaviour (roughly corresponding to his work in the 1960s); secondly, he will consider the forms of power that take hold of our behaviour (roughly corresponding to his work in the 1970s); and thirdly, a moment that is added only in the early 1980s, he will consider the modes of relation to self which our sexuality promotes and builds on. It need hardly be pointed out that even though this first, second and third followed that sequence in his own development, once all three approaches become available they are inextricably linked and have no chronological hierarchy. As Foucault points out in a late interview, 'these three domains of experience can only be understood one in relation to the others and cannot be understood one without the others' (1984g: 243[697]). Indeed, if the second phase doesn't so much add power to knowledge as introduce a new concept – power-knowledge – we could say that the final phase introduces another new concept – power-knowledge-self. What is important for us, however, is that this new tripartite concept can in fact be given a more simple name – experience.

In Foucault's mature thought, therefore, we can undertake an historical analysis of experience in terms of its three constitutive axes, which we can call knowledge, power and self. Or, in a later formulation, the domains of objectivation, coercion and subjectivation.

## The Transformation of Experience

Foucault begins to be explicit about the centrality of the idea of experience from the late 1970s; initially in an interview conducted in 1978 (1980a), and later in the various versions of the Preface to the second volume of the *History of Sexuality*. In the 1978 interview, the interviewer presses him to clarify his relation to the whole constellation of French intellectual life after World War Two, from Marxism and phenomenology to existentialism and literary modernism. What emerges most clearly from his responses is the sense that, at least at this stage in his thought, Foucault takes a certain notion of experience as the guiding thread linking multiple aspects of his intellectual and personal trajectory. We have already seen how this interview prioritizes what he calls the 'limit-experiences' which for him are represented by Bataille and Blanchot – those experiences which serve to 'tear the subject away from itself' and ensure that the subject will not remain as it was before (1980a: 241[43]). And we also saw that he wishes his own books to have this kind of effect, both for himself and for his readers – he wants them to be 'experience-books' rather than 'truth-books' or 'demonstration-books' (1980a: 246[47]).

This interview also gives us a way of understanding how these limit-experiences relate to the other kind of limit-experience: those which, as we saw, arise from the foundational gesture by which a culture excludes that which will function as its outside – for example madness (2006b: xxix[161]). Foucault speaks of these moments of rupture, or division, as giving rise to a certain experience in which a subject emerges as a concomitant to a field of objects. Thus, the process by which the object 'madness' emerges in the late nineteenth century also involves the process of emergence of a subject capable of knowing madness (1980a: 254[55]). This qualifies as a kind of limit-experience because it involves a transformation in a form of subjectivity, through the constitution of a field of truth. However, for Foucault a book which uncovers this history would itself endeavour to provide an experience which, in its own way, is also a limit-experience for the reader. Hence, 'the experience through which we manage to grasp in an intelligible way certain mechanisms (for example imprisonment, penalty, etc.) and the way in which we manage to detach ourselves from them by perceiving them otherwise, should be one and the same thing. This is really the heart of what I do' (1980a: 244[46], modified). What we find, then, is that Foucault uses the concept of limit-experience on, as it were, both sides of the analysis: it is both the object of the historical research and its objective. As he admits:

'it's always a question of limit-experiences and the history of truth. I'm imprisoned, enmeshed in that tangle of problems' (1980a: 257[57]). Alongside the
many attempts Foucault made to characterize his own work (in terms of knowledge, power/knowledge, or knowledge-power-subject), we can place this as an
additional and perhaps useful formula: his work continuously strives to understand and disentangle the connections between forms of experience and forms
of knowledge, between subjectivity and truth. And it strives to do so in a way
that makes it possible for readers to transform their own relation to these frame-
works of experience.

In the earliest version of the preface to the second volume of the *History of
Sexuality*,[9] Foucault explains the relation between his new interest in subjectivity
and his earlier focus on discourse and power, in terms of a general project of
the critical history of thought. This would mean the history of the forms of
objectivation, subjectivation and coercion which, at a certain time, for a particular set of people, constitute what he calls 'the historical *a priori* of a possible
experience' (1984e: 460[632]). These forms, which operate at multiple levels
of discourse and practice, constitute the limits of what can be known or thought
at any given time. They differ from the Kantian notion of an *a priori* of experience in that they are historically constituted and are, therefore, modifiable.[10]
Adopting the perspective of *History of Madness*, therefore, we could say that for
certain people in the eighteenth century, the experience of madness was made
possible by a historically specific combination of forms of objectivation, subjectivation and coercion. These forms, these structures of experience, determined
the way that insane, irrational people were seen, conceptualized and related to,
by those who considered themselves to be sane and rational. In the second version of this Preface (1984f), Foucault explains that to treat sexuality as a historically singular form of experience means to treat it as 'the correlation of a
domain of knowledge, a type of normativity and a mode of relation to self'
(1984f: 333[579]). In order to carry out a critical history of this 'complex experience' (ibid.), however, he must have the methodological tools for investigating each of these areas, and it is for this reason that, in the early 1980s, he tries
to work out a way of understanding the third domain – that of the self and its
relations. It is interesting to note that in this Preface, referring back to his very
earliest work, he mentions his dissatisfaction with the method of existential psychology (represented for him by his work on Binswanger: Foucault 1954) – a
dissatisfaction which arose, he now says, from that method's 'theoretical insuffi-
ciency in the elaboration of the notion of experience' (1984f: 334[579]). One
of the key differences then, between what we could call Foucault's pre-critical
and his critical phases is that the later phase will have to work out a sufficiently
complex notion of experience.

A key part of this notion is, as we have seen, the idea that our experience –
in the everyday sense of the term – is determined by forms of knowledge, power
and relation to the self which are historically singular.[11] And now we can add

that these forms, as a whole, constitute what Foucault calls thought – that is, the critical history of thought simply *is* the history of the forms, or structures, of our experience. Indeed thought, on this account, is what constitutes the human being as a subject.

'By 'thought', I mean that which institutes, in diverse possible forms, the game of truth and falsehood and which, consequently, constitutes the human being as a subject of knowledge; that which founds the acceptance or the refusal of the rule and constitutes the human being as a social and juridical subject; that which institutes the relation to self and to others, and constitutes the human being as ethical subject.' (1984f: 334[579])

Thought is, therefore, at the basis of the constitution of the human being as a subject in the three domains of knowledge, power and self – which are, as we have seen, the three fundamental domains, or axes, of experience. Of course, on this account thought is not something to be sought exclusively in the theoretical formulations of philosophy or science. It can, rather, be found in every manner of speaking, doing and conducting oneself. It can be considered, in fact, Foucault says, as 'the very form of action' itself (1984f: 335[580]). As we can see, Foucault is now working with a multi-layered notion of experience; and it is one which is not accessed through individual awareness, but through an analysis of what he now calls practices, or the modes of action in which people engage. We can study the forms of experience, he says, through an analysis of practices – as long as we understand practices as 'systems of action . . . inhabited by forms of thought' (ibid.). And this is precisely what he does in his histories of madness, the prison and sexuality.

The Kantian echoes of this critical project have no doubt been resonating clearly: Foucault was awoken from the slumber of existential psychology by his encounter with Nietzsche, and emerged into a critical phase in which he sought the *a priori* of experience. However, it wasn't the Kantian *a priori*, but the historical *a priori* that he sought; and not all possible experience, but historically singular experience. Foucault's project, then, differs fundamentally from that of Kant not just because of this historicizing of both the *a priori* and experience (and of course of the knowing subject), but also because it sets itself the task not of identifying unbreakable limits of reason, but of identifying singularities and working towards their transformation. Which is to say that it is critical in the Nietzschean, not the Kantian sense. What this means for experience is that the critical project aims not simply to understand the historical grounds of our experience, but to see to what extent it would be possible to change that experience – to transform it, through a critical work of thought upon itself. In the final version of the Preface to the second volume of the *History of Sexuality*, Foucault situates this project in the context of a possible history of truth – a history of the 'games of truth, the games of the true and the false, through which

being is constituted historically as experience; that is, as something that can
and must be thought' (1984a: 6–7[13]). It is these games of truth, and through
them these historically singular forms of experience, which can – perhaps – be
transformed.

Now that we have reached this idea of the transformation of experience, let
us return to the two senses in which Foucault uses the term. On the one hand,
as we have just seen, experience is the general, dominant form in which being
is given to an historical period as something that can be thought. But on the
other hand, experience is something which is capable of tearing us away from
ourselves and changing the way that we think and act. Throughout his work,
and his life, Foucault valorized those experiences which take us to the limits of
our forms of subjectivity. This was the attraction of writers such as Bataille, Blanchot and Nietzsche in the 1960s; it was the attraction of the sado-masochistic
practices which he discussed in interviews in the early 1980s; and it was also the
attraction of his more sedate engagement with the Stoics and the Cynics of late
antiquity. There was no point, he believed, in writing a book unless it was an
experience which in some way changed oneself. As he says at the end of the
early version of the Preface to the *History of Sexuality*, 'the pain and the pleasure
of the book is to be an experience' (1984f: 339[584]). But how can the experience of, for example, reading a book intervene to modify a general dominant
background experience?

The difficulty of answering this question, which can be related to the difficulty of explaining historical change, is something that, in different forms,
animated Foucault's entire theoretical trajectory. And it is a difficulty of which
he was well aware. Let's look at one example, from *The Order of Things*, where he
raises the question of the legitimacy of establishing discontinuities and periods
in a history of thought. How can we justify defining the limits of an age for
which we claim a certain coherence and unity – such as the classical age, for
instance? Isn't this simply setting an arbitrary limit in 'a constantly mobile
whole' (1966a: 55[64])? And, having established this continuity, how can we
then explain the collapse or disappearance of this coherent system? If this age
contains within itself a principle of coherence, then from where would come
'the foreign element [*l'élément étranger*]' which undermines it (1966a: 56[64])?
'How,' Foucault asks, 'can a thought melt away before anything other than
itself?' (ibid). How can we explain the fact that 'within the space of a few years
a culture sometimes ceases to think as it had been thinking up till then and
begins to think other things in a new way'? (ibid). The best answer that
Foucault can give is to say that this kind of discontinuity begins 'with an erosion
from outside' (ibid), an erosion which is made possible by the way in which
thought continuously 'contrives to escape itself' (ibid). The task of investigating these modes of escape, however, is one which Foucault says he is not yet
prepared to undertake. For the moment, he says, we will simply have to accept
the posited discontinuities – in all their obviousness and their obscurity.

Even though, in this context, Foucault backs away from further consideration
of this outside of thought, in another sense we can say that all of his work was

an attempt to investigate the ways that thought 'contrives to escape itself' through contact with such an outside. And at every renewed turn of that effort, the guiding thread was the idea of the strange, the foreign, the alien; and the question of its provenance and its effects. Summarizing briefly, once again, we could say that each of the three periods into which we can divide Foucault's work carries with it a different conception of the outside.[12] In the 1960s, that conception is bound up with his engagement with literature and, in particular, with the ideas of transgression and the outside which he gets from Bataille and Blanchot. In a series of essays published in literary journals at this time, as we have seen, Foucault demonstrated the influence which, for example, Blanchot's 'thought of the outside' had on the development of his own approach to this set of questions. In particular, Blanchot's literary-critical writing allowed him to formulate the connection between a certain crisis of subjectivity and the experience of an outside which comes to us in a subjectless language. In the 1970s, with the turn to politics and the question of power, we could say that the outside of thought, the engine or motor of change, is conceptualized as resistance which, perhaps, has its source in the forces of the body. While in the 1980s, with the final turn, the outside becomes, in a strange way, the inside of subjectivity itself; in other words, the potential for change emerges out of a folding back of the self upon itself.

One of the constant elements in this development is the way that the term *'étrange'* [strange/foreign] keeps reappearing in all its forms. We have already seen the line from René Char that Foucault includes in the first Preface to *History of Madness* – *'Développez votre étrangeté légitime'*. Several years later he turns this around, in a display of ironic self-deprecation, while responding to critics of *The Order of Things*. In response to their criticism he speaks of his sense of his own *'bizarrerie* [bizarreness]' – and what he calls his *'étrangeté si peu légitime* [his so little legitimate strangeness]' (1968: 53[674], modified). In *The Order of Things* itself, he speaks of literature as a form of discourse which has become, since the sixteenth century, 'most foreign' to Western culture (1966a: 49[59]); and speaking of the figures of the madman and the poet, he says that they find their 'power of foreignness [*leur pouvoir d'étrangeté*]' at the limits, the exterior boundaries of our culture (1966a: 55[64]). Much later, in the early 1980s, he can say that the whole – and only – point in writing a book, or doing philosophy, is precisely to introduce an element of the foreign into our ways of thinking. What would be the point in writing a book, he asks, if it didn't allow the person who wrote it to 'establish with himself a strange and new relation'? (1984f: 339[584]). Indeed, according to the final volumes of *The History of Sexuality*, it is the task of philosophy to see to what extent it can think otherwise, by 'the exercise which it makes of a knowledge which is foreign to it' (1984a: 9[15]).

Returning to the question of how certain experiences can intervene with a transformative force in our background experience, we can now say that this possibility always arises out of something that functions as an outside. There is nothing constant or universal about this outside, however, since it is always relative to the dominant forms of a given regime of thought and practice. We have seen that for Foucault the locus of the outside changes as his general methodology develops. In the 1960s it is something which is experienced and conveyed through certain works of literature, and also in the foundational gestures of exclusion, while by the 1980s it is something which makes itself felt, for example, in the cultivation of transformative techniques of the self. At this stage Foucault has, apparently, left behind his interest – and his faith – in literature as one of the ways in which thought 'contrives to escape itself'. In his late work, his experience books are no longer by Beckett, Blanchot or Bataille, but by Seneca, Diogenes and Plato. And they are also, of course, his own books – especially *History of Madness, Discipline and Punish* and the first volume of the *History of Sexuality*. We must, however, resist the temptation to see this shift as a progressive development which would leave behind each earlier phase. Rather, it would be much more productive if we were to maintain all three levels simultaneously. In that case, we would consider the work of transforming experience as something that can, at different times and in different ways, be effected through works of literature, through a resistance whose source is in the body, and through a re-elaboration of relations to the self. For us, it would then become possible to combine Foucault's conceptualization of the foreign, or the outside of thought, with his notion of experience and its possible transformation, and to use this framework as a way of understanding one of the effects of which literature is capable.

## Fiction, Experience, Experiment

Reading Foucault's work for its analysis of experience, therefore, gives us a way of answering our question about the conditions of possibility of the transformation of experience. The forms of human subjectivity and experience are built up historically in such a way that they are in a constant state of change and modification. We can analyse these forms in terms of three domains, or axes, that Foucault calls knowledge, power and self. Since these axes are constituted historically, both individually and in their complex inter-relations, they are inherently open to modification, both from outside and from within. My premise, and in fact the premise of Foucault's intellectual endeavour, is that there are certain books that can contribute to the modification of these modes of experience and subjectivity. However, I also want to show that Foucault's analysis gives us a way of establishing the transformative potential of specifically literary works. In other words, I want to show that it gives us a way of understanding the capacity of literature, as opposed to philosophy or science, to act as an experience-transformer. Foucault's analysis does this, initially, through the role it gives to fiction.

We have already seen (Chapter 3) that in the 1960s Foucault had defined literature in terms of the nature of the fictive use of language. The fictive, in this sense, is the capacity of language to bring us into contact with 'that which does not exist, in so far as it is' (1963c: 280). And, according to Foucault, any form of language which explores the distance between that which does not exist and that which is – whether it is prose, poetry, novel or 'reflection' (presumably including philosophy) – is a language of fiction (1963c: 280–1). While Foucault was to leave behind this core interest in literary fictions, the general understanding of fiction itself survived into his later work. If we read this 1960s statement alongside a comment he makes in one of his last interviews, we can see yet again how Foucault's trajectory inscribes a spiral rather than a straight line. In this interview from 1983, Foucault suggests that the task of the philosopher-historian is to carry out a diagnosis of the present by focusing on the 'lines of fragility' which make possible 'fractures' in our contemporary reality. By following these lines we would be able to grasp those elements of our present which are open to change. The role of the intellectual would then be to 'say that which is, in making it appear as that which may not be, or may not be as it is' (1983b: 450[449]). This is an interesting echo and reversal of the earlier characterization of fiction: fiction says that which is not, in so far as it is; while the intellectual says that which is, in so far as (potentially) it is not. But, of course, this is not so much a reversal as an alternative expression of the same suggestion: that fiction (in the broadest possible sense) relates to reality by opening up virtual spaces which allow us to engage in a potentially transformative relation with the world; to bring about that which does not exist and to transform that which does exist. The insight Foucault is expressing in the 1960s essay is that this possibility, the possibility of bridging the distance between that which is and that which may be, is given for us in the very nature of language.

There is no doubt that Foucault in general understood his own works of 'reflection', that is to say his works of historico-philosophy, as operating within this field of the fictive. In a discussion of his *History of Sexuality, volume I*, for example, he responds to a question about the dramatic nature of his works by saying, 'I am well aware that I have never written anything but fictions' (1977a: 193[236]). A fiction, however isn't necessarily outside of truth. It is possible for fiction to induce effects of truth, just as it is possible for a discourse of truth to fabricate, or to fiction, something. Since fiction is not defined in opposition to truth, therefore, Foucault's statement cannot be read as an admission of historical inaccuracy. It is, rather, a claim about the creative or productive power of the book in the context of a particular historical moment. This book, in fact all his books, are fictions in the sense that they aim to bring about, or to fiction, a transformation. 'One "fictions" history,' Foucault says, 'starting from a political reality which makes it true,' and 'one "fictions" a politics which doesn't yet exist starting from a historical truth' (ibid).

It may be helpful, in this context, to think of fiction in the same way we think of *poesis*; that is, as a fundamentally productive engagement with the world. To fiction is to fabricate, to produce, to bring into existence. The distinctive

feature of Foucault's histories, the feature which gives them their transformative power, is the fact that they are not only descriptions of the past, but attempts
to modify the present through a transformation, or a fictioning, of experience.
And all experience is, at a certain level, something that we produce or fabricate.
In a discussion of *History of Madness*, in the context of his idea of an experience-
book, Foucault underlines again the importance for him of inducing an experience in the reader which would have a transformative effect. This effect,
however, must be based on historically accurate research. 'It cannot', as he says,
'exactly be a novel' (1980a: 243[45]). But what matters most is not the series of
true, or historically verifiable, findings; it is, rather, the experience that the
book makes possible. And this experience is neither true nor false; like every
other experience, it is a fiction. 'An experience', Foucault says, 'is always a fiction; it is something which one fabricates for oneself, which doesn't exist before
and which happens to exist after' (ibid, modified). Nevertheless, this fabricated
experience maintains a complex set of relations with the truth of historical
research. The experience that the book makes possible is founded on the truth
of its findings, but the experience itself is a new creation which may even, up to
a certain point, destroy the truth on which it is based. It is not surprising then,
that Foucault admits that 'the problem of the truth of what I say is, for me,
a very difficult problem, and even the central problem' (1980a: 242[44]).

   But what of this idea that every experience is a kind of fiction, or is something
that we fabricate for ourselves? How can we make sense of this suggestion?
We have already seen (in Chapter 1) that the term experience is itself closely
connected to notions of experiment and a perilous engagement with the world.
And we have seen the idea, presented by Dewey, that experience is both a doing
and an undergoing. Similarly, the idea that experience can be an activity, rather
than something to which the individual is passively subjected, is already contained within the structures of the French language – in a way which is not the
case in English. In French, to have an experience is *faire une expérience* (literally,
to *make* or *do* an experience). In a similar way, just as in English we would say
that we have a dream, in French one makes a dream (*j'ai fait un rêve*). In the
case of experience, what this means is that when we read in English of Foucault
discussing having an experience, more often than not in French he is using the
phrase *faire une expérience*. The significance of this difference is that this is a
phrase which could, almost as easily, be translated into English as 'doing an
experiment'. In Foucault's use of the term, therefore, the idea that experience
is an active and experimental engagement is never far from the surface. Let me
give one example of how this semantic richness is sometimes lost in translation.
In the interview I've been quoting from, Foucault says: 'Mon problème est de
faire moi-même, et d'inviter les autres à faire avec moi ... une expérience de ce
que nous sommes ... une expérience de notre modernité telle que nous en
sortions transformés' (1980a: 242[44]). The English translation, unfortunately,
reduces this sense of engaging in a transformative experiment by speaking

simply of 'sharing an experience'.[13] For Foucault, however, to invite others to 'do this experiment/have this experience' with him, means that we would embark upon a shared testing of the limits of our modern forms of subjectivity. This is the kind of test that the experience-book makes available for its readers. On the basis of this understanding, we can now link up the idea of fiction, in its broadest sense, with the idea of experience. We can do this through the concept of experiment, which is the element that, under certain circumstances, they have in common. So, when Foucault says that all his works are fictions, we can understand him as saying that they are fictions because they are experimental and, similarly, they are experimental precisely because they are fictions.

On the basis of Foucault's analysis of experience, therefore, we can distinguish between two uses of the term which will play a key role in our account of the transformative potential of literature. We can distinguish between, on the one hand, something that we will call 'everyday' or 'background' experience and, on the other hand, something that we will call 'transformative' experience. In *History of Madness*, for example, we could say that Foucault was describing aspects of the everyday experience of madness in the classical age and the way that experience was quite abruptly transformed at the beginning of the nineteenth century. However, we have to bear in mind that this everyday experience incorporates a whole range of elements (epistemological, normative, etc.) of which any given individual may be unaware. It is not everyday, therefore, in the sense of being commonly understood, but in the sense that it forms a constant, albeit constantly changing, background to our ways of perceiving, understanding and acting in the world. This form of experience is what Foucault finally analyses in terms of three axes: knowledge, power and self. On the other hand, we can distinguish the category of transformative experiences, which comprises not only the Bataillean limit-experiences of the 1960s and the more sedate experiences provided by Foucault's own books, understood as experience-books, but also the sort of experiences that many works of literature open up for their readers. These are experiences which stop us in our tracks and make it more difficult for us to continue to think and act as we had done before. In other words, they make it more difficult for us to carry on unthinkingly in the forms of our everyday experience. It's important to note that when I speak of everyday experience here I am speaking of experience in general; and that, in an important sense, is ongoing and continuous. However, when I speak of transformative experiences I am speaking of something that is, at best, occasional and discrete. Now, my suggestion is that these discrete, punctual events are capable of intervening in and interrupting our ongoing, everyday experience. That is, they are not just high points, or moments of intensity, in the everyday flow of experience; rather, or in addition, they are events which leave the background experience transformed. If we call this kind of experience transformative, then, it is because it can modify our everyday experience by bringing about a shift, or a re-configuration, somewhere along its three axes:

knowledge, power and self. My suggestion is that a transformative experience, whether it comes in the form of a work of philosophy, fiction or history – or in any of its other multiple possible forms – will therefore leave the individual no longer the same as before.

It may help, at this point, to contrast this position with the closely related one which Dewey developed. An experience, such as the reading of a certain kind of book, is distinctive in that it intervenes in, and potentially undermines, the general form of experience that is given as its background. It has the power to do this, precisely because it constitutes what Dewey would call *an* experience. But the background of ordinary experience is also what makes possible this intervention – since, for example, it is only within a certain historically singular form of experience that a work of literature could have a transformational effect. It might seem then, that the distinction for Foucault is the same as the one Dewey makes between the general run of inchoate experience, and the kind of experience which a work of art – or a game of chess – can convey. The crucial difference, however, is that, for Foucault, the extra-ordinary experience is an *intervention* in the conditions that make ordinary experience possible – it is always valorized for its capacity to shake the grounds of our everyday, unthought experience. For Dewey, on the other hand, the idea of an experience does not necessarily carry this value. Even though, as we have seen, there is a conceptualization of the capacity of those experiences that art makes possible to continue to work within the audience's experience long after the work has been seen, Dewey does not seem to share Foucault's fascination with, and his demand for, a modification of subjectivity. Employing Foucault's vocabulary, then, we can say that a work of literature might be capable, perhaps through a particular quality of its language, or the structure of its narrative, of intervening in the everyday experience of an individual or a group, and bringing about a shift in their form of subjectivity. It might be capable, that is, of helping us to detach ourselves from ourselves, of helping us to think otherwise.

## Fictional Experiments

At the beginning of this chapter, I said that the question I wanted to address is, what is it about our forms of subjectivity that makes a transformation through works of fiction possible? The first part of my answer was to point out that since these modes of experience and subjectivity are historically constituted, they are always potentially modifiable. The second part of my answer is to suggest that literature can contribute to this process of transformation through its fictive nature in so far as it resonates with the productive, creative nature of all experience, and introduces something that can function as an outside in relation to the everyday experience of a reader. It is important to point out, however, that literature, like philosophy, isn't always or necessarily on the side of transforma-tive as opposed to everyday experience. It is just as likely, in fact much more likely, that what we call literature will bolster and reinforce accepted modes of experience and thought, than that it will undermine and transform them. These works are always tentative and experimental in nature; there is no guaranteed way to transform everyday experience, just as there is no way to accurately predict the effect or potential of any such work. And it is equally important to remember that such modifications are always small, fragile and uncertain; especially, we must admit, those which literature is capable of effecting.

Notwithstanding all these caveats, I would like to give another example now of the way that a particular work of literature can begin to effect this kind of change. I want to return to the work of Beckett; not to *Waiting for Godot*, which was so important for Foucault, but to the novel *The Unnamable*, the final novel in Beckett's *Three Novels* from the 1950s.[14] What can we say about the potential effect of this novel? What kinds of transformation is it capable of effecting? One of its potential effects is to make it more difficult for the reader to carry on with a certain understanding of themselves as a centre of rationality, language and experience. Speaking very schematically, we could say that the everyday experi-ence of self which this book undermines is one that is, philosophically, based upon the Cartesian *cogito*. Descartes can doubt everything, except his own exis-tence as a thinking, and therefore rational, being. But Beckett can doubt even this. And in fact what this book makes possible, through the fictional world it creates, is for the reader to share in an experiment in which this conception of the self is put to the test and, perhaps momentarily, exploded. In a discussion of the art of the novel, Milan Kundera makes the point that a fictional character is not an imitation of a living being, but 'an imaginary being. An experimental self' (1988: 34). We shouldn't see this as primarily an alter-ego for the author, but more as an experimental self for any reader of the work. With regard to Beckett's novel, however, we can say that his characters are experimental in a double sense: not only are they an experiment that the author sets up and allows the reader to participate in, but they continuously engage in experimen-tation on themselves. At times this can appear to be similar to the thought experiments that philosophers – such as Descartes or Husserl – use, but Beck-ett's characters typically move in a contrary direction. That is, not through doubt to a new foundation for certainty, but from certainty, through doubt, to a splintering of the self and its hold on the world.

Early in *The Unnamable*, for example, the narrator (if we can call him that) begins a process which seems to be decidedly Cartesian: 'I, of whom I know nothing, I know my eyes are open . . .' (U, 304). But this one certainty will not be allowed to form the basis for any other knowledge. How does he know his eyes are open? 'Because of the tears that pour from them unceasingly' (ibid.). He continues:

Ah yes, I am truly bathed in tears. They gather in my beard and from there, when it can hold no more – no, no beard, no hair either, it is a great smooth ball I carry on my shoulders, featureless, but for the eyes, of which only the sockets remain. And were it not for the distant testimony of my palms, my soles, which I have not yet been able to quash, I would gladly give myself the shape, if not the consistency, of an egg, with two holes no matter where to prevent it from bursting. (U, 305)

It is important to notice that the process by which the speaker gives himself a form here is essentially fictive in nature. He doesn't ascertain his shape through introspection or self-examination; rather he gives himself a shape, he fictions himself, through his own speech. 'I would gladly give myself the shape . . . of an egg,' he says, and later even the tear-filled eyes will be transformed: 'I'll dry those streaming sockets too, bung them up, there, it's done, no more tears, I'm a big talking ball, talking about things that do not exist, or that exist perhaps, impossible to know, beside the point' (U, 305). Whether or not such things exist is beside the point because, nonetheless, they are there for us, the readers of the novel. They attest to the power of language to convey 'that which does not exist, in so far as it is' (1963c: 280).

Blanchot has observed that 'What most threatens reading is this: the reader's reality, his personality, his immodesty, his stubborn insistence upon remaining himself in the face of what he reads' (1982: 198). We can take it, therefore, that every work of literature will have to overcome the stubborn resistance of its readers if it is to carry out a transformation. Beckett does this by matching the stubbornness of the reader with his own stubborn insistence upon engaging in an experimental disaggregation of his characters. The transformative experience this makes possible for the reader is for them, too, to lose their heads, to see if they couldn't also do without these organs, 'all the things that stick out' – 'why should I have a sex, who have no longer a nose'? (U, 305). After all, why do we need organs? What is their function? As the speaker asks a little later about the mouth, 'Would it not be better if I were simply to keep on saying bababababa, for example, while waiting to ascertain the true function of this venerable organ?' (U, 308). In this way the novel opens up the individual as an embodied, thinking, speaking being, and stubbornly insists that the reader no longer remain him/herself in the face of what they read. And this, to borrow Foucault's words, would be the pleasure and the pain of the book. My suggestion, then, is that if we situate ourselves in the perspective of Foucault's late work, drawing upon the analysis of the notion of experience which I have outlined here, we can give an effective account of how literature is able to bring about a transformation of experience. My claim is that works of literature are capable, not so much (or, not only) of expressing an experience, but of transforming an experience. And they do this by experimentally intervening in and modifying our modes of thought – where thought is understood in the very

broad sense outlined above. In other words, we can understand works of literature as experimental, transformative interventions in the reader's everyday
experience – where everyday experience is understood as being constituted
along the three axes that Foucault's account lays open.

I will return to a more detailed discussion of Beckett's *Three Novels* in a later
chapter, but for now I want to address two related questions that are raised by
this way of formulating the effect of literature. As we know, Foucault's analysis
involves separating (at least in theory) three aspects or axes of experience: these
are the axis of knowledge, of power, and of self or ethics. The first question that
may arise, therefore, is whether we can speak of significant transformation occurring if only one of the three axes is affected. In the first place, we have to remember that Foucault himself, in thinking about individual and social change, always
recognized both the necessity and the value of partial, non-totalizing practices,
and there is no reason to suppose his attitude to literature would be any different. In any case, it is safe to suggest that a work such as Beckett's *The Unnamable*
can be effective in these Foucauldian terms, without having to modify our experience along all three axes. And, in fact, any change on any one of the axes will,
necessarily, lead to a modification of the overall mode of experience. But that
still leaves a second question: whether works of literature are only, or particularly, suited to having an effect on a single axis – which would, presumably, be
the axis of self or ethics. Following this line of thought we might suggest, for
example, that a work such as Charles Darwin's *Origin of Species* (1859) had a profound transformative effect on our experience at the level of knowledge, whereas
a work such as Dostoevsky's *The Brothers Karamazov* (1879) was (and continues to
be) more capable of effecting an ethical transformation. This would be to claim
that ethics is the domain in which literature is most likely to be effective, or is
even the only domain in which it is capable of having an effect. There is no
doubt that these are attractive and, in a way, easy assumptions to make. But the
problem is that they too easily compartmentalize the three axes of which Foucault speaks. Can we really say, for instance, which axis is most affected by Darwin's work? Did it not profoundly alter our self-understanding in terms of
science, religion, and ethics – in fact all three axes of our experience? And, similarly, could we not say that the value of Dostoevsky's work comes from his insight
into human behaviour – and the knowledge we learn from that – as much as
from its ability to modify our relation to ourselves? Going further, we could in
fact argue that it modifies our relation to ourselves precisely in so far as it modifies what we take to be facts about human behaviour. What this implies for the
case of literature is the extreme difficulty, if not the impossibility, of clearly
delimiting the axis along which an effect takes place, given the reverberating
consequences of such effects along the other axes. In other words, to be brief,
we have to take seriously Foucault's insistence that these three axes are intimately intertwined and that they 'can only be understood one in relation to the
others and cannot be understood one without the others' (1984g: 243[697]).

Rather than attempting to give a final, definitive account of the complexities of these relations here, it would perhaps be better to simply maintain an openness to the multiple effects of works of fiction, regardless of the axis, or the combination of axes, along which they resonate. All we need to conclude for now is that the schema I have outlined here gives us a way of arguing for the suggestion we started from: that certain works of literature can compel us to think otherwise. Because, while it is true that works of literature are, in a fundamental way, products of their time, this must be balanced  with the insistence that they can act, in the manner of an experiment, both within their time and against their time.

Chapter 6

# Re-making Experience:
# James Joyce

In a discussion of Joyce's relation to Irish nationalism, Seamus Deane suggests that Joyce is a writer who discovered the fictive nature of politics and whose work consequently becomes 'an examination of the nature of the fictive' (1982: 181). In this chapter we will see that, at least in *A Portrait of the Artist as a Young Man*,[1] his work is also an investigation into the fictive nature of experience in general. Joyce's semi-autobiographical novel can be read as an exploration of the complex intertwinings of what, following Foucault, we have called the three axes that constitute experience: knowledge, power, and self. The novel shows us the protagonist, Stephen Dedalus, making a series of attempts to understand and untie these restrictive threads of experience, while also engaging in the difficult task of re-making them in less constricting ways. The novel is of interest to us in two important ways. First, it vividly demonstrates the historically constructed nature of experience and the difficulty of escaping from those forms of experience which are, in varying ways, imposed on us. It gives us, in other words, a portrait of human experience that is both rich in its complexity and precise in its detail. Second, as a work of fiction itself, it invites us to participate in an experiment that may provoke us to engage in a similar labour ourselves; a labour of understanding and re-formation. In order to draw out these aspects of the novel I will appeal not only to the Foucauldian framework established in previous chapters, but also to some elements of Hans-Georg Gadamer's (2003) analysis of experience as *erlebnis* and *erfahrung*. Gadamer will be a helpful addition here because, while these two thinkers are in many ways poles apart, they share a fundamental recognition of the social, communal aspects of experience and of its resulting historical, and potentially modifiable, nature.

Towards the end of *A Portrait*, Stephen Dedalus makes an entry in his diary, before he leaves Dublin, in which he welcomes 'life' and writes that he goes 'to encounter for the millionth time the reality of experience' (P, 275–6). Experience is certainly something we encounter a million times, or rather, in a continuous stream, but it is also true that these encounters are not all equal.

This is because, as we have already seen, the encounter with experience is always something which puts us at risk and in peril. Gadamer is one philosopher who has focused on the fact that experience (or, at least, what he calls 'genuine experience') always has a negative and corrective aspect (2003: 353). Our experience in the present corrects, in a way which may be painful, our expectations which are based on previous experiences. Even though, generally speaking, our experience follows a smooth path of recognition and confirmation, then, to open ourselves to the world and to its inevitable shocks and assaults is to accept experience in its perilous aspect. In this chapter, I want to explore the relation between these two aspects of experience; on the one hand its everyday familiarity, and on the other hand its arresting strangeness. Such an approach opens up the possibility of thinking in more detail about the historicity and malleability of experience and, consequently, about the ways it may be changed through encounters with works of literature.

A novel invites us to engage in a test, an experiment, which not only teaches us something about the world but also promises to leave us transformed, in however small a way. If we say that our experience of the world is conditioned by a complex set of background modes of thought and action, then the novel as a particular experience is capable of transforming that everyday experience by challenging, undermining, or simply exposing to view, those background modes. It works, therefore, by allowing us to engage in an experiment on our own forms of experience, which both confronts us with new knowledge of the world, and challenges us to see how far it would be possible to think and act otherwise. Joyce's *A Portrait* is a valuable illustration of this potential, because the particular experiment it makes possible is largely focused on the nature of experience itself – from its supposedly raw form in sensation, to its mediated forms in language, thought and emotion. What's more, the novel presents us with a central character, Stephen Dedalus, whose development as an individual is intimately bound up with his attempts to question and reject the modes of experience which are offered to him (or forced upon him) by his culture.

This particular novel is experimental, therefore, in the sense that it engages in an experiment which is both investigative and transformative in nature. On the one hand, the fictional Stephen is placed under the microscope; Joyce engages in a vivisective examination of this character in his struggle with the world into which he is born.[2] And since vivisection is by its nature an investigation of a living subject, the portrait that emerges (as many critics have noted)[3] is a dynamic, moving image in which Stephen's transformations are portrayed in all their complexity. On the other hand, the novel itself is also an experience which the reader undergoes, and an experience from which we perhaps emerge transformed. Therefore, we have to try to understand the relation between, on the one hand, the growth of experience on the part of the character Stephen and, on the other hand, the transformation of experience that the novel makes possible for the reader. In other words, we will explore what the novel tells us about the nature of experience and we will try to understand how it potentially intervenes in our own experience of the world. In developing this exploration, my reading of the novel will focus on three themes – language, identity, and freedom; but first I want to address the role of sensation in experience.

## Original Sensation

We may think it is natural to assume that sensation is the primary, or primal, form of experience. Even though we can admit that as adults our experience, including what we get through our senses, is inevitably conditioned by myriad past experiences, we still tend to think that sensation is, in some sense, experience in its raw form. And if as adults we doubt whether we can really have such raw experiences, we can easily imagine that infants and young children, in all their innocence, are still capable of sensing the world with an unspoilt immediacy. Giorgio Agamben (1993), in fact, goes even further and argues that the only true or authentic experience would be one which precedes our linguistic subjectivity: hence, it is something which only the *infant* (the being without language) could undergo. This is a form of experience which, by definition, nobody could ever say they were having, and yet it is a form for which Agamben shows a distinct nostalgia.[4] But is it really possible, even in this nostalgic mode, to continue to speak of experience in this case? Is it possible to experience our senses in a pure, pre-subjective way? James Joyce, I would say, thinks not.

Early in *A Portrait*, the young Stephen Dedalus remembers his participation in a religious procession from the chapel in Clongowes Wood College to a small altar in the woods. The preparations had begun in the sacristy, where Stephen was the boatbearer – that is, the boy who carries the small quantity of incense that will later be placed in the censer by the priest. He remembers this experience in a passage that evokes the holy and mysterious sounds, smells and sights of the darkened room:

> He thought of the dark silent sacristy . . . It was not the chapel but still you had to speak under your breath. It was a holy place . . . A strange and holy place. The boy that held the censer had swung it gently to and fro near the door with the silvery cap lifted by the middle chain to keep the coals lighting. That was called charcoal: and it had burned quietly as the fellow had swung it gently and had given off a weak sour smell. And then when they were all vested he had stood holding out the boat to the rector and the rector had put a spoonful of incense in it and it had hissed on the red coals. (P, 40–41)

Let's assume that this passage is an accurate portrayal of the experience of a young boy in a particular situation. What is the nature of the experience? What strikes us at first is its strong sensual character: all the boy's senses are engaged, and all are given their place in the recollection. First of all, vision gives us the dark sacristy, the silvery cap and the red coals. Hearing gives us the hushed silence and the hissing coals. Smell gives us the weak sour smell of the charcoal and also, at least by implication, the strong smell of the incense. And even touch, I would suggest, can be discerned in the clause 'when they were all vested'.[5] It would seem to be obvious then, that Stephen's experience of the sacristy on this particular occasion comes to him through his senses. In fact, one might go so far as to say that all our experience ultimately arises from our sense perceptions. And if that was the case, we would be tempted to say that experience is a fundamentally individual – albeit communicable – phenomenon, something that is strictly an occurrence between our bodies (and our minds, if we want to be Kantian) and the world.

Despite the richness of Joyce's evocation of this individual sensuous experience, however, I would suggest that this simple assumption is one of the targets of the novel; because for Joyce, just as for Foucault, experience is an inherently social and collective phenomenon that is not reducible to individual sensation. In fact, in the short passage quoted above, we can already see that Stephen's experience of the sacristy is irremediably mediated by social and historical forms. The fact that the sacristy seems to him to be a strange and holy place is the product of centuries of Catholic tradition. The particular quality of its silence, and of the hushed voices, are determined by an awareness that the altar, containing the Blessed Sacrament, is close by. The smell of the charcoal, the touch of the vestments, the gentle swaying of the censer, and the actions of the priest, are all presented to Stephen's senses in a way that could only happen in a late-nineteenth-century Irish Jesuit college. What this means for Stephen, as we will see, is that there is an important sense in which his experience – like everybody's experience – is not his own. And one of the problems he sets himself in his adolescence is to see to what extent he can create, or at least give shape to, his own experience independently of the social and historical forces which try to mould him. The dual nature of experience, therefore, as both individual and shared, is one of the central, although unstated, themes of the novel.

Despite these doubts, however, it is still tempting to take the very first pages of *A Portrait* as a representation of a young child's immersion in the world of pure sensation. The young Stephen sees, hears, smells and tastes, all in a way that seems to have the freshness and innocence of newly experienced sensation. This way of reading the opening pages of the novel would seem to be supported by the fact that there is a marked shift in the presentation of experience as Stephen grows older. Simplifying, we could say that his childhood experience tends to be much closer to the physical, although linguistically mediated, world of sensation; whereas in later adolescence, his experience tends to become intellectualized and, for want of a better word, spiritualized. Despite this shift, however, I would suggest that what the opening pages show us is, in fact, the impossibility of attaining to an experience which is pure or innocent in the sense of being pre-linguistic, pre-subjective, or pre-social.

One preliminary point must be made before looking at these pages in detail, however: we have to remember that this novel is not an attempt to record the growing sensations, experiences and thoughts of James Joyce. It may indeed by a *bildungsroman*, a novel of development; and it may indeed draw upon the experience of Joyce himself; but it is primarily a *novel*, a work of fiction. The point here is that, like every other novel, it is not so much a recording of experience, as an experiment on experience; an experiment which has both an investigative and a transformative end. Indeed, its fictionality is something that the work itself insists on right from the beginning. Its title clearly announces that this is a work of *art*; it is a *portrait*, and a portrait not of the author or of a novelist or a poet, but of an *artist*. In fact, not the portrait of *an* artist (who may be Joyce himself), but *a* portrait of *the* artist. On one possible reading, this would be a portrait, we might say, of the artist-type, of the male artist-type, of the young male artist-type, to be precise.[6] If this isn't enough to alert us to the fictional status of the text, the opening words are unmistakable: 'Once upon a time, and a very good time it was . . .' (P, 3). That is, the novel begins in full fairytale mode with a story about a little boy. To insist on the novel's fictional status, however, is not to say that it is disconnected from life, or from what we call reality. In fact, the significance of the novel is its potential to bring about a shift in our relation to the world, and thereby to bring about a modification in the world itself. But the tools Joyce chooses to carry out this experiment are the tools of fiction. Ultimately, therefore, what matters is not that he tries, or pretends, to reflect or re-present the sensations and experiences of his protagonist or of himself. Instead, what is important is that he presents us with something that *we* experience in a way that makes it more difficult for us to continue with our habituated and ingrained forms of experience.

Let's turn now to the opening pages of the novel: the passage in question comprises the first one-and-a-half pages and it begins, as we have already seen, in the style of a fairytale about a young boy walking down the road and meeting a 'moocow' (P, 3). Stephen reports that his father, who looked at him through 'a glass' and had 'a hairy face', had told him that story. Here, it seems, the senses are galvanized into activity for the first time: the young boy hears the story, he sees his father's hairy face, and soon he tastes the lemon candy, he wets the bed, he feels the warm urine turning cold, he smells the oilsheet, he dances, he claps and he sings. The sensuous world of the child is presented to us in all its innocent, rich complexity. However, even before the end of the first page, clouds are already beginning to gather. We are made dimly aware of the complexities of late-nineteenth-century Irish politics, in the form of family friend Dante's maroon and green brushes; we are told that the boy has, apparently, fallen in love with his neighbour Eileen; and we witness the aftermath of some misdemeanour he has committed. We don't know what this sin is, but we can surmise that it has something to do with his plan to marry Eileen when they grow up; and we later learn that Dante doesn't like Stephen to play with Eileen because she is Protestant (P, 35). In any case, at this moment, he hides under the table as Dante and his mother insist that he apologize: but if there is one thing Stephen Dedalus never does, it is to apologize.

His mother and Dante threaten him that his eyes will be pulled out by the eagle, but Stephen is stubborn.

This opening sequence can be seen, in musical terms, as an overture to the novel as a whole: it introduces all the major themes and most of the major characters, and it follows a pattern which is reflected in the whole work. That is, at one level, a fall from innocence, occasioned by illicit sexuality, and a subsequent demand and refusal to repent; and at another level, a fall from innocence into an adult world of politics and passion in which Stephen must find his way – without apologizing; or, at a third level, an emergence into a world which is already mediated by stories and songs, in which Stephen must in some way make these borrowed songs his own. In this sense, the young Stephen is in the same position as the community in Friel's Ballybeg: he is faced with the task of re-translating for his own use old, well-worn modes of discourse. It is far from certain, therefore, that the opening pages of the novel can be read as an evocation of a pure, innocent experience in which the world is given to the child through unspoilt sensations. In fact what these pages show, against Agamben's nostalgic wish, is that any such raw experience is an impossibility. We emerge into a world that is given to us by others, and we struggle to find a place in that world – partly by accepting it as given, and partly by trying to remake it as our own. And a large part of the way the world is given to us is through language; this, as we will see, is the kernel of the knowledge that Joyce's novel conveys to its readers.

## Language and Identity

Seamus Deane has emphasized the fact that in these opening pages, as in the rest of the novel, there is an inordinately high level of quotation. In fact, he calculates an average of more than ten quotations in every dozen pages throughout the book (1992: xvi). Everything from popular songs to prayers, political speeches and sermons are recycled by Joyce, culminating in the final extracts quoted from the protagonist's own diary at the end of the novel. This preponderance of quotation has important implications for both the reader and Stephen. For the reader, it leads to a growing awareness of the fact that the individual's experience of the world is always mediated and determined by what has gone before; that is, it leads to a growing awareness of the borrowed nature of experience. For Stephen, on the other hand, there is a tension between his tendency to ignore the extent to which his experience of the world is formed by processes of quotation, and his contrary acute sense of their effects. For example, there is the moment of epiphany in Chapter IV when he is about to realize that his destiny is to be an artist. He has observed some clouds that are moving westward across the sky, and he thinks of the Europe from which they have come: 'Europe of strange tongues and valleyed and woodbegirt and citadelled and of entrenched and marshalled races' (P, 181). Can there be any doubt that this sense of Europe is filtered through, perhaps unconscious, literary quotation? But Stephen himself seems to only dimly recognize this, when we read in the next sentence: 'He heard a confused music within him as of memories and names which he was almost conscious of but could not capture even for an instant' (ibid.). However, there are also times when Stephen seems to be acutely aware of the presence and power of already given narratives and tropes. In the very first page, for example, when we can assume the character is about three years old, we see him making an attempt to claim a song as his own:

*O, the wild rose blossoms*
*On the little green place.*

He sang that song. That was his song.

*O, the green wothe botheth. (P, 3)*

Apparently accepting the task of remaking these cited patterns as his own, Stephen has now claimed the song, by fundamentally changing it: not only in his lisping pronunciation, but also in his transposing of 'green' from the place to the rose itself. Even though we soon find out that Stephen has doubts as to whether there could in fact be such a thing as a green rose (P, 9), this strategy of claiming elements of the collective reality as his own continues throughout the novel.[7]

More importantly, however, Joyce's extensive use of quotation serves to highlight the fact that Stephen's experience, whether at the level of sensation or complex emotion, is profoundly determined by linguistic form. It is perhaps not surprising that a portrait of an artist who turns out to be a literary artist should focus on the power of language, but the phenomenon that Joyce draws our attention to is much more widely applicable than merely to adolescent poets. The sort of quotation that is in question here is not just the dominant form of quotation that Joyce uses (from sources such as songs, rhymes, poems, and so on), but also the quotation that arises when we take a reflexive attitude towards language; in other words, we might say, when we quote ourselves. An example will make this clearer. Here Stephen is perhaps eight years old and he has just been teased at school because he admitted to kissing his mother goodnight; and then teased again for denying it. Reflecting on what it means to kiss, Stephen gives us a precise, and very sensual, description of the act of kissing: his mother's soft, wet lips meeting his own raised, and no doubt equally soft, cheek.

But then there is a noise, the noise that his mother's lips supposedly make: 'they made a tiny little noise: kiss' (P, 11–12). The surprise for the reader is that the word 'kiss' is clearly not one of those onomatopoeic words that we think convey the sound of the action; so how can Stephen think that 'kiss' is the sound that a kiss on the cheek makes? It would seem that the young Stephen's experience of the kiss is already mediated, and to some extent formed, by the very word itself. It is as if the act of kissing, and its sound, come to conform in his experience to the sound of the linguistic term. Or, putting this the other way around, it is as if the word infuses its character into the action of the thing referred to. There are many similar examples of this phenomenon in the early part of the novel. Stephen's reflections on the words 'belt', 'suck', 'pock' and 'foetus' all attest to his sensitivity to the visceral, highly sensual effects of which language is capable.[8] And they also attest to his heightened sense of the materiality of language. In all of these cases, what is striking is not just that the words have a capacity to cause a physical reaction in his body, but that the word itself tends to be given a physical reality.

Probably the best example of this double phenomenon is the moment when Stephen, at roughly the age of 14, finds the word 'foetus' carved into a desk at his father's old university in Cork. On the one hand, Stephen's reaction to the word is instantly physical: 'The sudden legend startled his blood' (P, 95). And on the other hand, the physical reality of the word itself is emphasized within the space of several lines when the fact that the word is 'cut several times in the dark stained wood' is repeated in the phrase 'the word cut in the desk' and in Stephen's vision of a large student who was 'cutting in the letters with a jack-knife, seriously' (ibid.). It is only later, as an undergraduate student, that Stephen begins to become aware that this ability of words to cut and to be cut is also related to the phenomenon of colonization. In a conversation with the university's Dean of Studies, this English priest refers to the funnel with which an oil lamp is filled and Stephen remarks that, at least in Dublin, the item is called a 'tundish' and not a funnel. The priest responds to this in a way that Stephen takes to be condescending towards the local term – saying that he must look it up when he gets a chance – and this prompts one of Stephen's important insights into his relation with the English language:

> —The language in which we are speaking is his before it is mine. How different are the words *home, Christ, ale, master,* on his lips and on mine! I cannot speak or write these words without unrest of spirit. His language, so familiar and so foreign, will always be for me an acquired speech. I have not made or accepted its words. I hold them at bay. My soul frets in the shadow of his language. (P, 205)

Stephen's attention in this exchange focuses on the extent to which the language is for him an acquired speech, comprising words which he has neither made nor accepted. But it is not clear what contrast is being drawn here. Is he suggesting that English is an acquired language for him, in opposition to his 'native' language – Irish? Even though neither he nor his family are speakers of Irish, it is certainly possible that Stephen's thought is that at the level of his culture the native language has been replaced by an acquired speech. In that case, it would make sense for him – and his fellow countrymen – to re-adopt their native tongue. But Stephen, we know, is nothing if not hostile to the then emerging cultural nationalists who wished for a return to traditional ways – in language, sport and culture. However, he might also think the language is 'his before it is mine', simply because the English priest is a representative of what were the two dominant sources of power in Ireland at this time – empire and Church. Stephen's complaint, then, would grow out of an awareness not only of issues of accent and class, but also of what today would be called 'varieties of English'. Stephen knows that, even as a native English speaker, his use of the language will never be the same as that of the Englishman. On the positive side, however, one of the important things that he learns – or at least that Joyce was to learn – is that this position brings with it an enormous potential. This is so, firstly, because these local variants of English often preserve earlier standard forms of the language. So, in one of his later diary entries, Stephen remarks angrily that he himself has finally looked up the word tundish and has found that it is in fact an old English (Elizabethan)[9] word (P, 274). The second advantage is that this sense of foreignness in relation to a language has the effect of making one more alert to the complex, mutual conditioning that occurs between language and the world. And this conditioning, with all the confusion that comes in its wake, is a central element of our experience. For the writer, in particular, this can facilitate what we saw Deleuze and Guattari call the 'deterritorialization' of language (Deleuze and Guattari 1986: 16). It is not surprising, therefore, that for all his unrest with the English language, Stephen is never tempted to join the Gaelic revivalists.

At another level, however, Stephen's concern would probably apply to any language which he happened to be born into – precisely because he was born into it. All through his childhood, as we have seen, he has a heightened sense of the peculiarity of the relation between language and the world, and it is not surprising that this may have led to an equally strong sense of the fact that each individual is thrown into a language which exists before and beyond them. But what about the idea that he hasn't 'accepted' the language? It is here that Stephen's position differentiates itself from our everyday experience of the givenness of language, and it is here that his future path – as artist – makes itself felt: because Stephen is unwilling to simply adopt the forms of language which are given in his experience – the forms which are endlessly recycled in quotation. Indeed, he seems to hold out the possibility, at least in principle, of a language whose words he has made himself. If we allow ourselves, for a moment, to read *A Portrait* as an autobiographical novel, we could say that Joyce finally achieved this goal in *Finnegans Wake* (2000) – where he refused to accept a multiplicity of acquired speeches and instead made their words his own. But even here, of course, the apparently endless semantic possibilities that Joyce wields are already given in the languages which he uses. So, while it is certainly true that he does something with the language which had never been done before, we could perhaps say that that is true of every speaker of every language. Which brings us back to Stephen's sense of frustration with his relation to his own language: on the one hand he seems to be perfectly aware of the givenness of all language, but on the other hand he has a drive to re-create it as his own. In other words, a significant part of his forging of his own identity involves coming to terms with the exteriority of language in relation to his own experience.

This linguistically reflexive tendency on the part of Stephen, which includes, as we have seen, the drive to quote his own words, receives its final form in the last pages of the novel, which consist of extracts from his diary in the weeks prior to his departure from Ireland. These pages mark the shift from a third-person narrative to a first-person narrative (for the first time Stephen is an 'I'), and they seem to denote his coming into adult subjectivity on the eve of his exile. But we cannot forget that even this 'I' is a quoted text; somehow, some narrative force has chosen these (and only these) extracts to present to us, without introduction or explanation. This has the effect of reminding us again of the significance of quotation in the novel, especially in relation to Stephen's emerging sense of identity, or rather to his always fragile sense of identity. Once again, language is an important element in this sense, but in this case Stephen tries to bring language to his aid in helping to pin down, or hold together, a fragmenting sense of self. At the age of about 14, for example, he has a kind of crisis as he is walking in Cork city with his father. He feels disconnected from his surroundings and even from his own thoughts. In an effort to hold his sense of identity together he begins to name his surroundings:

—I am Stephen Dedalus. I am walking beside my father whose name is Simon Dedalus. We are in Cork, in Ireland. Cork is a city. Our room is in the Victoria Hotel. Victoria and Stephen and Simon. Simon and Stephen and Victoria. Names. (P, 98)

But these names, he finds, can guarantee him nothing. Trying to pin a sense of certainty on his own childhood memories, all he can grasp are names – 'Dante, Parnell, Clane, Clongowes' – but not the 'vivid moments' that lay behind them (P, 98). The experiences themselves have, in effect, been replaced by the names, and this is something that causes Stephen profound dissatisfaction.

Clearly, then, we can say that Stephen's experience of both himself and the world is intimately tied up with phenomena of language. And given a sense of identity which is fractured and unstable in this way, it is not surprising that he is open to a myriad possibilities of which his peers are unaware: because these lines of fragility, as Foucault calls them,[10] run through the culture in which he lives, as much as through him. Hence, for both the protagonist and the reader, there arises the question of freedom and transformation. That is, for anyone who is not satisfied to follow in the tracks of historically and socially sanctioned modes of experience, there arises the question of how to gain a certain freedom in relation to these conventions.

## Freedom

The question I introduced in Chapter 1, about which of our present possibilities will be ousted and which will be actualized, is essentially related to the question of freedom and authority.[11] It would be safe to say that for most readers, Stephen can be defined as the person who rebelled against authority in adopting Lucifer's motto '*Non serviam*'[12] and chose instead the freedom of exile in order to pursue an artistic career far from the forces of homeland, church and empire. However, if we accept this as the dominant line of the narrative, we can easily end up simply judging the character Stephen from our own safe and ironical distance, rather than engaging in the experiment that Joyce offers us.[13] This experiment essentially turns around the ways in which it is possible to gain a critical distance from our modes of everyday experience. Stephen, like Joyce and like the reader, has no simple ready-made answer to this question. Rather, his response to the forces in his environment is a complex mixture of resistance, acquiescence and flight. While it is true, therefore, that Stephen ultimately rejects authority and chooses exile, what is important is the experience of authority which he undergoes and the slow work he undertakes of freeing himself from its too-tight grip.

One of the most striking features of this experience is the predominance of external demands that Stephen should admit, confess and apologize. Indeed, the very first time we hear his name in the novel it is associated with such a demand: 'O, Stephen will apologize' (P, 4). But Stephen, from the start, is defined as an individual who does not apologize. He may indeed start out – and even end up – in a state of anxiety about his sense of identity, but he always stubbornly refuses to accept the demands and the schemas of thought which are thrust upon him by others. And in Stephen's experience, as in the experience of any other adolescent, these demands and impositions are legion. At one point in Chapter 2 he performs a quick inventory of these forces, and finds that they include voices telling him to be a gentleman, a good Catholic, a healthy young man, a true patriot, a hard worker and a good sport at school (P, 88); and this is before he is urged to consider joining the Jesuit order, and before he begins to consider the demands which the vocation of artist would impose on him. However, even though these voices, whatever their provenance, had already begun to seem 'hollowsounding in his ears' (ibid.), and even though we know that Stephen will ultimately adopt the '*Non serviam*' of Lucifer, it remains the case that for much of the novel he hesitates between rebellion and obedience.

In fact, he maintains a façade of quiet submission almost until the end, and we can see an early instance of the 'silence, exile, and cunning' strategy which he finally adopts (P, 269) in an incident which occurs before he goes on stage at a school performance, at about 14 years of age. Stephen is accosted by his friend Heron, who teases Stephen because Emma, who we are told is 'deucedly pretty', has just arrived to see the performance with Stephen's father. This teasing takes the form of a demand: 'So you may as well admit . . . that we've fairly found you out this time. You can't play the saint on me anymore . . .' (P, 81). Accompanying this demand, Heron strikes Stephen with a cane across the back of his leg, lightly, and then more strongly, as he repeats the demand: 'Admit!' Rather than responding angrily, Stephen adopts the strategy of mirroring 'his rival's false smile' as he bows 'submissively' and then proceeds to irreverently recite the *Confiteor*.[14] This strategy contrasts with an incident from two years previously, which Stephen now recalls as he recites the prayer. On that occasion he had earnestly resisted Heron's demands that he admit (that Byron was 'no good') and had ended up being beaten with the cane and a rotten cabbage stump, and was finally left on the street 'half blinded with tears, clenching his fists madly and sobbing' (P, 86). Now, however, outside the school performance, his strategy is more cunning and more effective, and even though he remembers the 'cowardice and cruelty' of his tormentors he finds that he no longer bears them any malice.

Here we see two possible ways of responding to, and exercising, authority, both of which Stephen rejects: on the one hand the pettiness of Heron, who makes much of minor points of honour and who easily mobilizes authoritative structures for his own cruel pleasures; on the other hand the intransigent refusal to acknowledge authority, the open rejection of all its demands, towards which Stephen himself has a strong tendency, but which has always been leavened by his 'habits of quiet obedience' (P, 88).[15] Maintaining these habits, however, is by no means easy; and Stephen continues throughout the novel to bounce from acquiescence to rebellion, and back again. The problem for Stephen is how to find a way of asserting his own freedom in relation to these structures of authority, but a freedom which goes beyond a mere 'No'. A significant moment in this search comes at the very end of the novel, when he finds that he is finally able to confess his own beliefs. In conversation with his friend Cranly, he expounds the principles by which he wishes to live: 'I will not serve that in which I no longer believe whether it call itself my home, my fatherland or my church' (P, 268). Taken aback by his own candour, and his friend's touch, Stephen declares with disbelief: 'And you made me confess to you . . . as I have confessed to you so many things . . . You made me confess the fears that I have' (P, 269).

This path of freedom, however, is much more difficult to pursue than either the path of obedience or the path of simple rebellion. This is partly because the power which Stephen must resist comes in the form of two equally formidable imperial masters: the Catholic Church and the British Empire. More importantly, however, it is because these are not simply external forces which could be easily rejected. If we take the idea of the *bildungsroman* seriously, then we have to say that Stephen's entire *bildung*, his entire formation, has been carried out according to the precepts of these two masters. There is a sense, therefore, in which he is fundamentally a Catholic colonial subject of the British Empire.[16] Despite the fact that his family has strong sympathies with Fenian politics, and his father and uncle abhor the role the Catholic hierarchy played in the fall of Parnell, there is no doubt that Stephen's experience is bound by these two masters. We see evidence of this grip, for example, in the fact that when he comes to work out an aesthetics which will lead him away from these masters, his primary source is St Thomas Aquinas. Indeed his friend Lynch comments that his theories have 'the true scholastic stink' (P, 232), and Stephen later refers to himself as 'a priest of eternal imagination' (P, 240). Similarly, the language in which he will come to express himself, as we have seen, is the language of the colonizer, albeit a language that the colonizer has partially forgotten or cannot understand.

There is, of course, nothing new or surprising in the idea that it takes a great deal of work to free oneself from one's early formation, and if there is any irony in Joyce's portrayal of Stephen it occurs most strongly here in his presentation of Stephen's attempt to free himself from all ties. It is easy, no doubt, to be amused by Stephen's oscillations between sordid sin and pious repentance, between flights of rapture and squalid reality, and between youthful rebellion and quiet respect for authority. To adopt such an attitude, however, is to participate in the same underlying cruelty which is present in all acts of vivisection. The suggestion I would like to make is that maybe it would be more productive, now that Stephen is lying squirming on the table, to treat this as an experiment which is also being carried out on us, the readers. We could then begin to raise questions such as: how do we open up a space of freedom in our interactions with systems of social and political power? Or, how is our experience of the world determined by systems of thought of which we are not aware? We may even begin to ask: is there anything that a novel such as *A Portrait* can do to help us in undertaking this work?

## 'buildung supra buildung'

To answer these questions, we need to return to the idea of the fiction of experience. This phrase conveys both the idea that a novel such as *A Portrait* presents us with a fictional account of the experience of its protagonist, and the idea that

the experience of the individual is always, in a sense, fictioned. Trying to understand the relation between these two fictions will help us to see what role the
novel plays in another kind of fiction; that is, in the fictioning, or transforming,
of the reader's experience in the act of reading. On the one hand, then, situating Joyce's novel within the *bildungsroman* genre, we can say that it portrays the
journey of a sensitive young man from childhood through various forms of
hardship to a late-adolescent realization of an artistic vocation. This journey
would involve the process of gaining new experiences while integrating them
into an ever-widening and more complex experience of the world. On this
reading, we would say that Joyce, having achieved a higher level of *bildung*, has
now gained the distance required to analyse and judge his younger self. This is
a perfectly legitimate way of approaching the novel, and it is one which highlights important features which we will discuss below, but it is also one which
I would like to push beyond. On the other hand, then, we have a novel which
not only portrays the developing experience of its protagonist, but also intervenes in the experience of its reader; in other words, a novel which contributes
to the fictioning, or re-fictioning, of the reader's experience. In order to understand this transformative potential, and its relation to the fiction of Stephen's
development, I will draw on both the Foucauldian framework that I have already
sketched, and on Gadamer's account of experience.

Starting with Gadamer, it is striking how well Joyce's novel seems to fit his
distinction between experience as *erlebnis* (immediate lived-experience) and as
*erfahrung* (an integrated life experience). In its structure, as *bildungsroman*, the
novel follows a pattern which could be identified as typical of the integration of
experience in the course of a life. Each chapter ends with a high point at which
Stephen has acquired a new understanding of his world, or a certain liberation
from its restrictions. However, the subsequent chapter always opens with a
crashing return to earth, from which the next high must be reached.[17] This
structure of personal development might be understood as a dialectical development comprising moments of shocking new experience, followed by periods
of recuperation, and once again by new experiential shocks. It would then be
tempting to say that we are constantly engaged in the process of converting
these intensely lived experiences (*erlebnis*) into the wisdom of our unified life
experience (*erfahrung*). However, at least in Gadamer's account, that is not
exactly the way the two forms relate. In fact, for Gadamer, it is difficult to say
if what is in question is the relation between two *modes* of experience, or the difference between two *concepts* of experience. In other words the question is, are
*erlebnis* and *erfahrung* two different kinds of experience which exist in a dialectical relation, or are they two conflicting, mutually incompatible concepts of
experience? Gadamer starts out with a critical exploration of the development
of the concept of experience (as *erlebnis*) from the late eighteenth century up
to the work of Dilthey, before going on to propose his own concept of experience (as *erfahrung*), which then plays a crucial role in his elaboration of the

nature of hermeneutic understanding. Even though he doesn't explicitly relate these as opposing modes or types of experience, his account does tie in with a long tradition in German philosophy of decrying the modern collapse of experience (as *erfahrung*) and its gradual replacement with a cheapened form of experience (as *erlebnis*).[18] In other words, it is assumed that these two modes of experience, one shallow and inauthentic, the other 'genuine', can exist side by side. For my purposes, therefore, I will take it that Gadamer is isolating *both* two forms of experience, and two concepts of experience.

Gadamer traces the concept of experience (as *erlebnis*) back to Kant's aesthetic theory, according to which the profound experiences of the genius are transmuted into works of art which then make these experiences available to an audience. Dilthey, according to Gadamer, built on this account as a way of counteracting the dominant scientific rationalism which threatened the human sciences at the end of the nineteenth century. For Dilthey, an experience (as *erlebnis*) is, as the word suggests, closely connected to the life (*leben*) of the subject; it is always what one has experienced (lived) oneself, and it comprises both the intense immediacy of a lived sensation and its long-lasting effect on the individual (2003: 61). Hence the importance of this concept in biographical (and potentially autobiographical) writing.[19] Gadamer however, in his attempt to establish an account of understanding in the human sciences, is dissatisfied with this way of understanding experience – and also, in fact, with this mode of experience. His criticisms of it focus on its inherently subjectivist limitations, on its paradoxical ahistoricism, and on its too close association with the specific forms of aesthetic experience. In particular, Gadamer associates Dilthey's concept with the ahistorical concept of experience and experiment which is operative in modern science: the problem is that this concept cannot take into account 'the inner historicity of experience' (2003: 346). This is a criticism which echoes the attitude of, for example, Walter Benjamin when he speaks of 'the increasing atrophy of experience [*erfahrung*]' in the modern world and denounces Bergson in particular for dressing up 'the passing moment (*erlebnis*)' in 'the borrowed garb of experience' (1999: 155, 181). The problem with the experience of the passing moment, for Benjamin and this whole critical tradition, is precisely that 'tradition is excluded from it' (1999: 181). And tradition is, for Gadamer, at the centre of hermeneutic practice in the human sciences. What Gadamer does, then, is to develop a concept of experience in which experience would be individual but also communal, in which it would be lived in the present but would also be aware of its own historically determined conditions, and in which it would give us a way of receiving, modifying and passing on a tradition that is essential to the forms of understanding that are operative in the human sciences.

This form of genuine experience (*erfahrung*) would then bear a close resemblance to the idea of accumulated wisdom which is operative in many (auto)biographical genres.[20] Indeed, Gadamer's account of this slowly

accumulated *erfahrung* could, as we have noted, be read as a sketch of the peri-
odic structure of Joyce's novel. If we can say that *erfahrung* involves a process of
integrating the endless flow of *erlebnisse* into an ever-widening unified experience which overturns and includes earlier perspectives, it resembles the process
which Stephen undergoes as we see him moving from chapter to chapter accu-
mulating his hard-earned experience.[21] However, it is important to remember
that for Gadamer, this dialectical concept of experience (*erfahrung*) doesn't
entail a final destination of closed certainty; rather, it is characterized by an
enduring openness to the perils of new experiences.[22] The process, in other
words, has no endpoint – or should have no endpoint – except in death. If we
read Joyce's novel primarily within the framework of the *bildungsroman* tradition, then it would seem that Gadamer's schema is particularly apt. Even though
Gadamer is himself suspicious of the concept of *bildung*, what's important for
him is the idea that a self is formed not by breaking with or repudiating the
past, but by practising an ever more complex integration of it, within the context of the recognition of one's own limitations and unsurpassable finitude.[23]
It is this valorized practice (of wisdom) at the level of the individual that
Gadamer will try to transfer to a more general level when he takes it as a model
for hermeneutic understanding – for what he calls 'historically effected
consciousness'.[24]

But, what if we want to read the novel primarily as an intervention in the
experience of the reader, rather than as a representation of the growing experience of its protagonist (or even author)? In other words, what if we read it as a
part of the historicity of *our* experience, rather than Stephen's? Even on these
terms, Gadamer still provides resources for beginning to do this. For example,
when he uses his concept of genuine experience (*erfahrung*) as a model for
hermeneutic understanding – or historically effected consciousness – he gives
us a way of re-conceptualizing the reading of texts handed down to us by tradition. According to this model, each event of reading will modify both the tradition in which the text has a place and the individual who is doing the reading.
The historical effect in question, therefore, is both a matter of the text having
an effect in the present, and of the present reading having an effect on the
text/tradition; forming what Gadamer calls 'a texture of reciprocal effects'
(2003: 283). It follows therefore that experience is profoundly historical – it has
an almost Heraclitean ever-changing nature: 'one's experience changes one's
whole knowledge. Strictly speaking, we cannot have the same experience twice'
(2003: 353).

The final model Gadamer chooses to elucidate this aspect of experience is
the model of the dialogue – in particular as he sees it presented in Plato's works.
What the Socratic technique demonstrates, for Gadamer, is the fact that participating in a dialogue, and reaching an understanding in it, involves a transformation of both participants: it 'is not merely a matter of putting oneself forward
and successfully asserting one's own point of view, but being transformed into a

communion in which we do not remain what we were' (2003: 379). Gadamer insists that the idea that the reader engages in a dialogue with a text is therefore not a metaphor, but is essentially what happens in the encounter: in other words hermeneutic understanding, when genuinely achieved, will modify the agent(s) involved.

This gives us a very rich set of tools for approaching the effects that works of literature can have on their readers. But one major worry, at least from the point of view of the approach I am taking here, is that Gadamer's entire project is committed to the pursuit of understanding and, despite its openness to the complexities of historical effects, it still maintains an appeal to the idea that a text, or a work, or an historical event, has a true meaning. Gadamer notes, for example, that temporal distance can aid the hermeneutic enterprise because such distance allows 'the true meaning of the object' to fully emerge. And even though he acknowledges that the discovery of this true meaning is never finished – 'it is in fact an infinite process' (2003: 298) – he still maintains the idea that there *is* such a meaning. In fact the aim of hermeneutics is, by the use of certain techniques (which are contrasted with the 'method' of science), to correctly understand the true, but ever-changing, meaning of tradition. In contrast, the approach I am taking here involves assessing the maximum transformative effect that a work can have in the present.[25] It is not a matter of understanding the work's true meaning within a continuous tradition, but of being open to the work's possible force in the present. On the basis of this approach, it is also difficult to simply accept Gadamer's distinction between a form of experience (*erlebnis*) which is narrow and superficial and a form (*erfahrung*) which would be 'real' and 'genuine' (2003: 357). Nevertheless, Gadamer's analysis can be helpful in trying to understand how a transformation of experience can happen. Even if we don't accept his judgement on the relative values of these two forms, his idea of a form of experience (*erfahrung*) which is inherently historical in the sense that it continuously accumulates, integrates and re-integrates past experiences can be put to work here.

We must be clear, however, how Gadamer's *erlebnis* vs. *erfahrung* distinction relates to the one I draw from Foucault's work, the distinction between our everyday, background experience and an interrupting, transformative experience. At first glance, it might seem that Foucault's background experience corresponds to Gadamer's *erfahrung*, while his transformative experience corresponds to *erlebnis*. This would be so, because Foucault's background experience has the characteristic of being a slowly accumulated basis for the many particular experiences we undergo, whereas his transformative experience has the characteristic of a shocking intervention which disrupts the flow of experiences and is capable of constituting a turning point for the individual. This set of parallels doesn't quite fit, however, especially when we remember that for Gadamer *erlebnis* is as much a failed concept as a discernible mode of experience. In fact, his own preferred concept (*erfahrung*) includes within itself both the shocks and jolts which new experiences bring *and* the integrative work which leads to a kind of wisdom, or 'insight' (2003: 356). It might be more accurate, therefore, to say that Gadamer's concept of experience (as *erfahrung*) comprises both what Foucault would call everyday and transformative experience. Understood in this way, we can say that Gadamer's concept of experience (as *erfahrung*) gives us a way of understanding both Stephen's developing experience within the novel, and the possibility that reading the novel might have a transformative effect on the reader. Combining Gadamer's analysis of experience (as *erfahrung*) with Foucault's privileging of transformation over understanding, we would then have the means to give an account of the relation between the fictional experience of Stephen and the fictioned experience of the reader.

## Anti-*bildung*

Let's return to the idea that, in *A Portrait,* Joyce presents us with a minutely detailed image of a young colonial Catholic's tortured attempts to free himself from the modes of everyday experience that his culture authorizes. Stephen's growing awareness of the complexity and insidiousness of this background experience – which is given to him in his language, his education, and his religion – is accompanied by his hardening resolve to evade these lures and traps. As he remarks to a fellow student,

> When the soul of a man is born in this country there are nets flung at it to hold it back from flight. You talk to me of nationality, language, religion. I shall try to fly by those nets. (P, 220)

The major action which Stephen undertakes in order to evade these nets is his decision to leave Ireland – to go, as he puts it, into exile.[26] For Stephen, this represents his ultimate *non serviam*, the final rejection of his formation, his *bildung*. However, as we have seen, it's not clear that even this self-imposed exile will be enough to allow him to evade those nets. Stephen is so formed by these discourses that even his attempts to escape from them are imbued with their characteristics. So, what kind of transformation is Stephen capable of, and how does it relate to the transformation which the novel makes available for the reader? What, in other words, is the relation between these two kinds of transformative experience – that is, the one(s) which Stephen may have undergone, and the one(s) which the reader may undergo?

I should make the point, first of all, that in general it is not necessary for a novel to actually portray transformative experiences in order for it to be able to effect them. However, in the case of *A Portrait* we might assume that its effect is indeed primarily conveyed by the way it portrays the transformation of

Stephen. Should we read this novel, therefore, as a portrayal, as well as an instance, of the kind of transformative experience that I am trying to analyse here? One obvious candidate for the source of this kind of experience in Stephen's world is the epiphany. This is a concept which Joyce developed at the time of writing *Dubliners* (1914),[27] and which he worked into the text of the first draft of *A Portrait* (posthumously published as *Stephen Hero*).[28] In that first draft, an epiphany is described as a 'sudden spiritual manifestation' of the precise nature or essence of a thing which shows itself forth in the most 'delicate and evanescent of moments' (SH, 216). These are moments in which, for any thing, 'its soul, its whatness, leaps to us from the vestment of its appearance', and for the early Stephen Daedalus[29] it is the task of the artist to record these moments with great care. This manifestation isn't confined to objects, however, and in fact the one example Stephen gives is an overheard snippet of conversation which, at least for him, reveals an essential truth about his fellow Dubliners. Building on this theme, we could then say that *Dubliners* is exactly the 'book of epiphanies' (SH, 216) which the young Daedalus had imagined.

However, if we take seriously the idea of an epiphany, we have to ask *to whom* the manifestation is made. It is true, for instance, that *Dubliners* can be read as a series of epiphanies, but these epiphanies are not always manifested to the character in question. In fact, generally speaking, we can say that the manifestation is revealed to the reader rather than to the protagonist. So for example, at the end of 'Grace', when the priest speaks of himself as a 'spiritual accountant' (D, 174), it is the reader and not any of the characters who witness a truth about the relation between nineteenth-century Catholicism and bourgeois order. Similarly, at the end of 'Two Gallants', when one of the friends reveals the gold coin in the palm of his hand, it is the reader who learns something essential about the hopeless pettiness of the two men's lives, not the protagonists.[30] It may be more accurate, therefore, to think of the epiphany as a product of the art of writing, rather than as a natural emanation from the world. That is, the epiphany in so far as it concerns us here is something which the author fictions; it is something which has an effect on the reader, not necessarily something which operates within the world of the story. Returning to the Stephen of *A Portrait*, the first point to make is that there are definitely moments for the character in which some kind of revelation is experienced – for example, as he swoons into the arms of the prostitute at the end of Chapter II; or the moment when his vocation as artist is revealed to him at the end of Chapter IV. But from the reader's point of view, it is more important that Joyce juxtaposes these events with their dissonant counterparts at the start of the following chapters. So, the moment of ecstasy with the prostitute is followed by the period of intense piety and devotion to religious ritual; while the moment of spiritual, aesthetic elation at the end of Chapter IV is followed by the 'watery tea' and 'greasy pawntickets' of the next page. In so far as something is manifested to the reader here, it is very different from what is manifested to the young Stephen – and that is not just because of Joyce's ironic distancing from his younger alter ego, but is a general feature of the way a novel does its work.

It is for this reason, therefore, that we would search in vain for a defining moment of transformation on the part of Stephen. And, in fact, it might be better to see this entire *bildungsroman* not so much as a novel of development, but as a novel of anti-*bildung*, or counter-*bildung*, a novel in which the protagonist is on a continuous course of resistance to the forces which try to mould him.[31] From the moment he hides under the table, refusing to apologize, to the final *non serviam* of his exile, Stephen is committed to this course, despite his strong tendency to obedience and acquiescence. And, as we have already suggested, it is the contours of this resistance which give the novel a great deal of its interest for the reader. Once again, then, the point is not to try to judge the effectiveness or authenticity of Stephen's own resistance, but to see what this experiment is doing to us as we read it. So, let's leave aside the question of how Stephen's transformation is effected, and turn back to those nets which he says are flung out to trap his soul. This metaphor is Stephen's way of expressing his sense of the limitations imposed on experience by the dominant discourses of his time; but these nets are by no means exclusive to Stephen's country, or to the late nineteenth century. In fact, we could say that the tightness of the grip which these forces exert, through the forms of our everyday experience, is an historical constant; but a constant of which we can only become aware with great difficulty. Stephen himself is only dimly aware of the extent to which even his resistance is formed by these already given patterns, but what the novel offers the reader is an insight into their historically conditioned ubiquity. And this is one of the things that makes it possible for the novel to have an effect.

But if these nets are no longer the same for us as they were when Joyce was writing, then how can his novel still be effective for us today? Here again we can draw on Gadamer's account of *erfahrung* to help us grasp both the mutability and the constancy of these limits. Gadamer insists that each reading of a text handed down by tradition will modify the text in the light of the present in which it is read. This, we saw, is one side of what he calls 'historically effected consciousness'. Drawing on this idea, we can say that a novel such as *A Portrait* will have an endlessly changing potential to have an effect, depending on the present in which it is read. What this means is that any particular reading of the novel, in any context whatsoever, may have the capacity to intervene in the reader's experience with a transformative potential. If it is true, as Gadamer says, that 'we cannot have the same experience twice' (2003: 353), then it is equally true that a novel (as an ensemble of text, reader and context) cannot be read twice. So, while Joyce set himself the task of having an effect on the Ireland of the early decades of the twentieth century, there is nothing to stop his novel from having related, although different, effects today. This possibility reminds us, if a reminder were necessary, how limited would be an approach that focused exclusively on authorial intention in understanding works of literature. But it also indicates how difficult, if not impossible, it is to determine in advance precisely what effects a novel could bring about. The most we can hope for, is to indicate potentials and general directions in which transformations may occur.

In the case of Joyce's *A Portrait*, these effects cluster around the lines of fragility which run through all historically given (which is to say, all) forms of experience. The novel presents us with a dynamic portrait that demonstrates the historical specificity, and therefore mutability, of the development of an individual. It investigates the forces which try to form it and to pin it down; and it exposes the drive to resist these forces in a counter-formation which falls into as many traps as it evades. In its development of the themes of flight and exile, it allows us to gauge the effectiveness of a certain style of resistance. But, just as importantly, it helps us to form an adequate assessment of the extent to which our everyday, background experience is given to us by pre-existing systems including religion, culture, narrative, and language itself. It is here that Joyce is at his most effective; if *A Portrait* is an experiment, it is one which successfully shows how far-reaching is the shared, collective nature of experience. Regardless of the outcome for Stephen, we can say that for the reader who has participated in this experiment, it is no longer so easy to imagine that our experience is truly our own, that the flight into exile is necessarily a flight into freedom, or that the sheer refusal of structures of power will allow us to escape them.

Turning back now to the modes of analysis that Foucault and Gadamer give us, we can say that the fictional experience of the novel is able to intervene in the fragility of our present experience by virtue of the fundamental historicity of experience. We see Stephen struggling to re-make his experience, in the domains of knowledge, power, and his relation to self; and our experience of this, as readers, potentially disrupts our own experience along the same three axes. That is, our future relation to the world, to others and to ourselves may be modified thanks to our reading of the novel. This fundamental historicity, and malleability, is something which Joyce demonstrates throughout his works, from the confused flight of Stephen Dedalus, through the wanderings of Leopold Bloom, to the all-encompassing histories of *Finnegans Wake*, in which all stories flow and counter-flow in an everchanging cacophony. But this is an insight whose effect only reaches its maximum intensity, in the reader's experience, when we give ourselves up to following these fictions in all their meticulous details; that is, when we allow the historicity of one to intersect with the historicity of the other.

Chapter 7

# Experimental Subjects:
# Swift and Beckett

The practice of vivisection is particularly cruel, yet the young James Joyce identified it as being characteristic of the 'modern spirit', especially in art (1991: 209). There is a sense in which, in his early work, Joyce – not afraid to turn this art on himself – carried out a live dissection of his own soul or, we might say, his own mode of experience. The carrying out of experiments on fictional characters is not, however, an exclusively Joycean practice; it is one that many novelists engage in to varying degrees, and it is one that particularly enables a testing of the limits of what it is to be human. It is when this fictional testing intersects with what may be a reader's testing of their own limits that a transformation in the reader's relation to the world and to self becomes possible. Here I want to examine two works, by Jonathan Swift and Samuel Beckett (*Gulliver's Travels* and *Three Novels*),[1] that subject their characters and, by extension, their readers to a series of experiments in which modes of experience are tried out, discarded, and transformed.

## The Voyage as Test

At the end of a series of long voyages, Lemuel Gulliver returns home to find that his wife and children disgust him as much by their smell as by their appearance. Even the sight of his own reflection is painful to him, because it reminds him that he is nothing but a Yahoo gifted with language. In emulation of the Houyhnhnms, he begins to adopt the gait of a horse, he speaks with a pronounced whinny, and taking refuge from his family he finds that only his two newly purchased horses, with whom he converses for four hours a day, understand him. Having been shrunk and stretched, shipwrecked and humiliated, Gulliver is ready at last to settle down in his garden and keep humanity at a comfortable distance. The journey made by Jacques Moran, in Samuel Beckett's *Molloy*,[2] is much shorter but equally transformative. Moran sets out on an ill-defined mission to find Molloy and quickly slides from being a respectable man of rigid habits and clear thought, to a ragged, half-crippled tramp who is harassed by suspicious farmers. Unable to find Molloy and abandoned by the son he had mistreated, he spends almost a year trying to return home on foot, travelling by night and avoiding roads. Arriving home, he finds his house in a state of neglect which he decides not to remedy. He mourns his beloved bees who have died during the winter and he moves out to live in the garden, where he tries to understand the language of the birds: 'I have been a man long enough,' he says. 'I shall not put up with it any more, I shall not try any more' (M, 175).

Here we have two journeys which, despite their differences, both undercut the expectation that a quest will end in conquest, whether of the world or of oneself. If Gulliver and Moran have achieved anything at the end of their travels, it is a certain diminishment; a stripping away of certainty and vanity, a loss of self-assurance. Gulliver, it is true, has accumulated a modest fortune after his fourth voyage, but he is reduced to conversing with his horses and he seems to be acutely aware of the general worthlessness of human society. Jacques Moran, for his part, hasn't travelled so far but he has been equally unsuccessful; rather than finding his quarry, Molloy, he seems to have transformed into him through a slow process of collapse and decay. And, like Gulliver, he ends by rejecting his own kind and taking refuge among animals. His loss of self-possession is so severe that when he sits down to write his report on his travels he does so only because an anonymous voice, which he has been hearing and trying to understand for some time, tells him to do so.

My intention here is not to bring Swift and Beckett together in a study of literary influences.[3] Instead, I want to draw upon an affinity that exists between *Gulliver's Travels* and Beckett's series of three novels, which includes *Molloy*, in order to illustrate the kind of transformative experiment that fiction makes possible. Each of these novels, in its own way, engages in an experiment that tests the limits of what it is to be human. We can read Beckett's three novels as a twentieth-century inflection of Swift's eighteenth-century forcing of the boundaries of Gulliver's mind and body. Swift's aim seems to be primarily to satirize the pride, vanity and stupidity of human beings by showing them to us through a series of distorted and distorting images. While it is much more difficult to make a simple hypothesis about Beckett's aims, we will see that his approach involves an even more fundamental undermining of our cherished certainties. Swift and Beckett achieve these effects through the experiments they carry out on their characters. If, as Kundera suggests (1988: 34), a fictional character is an 'experimental self', then we can say that Swift and Beckett place both their characters and their readers in the role of experimental subject, and that this is a role from which we may emerge transformed. The nature of the experiment is, however, different in each case. A major source of this difference is the fact that Beckett suffers from, or perhaps we should say enjoys, a profound epistemological anxiety; an anxiety which is not, at least to the same extent, shared by Swift. In fact Swift seems to know a great deal, especially about the vanity of human beings, whereas Beckett apparently knows very little. So, even though Swift does make fun of scholarly activity (for example in his account of the Academy of Lagado during Gulliver's third voyage to Laputa), his more general satire requires that he maintain a certain level of conviction in his opinions; otherwise there would be no basis for his 'savage indignation'.[4] Beckett, on the other hand, is prepared to give up much more of what we take to be human, so the experiment carried out in his works is more far-reaching than that of Swift.

The idea that there may be aspects of our current modes of being human that are in some sense expendable, is one that animates Foucault's final conception of critical philosophy. According to Foucault (1984c: 306), modern critique grows out of the Enlightenment challenge, formulated by Kant in the motto *sapere aude* (dare to know), to subject our most self-evident prejudices to scrutiny. The modern critical attitude is one that seeks out those aspects of ourselves that are no longer necessary, or desirable, and attempts to imagine them otherwise. For Foucault, in his own practice, this gives rise to the project of a 'critical ontology of ourselves' (1984c: 319), a project that has both a theoretical and a practical side. On the one hand, it is a matter of engaging in a philosophical and historical analysis of the forms of subjectivity that we now inhabit. This requires understanding of both the provenance of these forms and the nature of the limits that they impose on us.

We can take Foucault's *Discipline and Punish* as an example of this kind of historical ontology, in so far as it relates to modern forms of power. On the other hand, it is a matter of attempting to breach those limits, not in a spirit of defiant transgression, but in a slow and patient effort to modify the forms in which we live. Here we can take feminism and gay liberation as examples of social movements that have brought about significant modifications of the social forms in which we all live. In Foucault's conception, therefore, critical philosophy is essentially a form of thought that wrestles with the question of our historically imposed limits, and tries to connect up with practices that push beyond those limits. Without wanting to reduce the many effects of literature to the terms of such a project, we can nonetheless take this conception as a useful way of understanding *one* of the things that works of fiction may do. It is possible to read Swift and Beckett as engaged, albeit in very different ways, in a test to see to what extent a certain way of being in the world is unnecessarily constricting and limited. In the case of Swift, we can characterize this as the way of being that is moulded by the dominant political and social forms of eighteenth-century England, whereas in the case of Beckett we could say that the object of his interest is the experience of modern subjectivity, as identified by Descartes and as lived in the tumult of post-war Europe. In both cases, however, the possible impact of the work of literature is by no means limited to audiences which embody these forms of experience. Swift's satire is, at least at a certain level, as effective today as it was in 1726, while the effect of Beckett's works is capable of ranging across many cultures and times.

In Foucault's characterization of his critical project, the second aspect of that project, its testing of the possibility of going beyond certain limits, is said to embody an experimental attitude: it involves a 'historico-practical test of the limits we may go beyond' (1984c: 316). One of the achievements of works such as these by Swift and Beckett is that they engage in precisely this kind of experiment, and that the experiment is carried out on both the fictional characters and the audience. It is important, however, to realize that these experiments, by their very nature, are never completed once and for all. Each reading of the book is a renewal of the experiment, and one that may end in failure. But even in the case of a successful experiment we have to recognize, as Foucault points out, that the possibility of going beyond our historically imposed limits is always itself limited and determined; thus, Foucault says, 'we are always in the position of beginning again' (1984c: 317). This is part of the reason why the time of literature, which I discussed in Chapter 1, has more than one dimension; the work is continually renewed in the time of the reader, while it also follows its own trajectory and ages, for example in the way that Swift's work has aged. However, this ageing and distancing of a work is as likely to modify or intensify as to diminish its potential effects in the present. Now let's look more closely at some of these potential effects in these works by Swift and Beckett.

## Gulliver's Well-travelled Body

Focusing on *Gulliver's Travels* (2003)[5] first of all, we can imagine Lemuel Gulliver as the victim of a series of experiments carried out by a particularly cruel author. Each voyage brings a new set of humiliations and challenges that directly undermine his sense of himself as a man. There is, no doubt, a gratifying sense of power in being a gargantuan in Lilliput, but in the voyage to Brobdingnag he is shrunk to less than a hand's height, is carried around in a padded box, is forced to do battle with rats, and suffers the ignominy of being balanced on the nipple of a female servant. And given Swift's enjoyment of scatological humour, it is not surprising that Gulliver is pelted with excrement by Yahoos, has his clothes soiled by a young Yahoo's diarrhoea, and urinates on the queen's chambers in Lilliput in order to extinguish a fire. Swift's novel is of course very funny, and equally so whether we are laughing at Gulliver's predicament or at the satirical comments on human society that are lent to Gulliver's pen. One of the great advantages of the form of this novel is that every time Gulliver arrives in a new land he describes England and Europe to his hosts in words that convey Swift's own disgust and anger. In fact, the descriptions are so strongly critical that one of their hearers, the king of Brobdingnag, replies: 'I cannot but conclude the bulk of your natives, to be the most pernicious race of odious little vermin that nature ever suffered to crawl upon the surface of the earth' (G, 123).

But the experimental effect that I want to focus on doesn't arise from the details of Swift's criticism of his own society, or from the humour that this generates, but from the way his treatment of Gulliver is echoed in his treatment of the reader. Reading this first-person account of a series of extraordinary voyages, the reader is placed to a large extent on a par with Gulliver, the narrator. We share his hopes, his fears, and his humiliations. Even though we may have a strong sense that Swift the satirist is guiding Gulliver's pen, there is a sense in which we share Gulliver with Swift. And to that extent, we also undergo the experiment that Swift has set up; an experiment that successively shrinks, expands, distorts, and perhaps clarifies our perception both of others and of ourselves.

In the first two voyages recounted in *Gulliver's Travels*, this experiment takes the form of a playing with perspective that serves to defamiliarize Gulliver's (and our) experience of the world. Gulliver begins the story of his travels with a brief account of his family background, his education, and his marriage. He clearly prides himself on his straightforward, practical attitude to life. Being the third of five sons in a not very wealthy family, he makes the sensible decision to train as a surgeon, and studies navigation and mathematics in order to prepare himself for a life of travel. Having taken a voyage as a ship's surgeon he returns home and, on the advice of his friends, he marries. The marriage, like all the other details so far, is couched in terms of money: 'being advised to alter my condition, I married Mrs Mary Burton, second daughter of Mr Edmund Burton, hosier, in Newgate Street, with whom I received four hundred pounds for a portion' (G, 22). Gulliver is set up by Swift, then, as a sensible and practical man, the sort of man whose fantastic travel account we can trust. He is a kind of Robinson Crusoe shipwrecked in a Jules Verne novel. Even when he finds himself shipwrecked in Lilliput, Gulliver maintains his usual level-headed approach to the world. He patiently waits until he has gained the trust of the Lilliputian king, he observes and records the customs and practices of the people, and when he finally earns the right to leave the kingdom, he brings away with him samples of their animals (in his pockets) for his own future gain. In fact, he is so meticulous that he tells us he made a 'considerable profit' from exhibiting these tiny sheep and cattle when he was back in England, before selling them for £600 (G, 75). In the same spirit, he then gives us a detailed summary of his new financial situation, clearly content that despite the strangeness of his adventures everything had been turned to a handsome profit.

There is, no doubt, something stubborn about Gulliver in his resistance to forces that would modify his view of the world; but he is not at all unusual in this. However, at the same time as Swift is assaulting his character with a series of bizarrely challenging situations, he is also confronting the reader with a set of alienating shifts of perspective. The central technique of the first two parts of

*Gulliver's Travels* is of course this amusing juxtaposition of microscopic and telescopic vision. But the potential effect of this juxtaposition goes beyond its entertainment value. One of the simple points that this shift of perspective allows Swift to make, is that the jockeying for influence and power that motivates so much social and political activity is fundamentally petty and inconsequential. When he shows us toy-sized courtiers and ministers practising somersaults on fine threads in order to impress the king and gain advancement, the implied judgement on our own (or eighteenth-century) politics is clear. However, in a scene such as the searching of Gulliver's pockets by two Lilliputian officers, Swift achieves a more impressive effect. Here, the contents are described from the vantage point of the tiny, non-comprehending Lilliputians, and even the reader can find it difficult to understand what is the object in question. For example, in his right pocket they find 'a hollow Pillar of Iron, about the length of a Man, fastened to a strong piece of Timber, larger than the Pillar; and upon one side of the Pillar were huge Pieces of Iron sticking out, cut into strange Figures, which we know not what to make of. In the left Pocket, another Engine of the same kind' (G, 35). It is as if we too are fumbling in Gulliver's pockets, trying to understand these everyday objects which have become strange through a simple expansion in size. We later learn that these pillars of iron are Gulliver's pistols.

On his second voyage, when Gulliver is shipwrecked in Brobdingnag, he undergoes an experience which is the direct opposite of what had happened in Lilliput. The inhabitants of Brobdingnag are not strictly speaking, giants, since everything in this land is of equally enormous size. It would be more true to say that just as in Lilliput Gulliver had been expanded in size within an otherwise normally proportioned world, in Brobdingnag he is shrunk to less than six inches in a place that maintains the same proportions as our world. The result of this expanding and shrinking is that Gulliver gets to experience the world from both the microscopic and the macroscopic extremes. One of the most striking effects of this shift in perspective, in Brobdingnag, relates to Gulliver's perception of the human body. In Lilliput he had been impressed with the fineness and beauty of the inhabitants, but in Brobdingnag he is confronted with a magnified view of all their imperfections. Swift's habitual distaste for the female body takes a prominent role here as Gulliver is confronted, for example, with the sight of a woman nursing a baby: 'I must confess no Object ever disgusted me so much as the sight of her monstrous Breast . . . nothing could appear more nauseous' (G, 87). And later, in the street, he sees a woman with a cancer in her breast, 'swelled to a monstrous size, full of Holes, in two or three of which I could have easily crept and covered my whole Body' (G, 105). The image of Gulliver taking shelter inside the pores of an enlarged and cancerous breast is one that, despite its underlying misogyny, has an alarming effect.

However, alongside Swift's hostile attitude to the female body, Gulliver's own masculine pride is not allowed to escape mockery. When he was in Lilliput he had taken part in a military parade, to please the king. On that occasion he had stood with his legs apart, while thousands of foot soldiers marched under him. Despite the king's orders that the strictest decency should be observed, however, Gulliver noticed that some of the younger officers looked up as they passed between his legs: 'And, to confess the Truth, my Breeches were at that time in so ill a Condition, that they afforded some opportunities for Laughter and Admiration' (G, 42). But now that he is in Brobdingnag, he finds of course that comparisons of size are not to his advantage. Not only is he balanced on a girl's nipple, as if he were a toy, but he is particularly struck by his own diminutive size when compared with the queen. The queen holds him in her hand facing a mirror and, seeing their two bodies in full view, he realizes that 'there could be nothing more ridiculous than the Comparison: So that I really began to imagine myself dwindled many Degrees below my usual Size' (G, 101). Gulliver, however, is beginning to show signs that this changing of perspective is affecting his judgements about the world. He acknowledges to himself that the appearance of beauty is merely that, an appearance; and that it is dependent on a certain mutual compatibility of proportions. And while living in Brobdingnag, he realizes that the pretensions and vanities of his fellow Englishmen would appear as absurd at that moment as those of the Lilliputians had appeared to him on the earlier voyage.

It might be expected that a sensible man like Gulliver, having travelled to such fantastic worlds and learned the lessons that they have to teach, would return a wiser and more experienced person. In that case, the novel would be an elaborate demonstration of the truism that travel broadens the mind. But Swift's experiments on Gulliver do not stop there. Skipping over his third voyage, to Laputa, we find in his fourth and final voyage that Gulliver is confronted with the most extreme shift of perspective yet; he arrives in a land where the human beings are a degenerate breed of animals that are enslaved and despised by the supremely rational horses. The Yahoos are filthy creatures with no use of language and no control over their passions, while the Houyhnhnms lead clean, orderly and quietly controlled lives. At first Gulliver doesn't recognize the Yahoos as his own species, but the Houyhnhnms immediately suspect the truth, despite his covering of clothes and his apparent use of language and rationality. Eventually Gulliver has to acknowledge his affinity with the Yahoos, but this only drives him further in the direction of adopting the habits of the Houyhnhnms in order to distinguish himself from his fellow beings. At first glance it might seem that Swift, in pointing up the bestiality of the humanoid Yahoos, is recommending to us the example that the calm and rational Houyhnhnms offer; and if Gulliver could safely be taken to express the views of Swift, that would be a natural conclusion. However, Swift's treatment of Gulliver makes such an interpretation impossible to accept.

Bearing in mind the earlier image we have of Gulliver as a sensible man of business, courageous in his travels, and reasonably intelligent and meticulous in his observations of a range of fantastic societies, let's consider how he now appears in the land of the Houyhnhnms. He is dressed in clothes made from the skin of Yahoos, who are arguably members of his own species, he trots like a horse, he speaks to horses in a whinnying voice and lives in a stable, and when he attracts the sexual advances of young female Yahoos he is both repelled and ashamed in front of his new equine companions. Whether or not we admire the nobility, virtue and rationality of the Houyhnhnms, it seems undeniable that Gulliver's attempts to remake himself in their image reduces him to an absurd figure of fun. It is as if Gulliver, having been put through the mill one too many times by Swift, finally snaps; like Jacques Moran, unable to take it any more, he seems to renounce his humanity. If we treat this novel as an experiment that tests the limits of what it is to be human, we can make sense of this outcome as an indication of the poles between which human behaviour is capable of swinging. Swift, of course, is perpetually dissatisfied with the behaviour of his fellow creatures; but he seems to be equally dissatisfied with the behaviour of Gulliver, his experimental self. Confronted with the extreme contrast between a bestial humanity and a virtuous animality, neither of which, arguably, are intended to be attractive possibilities, Gulliver gives himself over entirely to the unfeeling rationality of the horse. While it is true that, once he has returned to England, he begins to try to tolerate his fellow Yahoos, this seems to be done more from necessity than from any appreciation for their company. In fact, in the last lines of the novel he asks that any Yahoos who have the vice of pride, in other words all human beings, should 'not presume to come in my Sight' (G, 271). Gulliver even includes himself in this prescription; he finds his own image intolerable, and sets himself the exercise of looking at his face in a mirror frequently in order to accustom himself to the repellent sight of a human being.

It is significant, however, that even though he is doing his best to have done with his life as a human being, this doesn't prevent him from including a savage satirical attack on colonialism in the final pages of the book (G, 269–70); an attack that presumably draws its energy at least in part from Swift's experience in Ireland. Despite the scathing attacks on human iniquity, therefore, behind which Swift is barely hidden, Gulliver never quite gives up on his fellow Yahoos. It is as if, in the course of the novel, Gulliver had been coming round to Swift's view of the world, and that his (Swift's) indignation towards injustice and idiocy was at the end enough to counter-balance his (Gulliver's) final disgust with human depravity. And, for the reader, it is possible that a similar shift will have occurred. We may, for example, be more aware of the ways in which we trim ourselves, both physically and psychologically, in accordance with our environment; and more aware of the ways in which we modify that environment to suit our own proportions. We may be more aware, if such a thing were necessary, of the vanity, pride and nastiness of our fellow human beings; while also being more unremitting in our hostility towards the effect these qualities have on others. And, having lived through the journeys made by Gulliver, we may have a greater critical distance from the lenses through which we habitually experience our world. In other words, by means of the experiment that Swift carries out on Gulliver, the book may have brought about corresponding changes in our own experience of ourselves, of others, and of the world.

## At the Limits of Humanity

At the end of his travels, Gulliver would like to be able to have done with his own humanity, and this is a goal that many of Beckett's characters also strive to achieve. But they, too, find it impossible to completely renounce either themselves or their fellow creatures. The experiment that Beckett sets up in his *Three Novels*, however, pushes this attempt to its most extreme limit by slowly taking apart his character's experience of human subjectivity. In the universe that is constructed in Beckett's work in general, and in these novels in particular, the individual suffers from existence. Sometimes they (usually it is a he) suffer stoically, sometimes they suffer with resignation, and sometimes they suffer defiantly, but they always find it impossible to make their suffering stop. As Malone says, 'there is no good pretending, it is hard to leave everything' (MD, 276–7). This is not a question of the difficulty of dying and of leaving the world behind (suicide is never seriously considered by Beckett's characters);[6] it is, rather, the difficulty of disentangling from both the world and oneself, in such a way that one understands what both the world and oneself were, before one leaves them behind. We can read the *Three Novels* as, in part, an investigation of the possibility that an individual consciousness might do this.

Just as Gulliver was, arguably, drawn back into human society through his (partially enforced) relations with his family, so Beckett's characters find that their relations with things and with people weave a web of ties that they struggle to loosen. However, the central tie, at least in the *Three Novels*, is the one that ties the individual to their own enunciations through the pronoun 'I'. The whole problem, as the Unnamable comes to realize, is one of pronouns: 'it's the fault of the pronouns, there is no name for me, no pronoun for me, all the trouble comes from that' (U, 404). The Unnamable can no longer ascribe the pronoun 'I' to himself without being undermined by a plague of doubts: 'I don't know who it's all about, that's all I know, no . . . it's about him who knows nothing . . . who cannot hear, cannot speak, who is I, who cannot be I, of whom I cannot speak, of whom I must speak, that's all hypotheses, I said nothing, someone said nothing' (U, 404). The drive to immediately undermine all affirmations and denials is the most characteristic feature of the discourses of all the narrators in the *Three Novels*. These characters are sure of nothing, not even of who it is that speaks when it is apparently they who are forming the words, and it is this perpetual doubt that makes it so hard for them to have done with the situations in which they find themselves. In this respect, they are in a position which is fundamentally different from that assumed by Foucault when he suggests that for him the whole point of writing (or reading) his books is to try to '*se déprendre de soi-même*', to detach oneself from oneself, or even to 'disassemble the self' (1984a: 8[14]).[7] For Foucault, the task of detaching from oneself is carried out through a philosophical and historical investigation of our limits; it is grounded, in other words, on a kind of knowledge. For Beckett, however, the task was always to achieve this from a position of ignorance. In a 1956 interview, shortly after the completion of these three novels, Beckett makes the point that unlike Joyce, who was a master of his material, he himself is 'working with impotence, ignorance. I don't think impotence has been exploited in the past'.[8]

Beckett's approach to the task is also distinctive in the conception of fiction, or artistic production in general, that it sets in motion. One of the questions that Beckett grappled with early in his writing career concerned the status of expression and representation in the modern art work. In a nutshell, Beckett believed that the traditional idea, that the artist expresses his or her own vision of the world by producing visual or verbal representations of that world, could no longer be sustained. Especially in the aftermath of the war, Beckett thought it was undeniable that this tradition was fatally beset by an anxiety about its own validity. In a discussion of the work of the painter Bram van Velde, for example, Beckett suggests to his interlocutor that the history of Western painting is the history of attempts to avoid and escape from the inadequacy of the representational and expressivist relation. It is only now (1949), he says, that this inadequacy has become clear to anyone who reflects on the matter. And, for Beckett, van Velde is the first painter to 'desist from this estheticized automatism, the first to admit that to be an artist is to fail, as no other dare fail, that failure is his world and the shrink from it desertion, art and craft, good housekeeping, living' (Beckett 1987: 125). In his own fiction, Beckett increasingly follows a similar path: rejection of representation and authorial expression, and an attempt to make something of value even when all accepted standards of value have been undermined. This leads to a form of writing that shares much with, for example, Robbe-Grillet, and with the idea, expressed by Foucault, that fiction doesn't so much represent the world as make it possible for the world to be perceived and experienced in the first place. Description, Foucault says in a discussion of Raymond Roussel (1964a: 422), 'is not at all the fidelity of language to an object'; in other words, it is not a matter of a representational relation. Instead of language following perceptions, for Foucault and for Beckett, 'it traces a path for them, and in its newly silenced wake, things begin to shimmer for themselves, forgetting that they had first been "spoken"' (ibid.). Beckett's approach to the project of disassembling the self, therefore, shares with Foucault's a common recognition of the centrality of the role of language; a role that is all the more important, given the impossibility of accepting the traditional schema of the relation between words and things. Despite the differences in their basic epistemological orientations, therefore, and in the restrictions of their chosen orders of discourse, for Foucault and Beckett the project of disassembling the self is a shared task.

Before looking in more detail at how Beckett approaches this task in *Three Novels*, it will also help to look at the formulation that Nietzsche gives to one aspect of the problem of the pronoun 'I'. In a notebook entry from 1885, Nietzsche rejects the idea that it is the 'I' that thinks; this is a prejudice that the philosophers, like the 'common people', have learnt from grammar. 'Up to now,' he says, 'belief in grammar, in the linguistic subject, object, in verbs has subjugated the metaphysicians: I teach the renunciation of this belief.'[9] Far from being that which thinks, the 'I' is itself a construction of thinking, a 'regulative fiction' through which constancy and knowability are 'inserted into, *invented into*' the world of becoming. For Nietzsche, therefore, the 'I' is one of the tools with which we fiction a world that better suits our human perspective. It is a mistake, therefore, to believe that in the 'I think' there lies something of 'unmediated certainty'. Just because that fiction is now, apparently, indispensable doesn't mean that it is in any way true: 'However habituated and indispensable this fiction may now be, that in no way disproves its having been invented: something can be a condition of life and *nevertheless be false*' (ibid.).[10]

Bearing in mind these claims by Nietzsche, we can read Beckett's *Three Novels* as an attempt to see to what extent this fiction really is indispensable. Or, if we assume that it certainly is indispensable, we could say that they gauge the form and the extent of the price we pay for this fiction. Molloy, for example, had warned that his use of 'I' was deceptive: 'And when I say I said, etc., all I mean is that I knew confusedly things were so, without knowing exactly what it was all about. And every time I say, I said this, or I said that . . . I am merely complying with the convention that demands you either lie or hold your peace. For what really happened was quite different' (M, 88). What really happened was that, for example, he heard a murmur, 'something gone wrong with the silence', and in response to this stimulus there would arise a certain kind of consciousness within him, which he would express by saying 'I said, etc.' (ibid.). Applying a Beckettian version of Ockham's razor, Molloy suggests the following as the simplest explanation of the phenomenon: 'simply somewhere something had changed, so that I too had to change, or the world too had to change, in order for nothing to be changed' (ibid.).[11] But of course, even this simple explanation, spoken as it is by Molloy, and inevitably employing the first person singular, is also a lie. Nevertheless it does at least rule out, in Nietzsche's words, the idea that the 'I think' can act as a basis for unmediated certainty because, at least in Beckett's universe, one cannot even be sure that it is 'I' who is doing the thinking.

Taken as a unit, these novels trace the decline and disintegration of a series of individuals who are all, at a certain level, collapsible into each other. Like Gulliver narrating his voyages, for these characters too authorship and veracity are constantly being called into question. But Beckett takes this process of collapse further, until even the 'I' of the narrator is almost effaced finally by a nameless voice: what the Unnamable calls 'the everlasting third party' (U, 375). Let's begin with a brief overview of this collapse as it unfolds across the three novels. The narrator of the first of the novels, Molloy, is a 'sordid wonder'[12] who spends the entire novel lying in his mother's room waiting to die, where the only task left to him is to write every day, although he doesn't know what he is supposed to write or who it is that reads it. What he does know, and this is one of his only certainties, is that all he wants now is 'to speak of the things that are left, say my goodbyes, finish dying' (M, 7). But before doing that he must write his story, a story involving several attempts, all of which end in failure, to reach his mother. Having begun his journey half-crippled, riding a bicycle, he ends it lying in a ditch, saying to himself: 'I longed to go back into the forest. Oh not a real longing. Molloy could stay, where he happened to be' (M, 91). At first glance, Part Two doesn't seem to have any connection with the narrative voice of Part One. However, we later find out that it is a report written by Jacques Moran recounting his attempt, which also ends in failure, to find Molloy. The ostensible connection between the two parts of the novel is not just that the narrator of the first is sought in the second; it is also that the narrator of the second part is, to a large extent, transformed into the narrator of the first part through the experience of his journey. And to that extent, as we have already seen, he is also pushed to the periphery of humanity. His own sense is of 'a crumbling, a frenzied collapsing' of all his defences, and a consequent dispossession of self (M, 148–9). With this collapse there also disappears the claim to veracity that any narrative makes; Moran's report had begun with the words 'It is midnight. The rain is beating on the windows' (M, 92). The report, and the novel, ends with 'Then I went back into the house and wrote, It is midnight. The rain is beating on the windows. It was not midnight. It was not raining' (M, 176).

The second of the three novels, *Malone Dies*, is also narrated by a man lying in bed in a closed room with almost no contact with the outside world. However, this narrator, Malone, is not being encouraged to write by others: he seems to be doing this simply for himself, in order to pass the time before he dies, which he expects to happen within a month or two. He decides that to pass the time he will describe his present state, tell three stories, and finally give an inventory of his remaining possessions, something that he has always wanted to do. With the expectation of an 'occasional interlude', this makes up what he calls 'a full programme' to fill the time before his death (MD, 182). Naturally, he doesn't quite follow this plan; his stories splinter and fragment, the interludes multiply, and his inventory is never finally established. And even whether he actually succeeds in dying at the end is open to doubt as his story comes to a stuttering halt. The third novel, *The Unnamable*, is stripped down even more severely than the first two. Now the narrator is no longer in an identifiable room; he does not write, either for himself or others; he simply speaks, occasionally telling stories as before, but mostly engaging in an internal monologue whose primary aim is to say whatever is necessary to make it all stop; to have done with it all, once and for all. But this attempt too ends in failure; the right words don't come, he can never be silent, he can neither stop nor continue. His story ends with the words 'you must go on, I can't go on, I'll go on' (U, 414).

Within this framework, Beckett carries out an unparalleled range of experiments on his characters. We can read the opening words of *The Unnamable*, 'Where now? Who now? When now?' (U, 291), as an indication of the three major focus points of these experiments. The first question concerns the possibility of fixing the coordinates of a body in space. Beckett's characters, especially in the *Three Novels*, devote a great deal of energy to assessing their own location, whether they are at rest or in motion between two (often unknown) points. In particular, they are prone to losing their sense of their own bodies as intact vessels for action in the world; and they constantly innovate, or wish to innovate, in their means of locomotion. The second question raises one of the central concerns of Beckett's prose works: the nature of identity, its relation to the possibility of using the first person singular, and the difficulty of negotiating encounters with an other. The third question can be read, perhaps a little more tenuously, as conveying a fundamental doubt about the nature of narrative, a doubt that spreads insidiously to threaten all forms of knowledge. These three areas of human experience – bodily integrity, the sense of self, and knowledge of the objects and events of the world – are the central points around which Beckett's fictional experiments cluster. However, since it is by no means possible to neatly separate these areas into isolated strands, I will approach them together, principally through a consideration of the experiments that Beckett carries out on his characters' bodies.

## The Disarticulated Self

If we imagine, at the end of Gulliver's travels, that he returns home weary, exhausted, and transformed from what he was before, then how much more do Beckett's characters suffer from and represent physical wasting, and the transformations it brings about. In the case of Gulliver, the fact of his well-travelled body is as much a result of accident as his own intention, whereas Beckett's creatures deliberately pursue their own bodily experiments, as a means of attaining alternative modes of human being. Beckett's pre-war novel, *Murphy*,[13] sets up this experimental approach in a way that offers a key to the later *Three Novels*. This novel opens with the central character, Murphy, sitting naked in a rocking chair, with seven scarves holding down his legs, his torso and his hands, so that 'only the most local movements were possible' (Mu, 2). Murphy, we are told, does this to give pleasure to his body which, once appeased, will allow his mind to become free. In order to achieve this he must block out the external or 'big world', restrict the movements of his body, and then rock the chair faster and faster until his mind is free to enjoy the internal or 'little world' of his own mind (Mu, 6–7). This little world, the mind of Murphy, is so strange that Beckett devotes an entire mock-serious chapter to describing the way it saw itself. First, Murphy was convinced that his mind and his body were completely separate entities; his mind was 'bodytight' and any communication between the two was a mystery to him, but a mystery that he had no interest in resolving. His mind saw itself as a hermetically sealed sphere that faded from bright light down towards half-light and, finally, utter darkness. In the first, bright zone there were the mental forms that had parallels in the physical, or big, world; but here these forms could be re-arranged. 'Here the kick that the physical Murphy received, the mental Murphy gave. It was the same kick, but corrected as to direction' (Mu, 111). The pleasure to be attained here was 'reprisal ... Here the whole physical fiasco became a howling success' (ibid.). In the second, half-light zone there were the mental forms that had no parallel in Murphy's physical world; here, for example, was the caress as opposed to the kick. The pleasure of this zone was the pleasure of contemplation; here he was free to move 'from one unparalleled beatitude to another' (Mu, 112).

The third, dark zone of Murphy's mind, however, leaves behind this kind of self-indulgence and makes possible a different form of experience. Whereas the first zone contained elements of the physical world that could be re-arranged at will, and the second zone contained states of bliss and tranquility, the third zone contained neither elements nor states, but forms that were in a constant state of becoming and flux: 'Here there was nothing but commotion and the pure forms of commotion' (Mu, 112). In the first and second zones, Murphy was still Murphy, although he was free, free to re-arrange and enjoy his experience; but in the third zone he was a mere speck in a greater freedom of constant change.

> Here he was not free, but a mote in the dark of absolute freedom. He did not move, he was a point in the ceaseless unconditioned generation and passing away of line.
>
> Matrix of surds. (Mu, 112)

While the other two zones of his mind gave him pleasure, how much more pleasant was 'the sensation of being a missile without provenance or target, caught up in a tumult of non-Newtonian motion. So pleasant that pleasant was not the word' (Mu, 112–3). It was this condition, a condition of utter loss of subjectivity and will-lessness, that Murphy more and more craved and sought through his physical experiments, such as the use of the rocking chair. However, this is a difficult condition to achieve, and even more difficult to maintain. The nearest Murphy seems to get to seeing it in a sustained form is in the inmates of the Magdalen Mental Mercyseat, where he gets a job as an orderly.

In accordance with Murphy's distinction between the big world of exteriority and the little world of interiority, the asylum patients are seen by him as stubbornly inhabiting the microcosmos against all the blandishments of the psychiatrists. Murphy would very much like to join them in their small worlds, but he is in fact too sane. In what is perhaps a subtle allusion to Gulliver's experience in Lilliput, we are told that Murphy felt 'as though the microcosmopolitans had locked him out' (Mu, 240). Ultimately, however, Murphy becomes a victim of an ironic literalization of his own experiments, when a gas explosion kills him during one of his rocking-chair sessions. Now his body is literally destroyed by the chaotic non-Newtonian motion of gas; he finally becomes a speck in the chaos of constant flux (Murphy had earlier hypothesized that the word 'gas' must be etymologically linked to the word 'chaos').

In the later *Three Novels*, Beckett's characters continue to pursue, or at least to undergo, the kind of experience that ruptures and fragments their bodily integrity. Readers who are familiar with the work of Deleuze and Guattari will see in these experiences echoes of the idea of the body without organs (BwO).[14] This is a body that throws off its organized structure and moves towards the pole of unrestricted, experimental lines of flight, as opposed to the pole of rigid, immobile strata that is characterized by the organs.[15] It is also a body that has clear affinities with the experience that Nietzsche described as the Dionysian as opposed to the Apollonian, and in this respect it connects up with a concern that Beckett expresses in one of his interviews. Briefly, Nietzsche's argument is that the Dionysian principle of disarticulation is opposed to the Apolline principle of individuation. The Dionysian undercuts and explodes our centred, stable forms of subjectivity, and it is experienced with both horror and ecstasy.[16] In the interview where Beckett discusses his wish to work with 'impotence and ignorance', he says that this places him at the opposite end of the spectrum from the Apollonian artist, which is a type that is 'absolutely foreign' to him (Graver: 148). Clearly, another way to characterize the non-Apollonian artist is to use this concept of the Dionysian artist (although Beckett himself doesn't make this connection). In that case, we would read Beckett as a writer who tries to make available to us the kind of fragmenting and dismantling of self that, as Nietzsche suggested, was at the core of the origins of Greek tragedy. In the *Three Novels*, an early and relatively gentle example of this process occurs when Molloy's journey has been interrupted by a stay in the house of a woman he calls Lousse. Molloy is lying in the garden of the house one night, listening to the almost inaudible sounds of the wind, when his body begins to merge with the forces of nature:

> And there was another noise, that of my life becoming the life of this garden as it rode the earth of deeps and wildernesses. Yes, there were times when I forgot not only who I was, but that I was, forgot to be. Then I was no longer that sealed jar to which I owed my being so well preserved, but a wall gave way

and I filled with roots and tame stems . . . But that did not happen to me often, mostly I stayed in my jar which knew neither seasons nor gardens. And a good thing too. (M, 49)

To forget to be is to inhabit a form of becoming, and in Beckett's universe these becomings often link up with phenomena of the natural world. In fact, much later, the Unnamable laments that 'they' have diminished his possibilities by taking away nature. If only they gave him a 'scrap of nature' he could escape his current predicament, which is to be trapped 'without anyone, without anything, but me, but my voice . . .' (U, 395). Molloy's experience in the garden, therefore, underlines the paradox of the enclosed space, the jar which is, perhaps, vacuum-sealed. This space preserves, but it only does so at the cost of excluding all contact with the outside, which is to say, with all possibility of becoming. It is for this reason that Murphy, Molloy, Malone, and the others are all drawn to experiment with the possibilities of self-fragmentation. However, they are also aware that the chaotic motion that is associated with becoming has its own pitfalls. As Murphy discovered, the Dionysian disarticulation of self can be both horrific and ecstatic. Even Molloy, in this passage, remarks that it was 'a good thing' that this letting down of his walls didn't happen very often.[17]

As a result, Beckett's characters are incapable of finally choosing between motion as potential becoming, and immobility as likely stagnation. Instead, they seem to be compelled to launch themselves into all sorts of improbable forms of motion, while also being tantalized with the possibility of immobility. Murphy, as we saw, greatly enjoyed the sense that only 'the most local movements' were possible when he was tied in his rocking chair (Mu, 2). Jacques Moran, in *Molloy*, dreams of the impossibility of motion, even when he is about to send his son away to buy them a bicycle: 'To be literally incapable of motion at last, that must be something! My mind swoons when I think of it' (M, 140). One of the characters in *Malone Dies*, Macmann, is likewise addicted to immobility: 'a good half of his existence must have been spent in a motionlessness akin to that of stone, not to say the three quarters or even the four fifths, a motionlessness at first skin-deep, but which little by little invaded, I will not say the vital parts, but at least the sensibility and understanding' (MD, 243). The Unnamable is also finally reduced to a similar state; for him, 'the days of sticks are over, here I can count on my body alone, my body incapable of the smallest movement and whose very eyes can no longer close as they once could' (U, 300–1). Yet to be incapable of movement, like its opposite extreme, the chaotic movement that Murphy sought, is something that can only be experienced as fiction, at the limits of the human: because the human condition, so far as Beckett's characters observe and undergo it, is defined by an incessant coming and going; a relentless movement and displacement from which we can only ever have temporary respite. Malone describes Macmann observing an evening crowd of people returning home from work, for example, and he comments on the necessity of such motion: 'Because in order not to die you must come and go, come and go, unless you happen to have someone who brings you food wherever you happen to be, like myself' (MD, 232). But even these motionless narrators, trapped inside their rooms, are still caught up in the necessity of motion; through the comings and goings of the characters they invent, through the endless round of thoughts and words in their heads, and even, in one case, through the comings and goings of their chamber pots.

Beckett's characters also experience a kind of rupture of bodily integrity that is directly related to this problem of motion. They often start out on their journeys travelling on foot or by bicycle; but they frequently end up reduced to crutches, crawling, or rolling on the ground. Molloy, for example, at the outset has such respect for his bicycle that he says he would never call it a 'bike' (M, 16). But when he rides it, with his crutches strapped to the cross-bar and his bad leg propped up on the axle, he cuts such a figure that he is finally arrested for disturbing the peace. Later, having lost the bicycle, he makes his way through the undergrowth of a forest in a way that transforms human locomotion out of recognition. His body is slowly disintegrating; he now has two bad legs, and the first bad leg is shortening, which makes efficient motion almost impossible. He limps, hobbles and stumbles through the forest, progressing by no more than 30 or 40 paces a day. More and more, during his rest periods, he lies down 'in defiance of the rules', sometimes prone, sometimes supine, on his right side, then on his left side (M, 82). This rule against lying down is the rule that human beings must walk erect, and not crawl on their bellies like a snake. But it is a rule that Molloy finally realizes he can break: 'And I still remember the day when, flat on my face by way of rest, in defiance of the rules, I suddenly cried, striking my brow, Christ, there's crawling, I never thought of that' (M, 89). Of all the modes of locomotion that Molloy has tried, he says, this one has the great advantage that when you stop you are already at rest; there is no need to sit down and get up again: 'he who moves in this way, crawling on his belly, like a reptile, no sooner comes to rest than he begins to rest, and even the very movement is a kind of rest' (M, 90). But even crawling will be deformed when Molloy tries to do it: he lies flat on his belly, swings his crutches forward into the undergrowth, and drags himself along with his arms. Sometimes he lies on his back, swings the crutches behind him, and drags himself backwards and unseeing through the undergrowth. In this way he finally arrives at the edge of the forest, a fact he only realizes when he falls into a ditch. His progress stopped by this feature of the external world, Molloy gazes out over the plain wondering how he can continue his journey to find his mother. Realizing that the absence of undergrowth in the plain will make his recent form of locomotion impossible, he wonders if he could roll across the plain, but doubts whether 'they' would allow him to roll right up to her door.

In this short journey, Molloy has gone from riding a bicycle using only one foot, to hobbling on crutches with two bad legs (one shorter than the other, one stiff), to dragging himself face down through a forest, and finally to wishing he could roll across a plain into town. This drive to bodily transformation is also present in Macmann, whose story is told in *Malone Dies*. At one point, when Macmann is caught in a rainstorm, he lies down on his belly and allows the rain to soak him. Then he turns on his back and, with his mouth open collecting the rain and his palms upturned, his long hair becomes drenched and churned up with the earth and the grass into 'a kind of muddy pulp' (MD, 242). Lying like this, merging with the mud through which Molloy had crawled, Macmann wishes that the rain would never stop and that he would never have to move again. But motion is forced on Macmann, as it is forced on all Beckett's characters; he is finally compelled to move when the 'élan vital or the struggle for life began to prod him in the arse again' (MD, 243). In this case, it is his discomfort that makes him rock from side to side as he lies in the rain, until almost by accident he begins to roll, and finds to his surprise that he makes good progress across the plain. So pleased is he with this form of locomotion that he forms a plan to continue rolling all night until he gets to the edge of the plain. But it is not only the pleasure of this means of travel that seems to appeal to Macmann, it is also his experience of this transformed body with its transformed mode of being in the world. He will never again have to 'hold himself erect in equilibrium'; he will simply 'come and go and so survive after the fashion of a great cylinder endowed with the faculties of cognition and volition' (MD, 246). So, even though he would still be condemned like all human beings to 'come and go', and even though he would still have the faculties of cognition and volition, he would be a giant cylinder, rolling unimpeded through the night, never again required to take the form of man (Macmann, of course, means 'son of man').

Another, more Swiftian image of the transformed human body is that of Malone, expanded to global proportions, shitting on the antipodes. At one point he feels that his feet have dropped away into the depths and his body seems to have expanded to gargantuan size. He believes that if he were to shit, 'the lumps would fall out in Australia. And if I were to stand up again, from which God preserve me, I fancy I would fill a considerable part of the universe, oh not more than lying down, but more noticeably' (MD, 235). So, even Malone clearly has his own Gulliver moments. However, the force of the experiment being carried out on Malone is undoubtedly much greater than the one to which Gulliver was subjected. This is clear, for example, in Malone's experience of himself as a splintered, liquefied body. Malone regularly feels that he is turning into a liquid, or mud, or that he is a small, contracted thing that would get lost in the eye of a needle (MD, 225). But more disturbingly, he also sees himself and the characters he creates as a small heap of granules or specks which could be 'removed grain by grain until the hand, wearied, begins to play, scooping us up and letting us trickle back into the same place, dreamily as the saying is' (MD, 224). He is familiar, he tells us, with the feeling of a hand 'delving feebly in my particles and letting them trickle between its fingers' (ibid.).

Sometimes this hand is plunged in up to its elbow, clutching and ransacking and 'avenging its failure to scatter me with one sweep' (ibid.). This is an extraordinary image of the human being, as a small heap of lentils perhaps,[18] being sifted and played with 'dreamily' by an anonymous and volatile hand.

In *The Unnamable*, this process of experimenting with the human form is taken to its most extreme limit. We have already seen that the narrator of this novel is, from the start, deprived of a body or of any stable, definable space in which to act. He is a voice that we hear, but a voice that doesn't know what it is itself, or even whether its words are really its own. It says 'I', and yet it does so always 'unbelieving' (U, 291). What is important is that he doesn't *know* anything. He doesn't know who he is, where he is, or what he is; and yet he must continue speaking in the faint hope that he will find out who he is, that he will say the words that must be spoken. Speaking in the guise of one of his creations (Mahood, a man without limbs who is propped up in a barrel outside a restaurant beside the abattoir), he implies that if he could be certain of his own existence then this certainty would allow him to be born at last. And, to a large extent, this novel records the Unnamable's attempts to be born, so that he can finally die and be done with it all. Even this creature without a body, however, still manages to engage in forms of physical experimentation. Sometimes he does this through a hazy awareness of his own physical sensations, and sometimes he does it by giving himself, by fictioning for himself, specific bodies. We have already seen that one of his early sensations is of tears falling continuously down his face; but he's not even sure that they are tears, and wonders if they might not really be 'liquefied brain' (U, 293). However, ultimately he loses even this sense of his own body. In one moment of crisis he realizes that he no longer feels his own mouth: 'I don't feel a mouth on me, nor a head, do I feel an ear, frankly now, do I feel an ear, well frankly now I don't, so much the worse, I don't feel an ear either, this is awful, make an effort, I must feel something' (U, 382). His sense of his own body has reduced to such an extent that the most he can say is that he feels he is a surface with no thickness, separating an inside from an outside. Rather than having a human body, he is a 'tympanum' that vibrates between the mind and the world, but belongs to neither.

Nevertheless, even in this reduced state the Unnamable still has the means to produce for himself a body, albeit a rather strange one. Feeling the need to scream, for example, he realizes that he has no mouth and so he decides to make himself one: 'I have no mouth, and what about it, I'll grow one, a little hole at first, then wider and wider, deeper and deeper, the air will gush into me, and out a second later, howling' (U, 384). But even this may be too great a task and so he wonders if he might not do well enough as he is, which he imagines now to be a kind of ball. All he needs to get things going is a little stir, an upheaval or subsidence, a small disturbance that would start the ball rolling. And, once started, the disturbance would spread and pretty soon all the forms of locomotion would be re-introduced to his static universe: 'trips properly so called, business trips, pleasure trips, research expeditions, sabbatical leaves, jaunts and rambles, honeymoons at home and abroad and long sad solitary tramps in the rain, I indicate the main trends' (U, 384). Everything from sabbatical leave to walking in the rain would re-appear, if only a little physical motion could be made to prod his non-existent body, like the ironic *élan vital* that re-motivates Macmann.

Running contrary to these attempts to fabricate for himself an intact body, no matter how strange that body would be, the Unnamable also shares with Molloy, Malone and the others the painful experience of a Dionysian splintering of self. As the monologue continues his questions pile up incessantly, more and more frantically self-contradicting, twisting and turning, but without exit. Since he is essentially an incorporeal being his reality is entirely made up of language, but one of his discoveries is that language is not adequate to the task of formulating, and therefore terminating, his existence. Words swirl around his non-existent head, coming from both the inside and the outside: 'the words are everywhere, inside me, outside me . . . impossible to stop them, impossible to stop, I'm in words, made of words, others' words . . . I'm all these words, all these strangers, this dust of words' (U, 386); even the air, the walls, the floor and the ceiling are all words, he says. In this swirl of verbiage, the Unnamable feels himself breaking up and scattering through his surroundings. Now everything begins to give way, to flow and swirl like a snowstorm in which the flakes are particles of him, 'meeting, mingling, falling asunder' (U, 386). Subjected to these experiences, the Unnamable realizes that the best response would be to simply allow himself to be taken up in these swirls. If, like Murphy in his rocking chair, he could abandon himself to this chaos of non-Newtonian motion, he would perhaps find some relief. All he would have to do, he realizes, is to allow himself to 'wander', to actually become every particle of the whirlwind of dust (U, 401). But such a response, which would essentially be a wandering from his own form of subjectivity, is something that is 'impossible' for the Unnamable (ibid.). The swirl of words, which are animated by the 'everlasting third party', and which make up the walls, the ceiling and even himself, is a swirl that continues on its own way, but also cannot disregard the narrator, and always finally re-imposes the 'I' on his wandering chaos. 'In the end,' he says, 'it comes to that, to the survival of that alone, then the words come back, someone says I, unbelieving' (U, 402). Here, at the end of the novel, we have an echo of the theme that the 'I' is spoken, but without being given any credence. At the start, we had read 'I, say I. Unbelieving' (U, 291), but now we read 'someone says I, unbelieving' (U, 402). It is no longer even the 'I' that says 'I', it is simply 'someone'. So, at the end of this long journey in which he hasn't moved, the Unnamable can no longer say 'I', but also he cannot avoid saying 'I', he cannot go on, but also he cannot avoid going on, he cannot speak, but also he cannot remain silent. And that, as he says, is 'where you're buggered' (U, 412).

Reading these novels as a series of experiments that test and evaluate the forms of humanity that we inhabit, we can say that they confront the reader with the difficult, if not impossible, task of breaching our own limits. These, as we have seen, are the limits imposed by body, meaning (knowledge), and subjectivity (the 'I'). Unfortunately, we cannot say that Beckett's characters are successful in surpassing these limits, since his characters seem to fail in all their endeavours. Despite their resilience and obstinacy, they only achieve momentary and often self-destructive flight from those limits. But if there is one form of success that they do attain, it is that they push at the limits in such a way that they perhaps give us, the readers, a chance to see the shape and contours of those limits in a way that would not otherwise be available to us. In other words, beyond anything that Nietzsche, or Deleuze and Guattari, or Foucault could achieve, these novels relentlessly further the task of leaving behind the 'I', of launching on a line of flight, and of surpassing the limits of our current forms of subjectivity.

## A Difficult Wandering

The desirability, and also the difficulty, of wandering from ourselves is something of which Foucault, especially in his late work, is very much aware. In fact, the turn towards ethics in the last phase of his work is premised on the idea that the value of the pursuit of knowledge, for example about the history of human practices of ethics, is to be found not so much in the knowledge generated as in the transformation of subjectivity that is thus made possible. 'After all,' Foucault asks, 'what would be the value of the passion for knowledge if it resulted only in a certain knowledgeableness and not, in one way or another and to the extent possible, in the knower's straying afield of himself?' (1984a: 8[14]). This 'straying afield' is, in French, *égarement* which means, quite literally, a wandering. We must wander from ourselves, therefore, in order to benefit from the transformative potential of the work in question. But wandering from ourselves is something that we rarely want to do, and when we want to do it, it can remain stubbornly difficult to achieve. Foucault's own intellectual project strives to achieve such a straying afield of oneself through the patient labour of investigation, reflection and practice. My suggestion is that novels such as those by Swift and Beckett can help us to achieve an analogous wandering by means of the experiments that they enact on their characters and, consequently, on their readers. As Blanchot points out, it is difficult to overestimate the stubbornness of the reader, and yet there are works that have a strong potential to overcome this resistance, even if their characters, such as Gulliver and the Unnamable, ultimately find the task too difficult. But even in these cases of failure, it is our participation in the process of wandering, despite our stubbornness, that is presented to us by the novel, which may in fact make possible a wandering, however slight it may be, on our own part.

Each of these novels by Swift and Beckett, therefore, makes available for the reader an experiment that tests the limits of what it is to be human. They are books from which the attentive reader might emerge with a modified experi-ence of themselves and their world; with an increased awareness of both the bodily and the linguistic limits of their modes of being; and, with a stronger sense of their own pliability. Hence, they are books that have the potential to further the ethical project that Foucault advanced using his own historico-phil-osophical techniques: the project to expand our range of freedom by testing and pushing beyond the imposed limits of our humanity.

# Chapter 8

# Ethics and Fiction

At the height of his interest in literature, in 1966, Foucault praised André Breton for the way he had used writing as 'a means of pushing man beyond his limits, of forcing him to face the insuperable, of placing him near to what is furthest away from him' (1966c: 172 [555]). We have seen that Foucault was later to adopt similar formulations to describe the ethical dimensions of his own philosophical project, and this raises the question (for us, if not for him) of the ethical significance of literature. This is a question, or a series of questions, that I want to address now. What is the relation between ethics and fiction? Can literature make a contribution to ethics? Could a particular ethics make a contribution to our reception, or understanding, of fiction? In the history of philosophy there has been a whole range of answers to these questions. We saw how Plato's assessment of literature, as a powerful yet frivolous force, made him both admire and fear it, and ultimately want to subject it to a strict regime. From the ranks of writers, we took Seamus Heaney as an example of the way that poets try to counter the Platonist rejection of poetry; in Heaney's case, by furthering the tradition, particularly strong in Ireland, of weaving poetry into the fabric of political debate. Plato's view, however, was more immediately countered by Aristotle, for whom poetry (in the form of tragic drama) was ethically significant because it made publicly available a catharsis (purgation, or clarification) of the dangerous emotions of fear and pity. As for contemporary Western philosophy, schematizing in the extreme we could say that two answers to the question of the relation between literature and ethics stand out. On the one hand there is a view, which often appeals to Aristotelian ideals, that literature (especially the modern novel) helps us to clarify our emotions and our moral concepts. On the other hand there is a view (partly inspired by Nietzsche) that the value of literature is, in a sense, the opposite: it complicates, it confuses, it splinters; it confronts us with the alien and the unknown, and tends to undermine rather than refine our perception of the world. It is to this way of thinking, of which we could take Deleuze as a representative, that my approach most easily belongs.

Despite their differences, we can take the work of Martha Nussbaum (1992) and Noël Carroll (1998) to be representative of the first of these contemporary approaches. Nussbaum holds that narrative literature (principally the novel) is required as a supplementary component to moral philosophy, and indeed moral education (1992: 23–9). On this view, complex works of fiction, such as the novels of Henry James, would help both ordinary readers and moral philosophers to acquire the skills needed for a more finely attuned perception of the world. Not only would they build up our ability to respond sympathetically and intelligently to the needs of others, but they would also help us to clarify our own moral understanding by showing us how those concepts may have undesirable practical consequences if too rigidly enforced (1992: Chapter 5). Reading and viewing these works would then be a necessary corrective, for example, to the over-rationalizing of much contemporary moral philosophy. Carroll argues, in a similar vein, that narrative art works (including the novel) are capable sometimes of deepening and clarifying our moral understanding and emotions; and this is an effect that such works, as opposed to philosophical treatises, are particularly good at (1998: 151). In this approach, then, we could say that literature is confined to the role of obliging assistant to moral philosophy, and to the project of moral education. Literature provides emotional training and allows a certain clarification of concepts through the complex fictional scenarios it presents to the reader. But it is never allowed to upset the conceptual apparatus; it is as if it has accepted Plato's offer of a truce with poetry, on condition that it produce only 'hymns to the gods and verses in praise of good men' (*Republic*, 607a).

The second of these contemporary approaches is one for which the value of literature is based on a much more hazardous potential that we find in fiction. We saw that in the 1960s Foucault was attracted to a form of literature, and to a way of thinking about literature, that prioritized the themes of transgression, the outside, and the dissolution of subjectivity. For those writers, the ethical significance of fiction was its capacity to pierce the veil of our ordinary experience of the world and of ourselves; to undermine our commonsense grasp of language and its relation to the world; and to convey an experience that in some sense takes both the writer and reader to a disturbing limit. A more recent example of this general approach can be found in the work of Deleuze, for whom there are significant works of fiction (principally by British and American writers)[1] that consist of a flight from the human in the direction of a risky and unpredictable becoming. We have already seen that Heaney has a similar sense of the capacity of a poem to open up a plane on which the poet is 'intensified . . . and freed from his predicaments' (1989: xxii; see Chapter 2, above). For Deleuze, as for Heaney, this idea of flight implies much more than an urge to escape. It designates a line of becoming that creates for itself weapons to combat the rigid structures from which it moves, while it flies off in unpredictable and potentially uncontrollable directions, towards the minor, the animal, the non-organic. In *Moby-Dick*, for example, Captain Ahab could be said to have constructed for himself a line of flight away from the human in the direction of a becoming-whale. In words that echo my earlier discussion of Beckett and Swift, Deleuze (1998: 1) suggests that 'the shame of being a man' is the major motivation for this kind of writer. For Deleuze, the experience of the writer-in-flight is also sometimes capable of producing a symptomatology of the social world in which the writer lives. According to this idea, an idea that is also present in Nietzsche's thought, we could say that Kafka identified and diagnosed the syndrome of modern bureaucratic life, while Sacher-Masoch delineated a set of symptoms that define a particular possibility of human sexuality. It is for this reason that, in his final work, Deleuze (1998) proposes an approach to literature that is both 'critical and clinical'. These ideas, of the writer as an explorer of new ways of being (non-)human and as a diagnostician of their time, give us a way of linking up literature and ethics that differs significantly from the first approach that we sketched above. On this second approach, we can treat works of fiction as exemplary demonstrations of the possibilities that could be explored if we left behind our present modes of being; and also as valuable assessments of the barriers and limits that our present sets up to prevent such flights. Fictional works can easily be connected, therefore, with forms of ethical practice that try to mould new forms of life. Indeed, Deleuze argues that the style of great writers (both literary and philosophical) always has an ethical dimension because it is not only a way of writing, but is also suggestive of a way of living; it is a matter of 'inventing a possibility of life, a way of existing' (1995: 100).

It is clear that the basic philosophical orientation of the present book has strong affinities with this second approach to the ethics-literature nexus. This is hardly surprising, given the closeness between Foucault and Deleuze on many fundamental issues in philosophy. However, it is also true that the approach I develop here departs in at least one significant way from that of Deleuze. It is a striking feature that, in his writings on literature, Deleuze tends to focus on the lines of flight of the authors and characters, rather than the readers, of the works he is discussing. Hence, he will discuss the importance of a writer's poor health (1998: 3–4), the writer's alcoholism or self-destruction (2002: 38), or the writer's experiments with new forms of perception (2004: 183). And he will discuss a character's path of becoming, as for example Ahab in *Moby-Dick* (2002: 42) and Gregor in *The Metamorphosis* (Deleuze and Guattari 1986: 14). But very little attention is given to the effect, if any, that these features of the works will create in the reader, or to the mechanism by which such effects could be realized. In particular, the idea that these works might function as a tool in the ethical self-elaboration of the reader is not explicitly considered. Now, having made a long journey through the writings of Foucault, Heaney, Beckett, and all the rest, I want to outline a way of conceiving the ethics-literature nexus that falls within this second approach, as opposed to what I would call the more timid approach of Nussbaum and Carroll, but that adds a way of understanding the role which fiction plays in the transformation of the reader. It is this transformation that I have been speaking of as a transformation of experience.

Within this framework, therefore, I will outline an understanding of the relation between ethics and fiction that prioritizes the transformative effects that such works can have on their readers. The basic supposition of this approach is that works of fiction can play an important role in the ongoing task of working out answers to the central question of ethics, 'how is one to live?' This question is as much practical as theoretical and so the task it confronts us with will comprise both practical experiment and theoretical exploration. The argument of this book is that works of literature have the potential to play an important role in helping us to undertake this task. And the key to this relation between ethics and literature is the element of experiment that characterizes both practices. If we follow Foucault in seeing ethics as requiring an experimental engagement with one's own modes of behaviour, both in order to understand them and in order, possibly, to modify them, then we have a basis for making a link at a fundamental level between these experiments in the art of living, and the experiments of fiction. Fiction, as we have seen, is not related to experiment merely in the sense that some novels or plays may be said to be 'experimental'; rather, it is experimental in the more fundamental sense that it draws the reader into a test involving their ways of seeing, feeling and judging the world and themselves. Fiction does this through its capacity to present to us (in novels and plays as well as in poetry) people, worlds, and modes of experience that, while they may not exist, are nonetheless capable of exerting a real influence on the world in which we live. When these experiments exert such an influence, they do this through the modifications they tend to effect in the experience of the reader or audience. In other words, it is possible that after the engagement with the text or performance the recipient will no longer experience their world in the same way as before. It is, however, essential that the reader should be both attentive and active in this engagement; as we have seen, a work of literature, like any work of art, will only have its full impact when the audience openly, actively and carefully interact with the experience that it makes available.

The idea that this interaction should be characterized by care provides an important hint about its ethical dimension. One of the features that Foucault admires in ancient Greek ethics, and the one that most clearly differentiates it from many modern approaches to morality, is the central importance it gives to the theme of the care of the self: *epimeleia heautou* in Greek, *cura sui* in Latin, and *le souci de soi* in Foucault's French.[2] In Greek, Latin and French, but not always in English translations, this implies a form of self-care that doesn't presuppose a substantive self (*the* self), but rather consists of a reflexive attitude, a turning back of care from the world in an act of self-scrutiny and self-elaboration. This conversion, or as Plato puts it, this turning around of the soul (*Republic*, 518d), is characterized by an attitude of nurturing and inquisitiveness. And, to be inquisitive, to display curiosity, is also to adopt an attitude of care (in both English and French the word derives from the Latin *cura*, care). In a late interview, Foucault praises curiosity as a quality that betokens an admirable orientation towards the world. It evokes, he says, 'the care one takes of what exists and what might exist; a sharpened sense of reality, but one that is never immobilized before it; a readiness to find what surrounds us strange and singular; a certain determination to throw off familiar ways of thought and to look otherwise at the same things; a passion for seizing what is happening now and what is disappearing' (1980b: 325[108], modified).[3] In other words, curiosity in its richest sense is not an idle or dangerous probing of things that should remain secret; rather, it is a way of paying attention to our world and of accepting a certain responsibility for our dealings with it. It is akin, perhaps, to the 'sense of wonder' that Aristotle identifies as the origin of philosophy.

Foucault's description of the attitude of curiosity adds, to the ancient idea of *epimeleia* and *cura*, the modern tendency to approach the present moment as something that can be transformed. It was Baudelaire, according to Foucault, who first identified the kind of attention to the world that characterizes the attitude of modernity: a valorization of the present which is 'indissociable from a desperate eagerness to imagine it, to imagine it otherwise than it is, and to transform it not by destroying it but by grasping it in what it is' (1984c: 311). Curiosity in this sense is 'an exercise of extreme attention to what is real', combined with a 'practice of liberty' in which that reality is both respected and violated (ibid.). This is a combination that we have already seen to characterize Foucault's conception of critical philosophy: a patient attention to the detail of our present (an ontology of ourselves) combined with an impatient effort to change that present through the experimental testing of our limits (a practice of liberty). Similarly, this is a combination that underlies the characterization of fiction as 'that which is not, in so far as it is'. To approach a work of fiction with care and attention is, therefore, to be open to the complexities of its relations with the non-fictional world. It is to allow this imagined reality to, as Heaney says, press back against the pressure of reality and therefore to play some small role in modifying that reality and our relation to it.

I have already made the point that, on this approach, there is not necessarily an unbridgeable divide between literature and philosophy. Foucault, we have seen, is willing to place his philosophical histories under the rubric of fiction; at least up to a certain point, and in a very precise sense (Chapter 5). That is, they give a particular account of 'what happened', but they do so in order to intervene in a contemporary reality in a way that will create, or fiction, a transformative effect. Using the conceptual framework that I have developed here, we would say that these histories are capable of transforming the experience of their readers. Let me give an example of what this might mean: when I teach a course on Foucault at the University of Hong Kong, I spend several lectures going through the details of Foucault's account of modern power in *Discipline and Punish* (1995). I describe the disciplinary techniques that were developed by, for example, the eighteenth-century Catholic educator Jean-Baptiste de La Salle. I try to show how these techniques are still functioning in the twenty-first century at an Asian university. The fact that some of my students have actually attended one of the De La Salle colleges in Hong Kong makes the examples even more effective. But what do I hope to achieve in doing this? Apart from hoping to familiarize my students with an important element of contemporary European philosophy, I hope to change their experience of the classroom. I would like it to be impossible for them to unthinkingly enter such a space again; I would like it to be impossible for them to be unaware of how simple realities such as the architecture of the room have effects of power that, among other things, tend to form their subjectivity in a particular way. In other words, I would like to transform their experience of that space.

This, however, raises an important question: since transforming their experience doesn't seem in any way to transform the room or the university, why is it valuable or significant? To answer this question we can appeal to the threefold analysis of experience that we discussed in Chapter 5. Drawing on this account, we can say that the students' experience has, potentially, been modified along all three of the axes, or domains, of experience. First, they now know something new about the origin and ubiquity of certain disciplinary technologies. Second, they have perhaps undergone a shift in their relation to the kind of authority that is exercised in a classroom; they may begin, for example, to devise more effective forms of resistance to the power effects that are generated in that context. Third, they may now have a modified sense of themselves, as subjects who are moulded in all sorts of almost indiscernible ways by their social surroundings. And this new sense may have any number of more or less direct effects on their behaviour. Clearly, no straightforward programme of reform or general political action can emerge from these changes. But, the minimal point to make is that such transformative experiences are valuable, first to the extent that they tend to open up a new space of freedom for the individual, and secondly, to the extent that the cumulative effects of such changes might lead to large-scale social transformations.

But, even if a book like *Discipline and Punish* can be said to be an experience book in this sense, can we really say that works of literature are also capable of similar or analogous effects? Perhaps the least promising genre of work from this point of view is lyric poetry, so let's look at one of the examples I discussed in the chapter on Heaney, the poem 'Damson'. In the case of this poem, and perhaps most poetry, I think we would have to admit that the first domain of experience, that of knowledge, is not directly affected by our reading. The poem doesn't aim to educate or inform us by imparting a truth in any ordinary sense. That is, it doesn't aim to produce a truth-effect. With regard to the second and third axes of experience, however, we can be more confident that a direct effect is possible. If we bear in mind that the second axis, which as a shorthand we can call the axis of power, also encompasses the ways in which we are constituted in relation to authority and the norms of society, we can say that the poem may provoke a re-alignment in our relation to these norms. It would do so by provoking a reconsideration of, for example, the norms of justice and retribution that govern our understanding of, and practice in relation to, inter-communal conflict. With regard to the third axis, concerning the relation to self in its ethical dimension, we can say that the poem may provoke a modification by, for example, encouraging a stronger sense of the ways in which our belonging to a given community can cause us to act in certain ways. Or, it may bring about a shift in our relation to ourselves as potential avengers and peace-makers who have a certain responsibility to make a contribution to the large-scale events by which we are surrounded. Moving beyond the specifics of these axes, however, we would also have to say that the very quality of the language and the images employed by Heaney are capable of leaving a lasting impres-sion, however trivial this may appear. For example, the phrases 'wine-dark taste of home' and 'jam ladled thick and steaming down the sunlight' are capable of continuing to resonate through such diverse experiences as returning home after a long absence, or reading Homer; while the 'packed lunch' and 'bloody knuckles' of vividly coloured memory help to give a visceral reality to the hun-gry ghosts of Heaney's imagination, thus bringing Hades before us in a way that makes us almost contemporaries of both Homer and the Irish bricklayer.

The sum total of these possible effects would be, as I have argued, that the reader will no longer experience their world in the same way as before. And if this is true in the case of a poem, it is even more demonstrably so in the case of other forms of fiction. In fact, works of narrative fiction and drama are, argu-ably, capable of having an effect even along the first axis of experience, that of truth or knowledge. Any drama or story set in a context with which the audi-ence is not personally familiar is likely to reverberate with all sorts of more or less reliable knowledge and assumptions that the audience do possess. In the case of a play such as *Translations*, for example, we might bring to our viewing of the play the knowledge that we have about the historical context in which it is set; or on the other hand we might be motivated, after seeing it, to inform ourselves about that context by reading political or social history. So, even though the play itself doesn't directly convey this knowledge, or at least not in a way that a careful viewer would accept unquestioningly, there is no doubt that its curious and perhaps unbelievable picture of nineteenth-century Irish peas-ants speaking Latin and Greek, is likely to provoke a series of questions that can only be answered with historical knowledge. Further, we can surmise that any subsequent research we did on that situation would be coloured by our previ-ous experience of the play. But, whether or not Friel's picture turns out to be accurate is not really what matters: what matters is that we have been motivated to seek this information, to think about how to interpret it in the light of a pres-ent political context, and to consider some of the complex relations that inter-twine fiction, politics, and history.[4]

In the case of the second domain of experience, narrative fiction is even more clearly effective. It is quite possible, for example, that as readers of Joyce's

*A Portrait* we will gain a new or heightened sense of the extent to which social and historical forces shape our personal experience of the world. Everything, from our experience of sounds and smells to the contours of our use of language, comes to us in ways that are shaped by a larger social context. And this context, as Joyce shows, is shaped by large-scale political, economic and religious forces. The relevant forces will differ for each reader, depending on the time and place in which they live, but for any reader Joyce makes available an experiment with one form of resistance to these forces. Clearly, this is not to say that some or any readers will emerge as replicas of Stephen (although such a response is possible). But attentive, careful readers may emerge with a keener awareness of the historically conditioned nature of their experience, of the constraints and opportunities this brings, and of the difficult choices to be made between acquiescence, obstruction and resistance. Even if it is only in a subtle and tenuous way, then, we can say that our relation to structures of power and authority may be changed through a reading of the novel; and this is something that we could describe as a transformation of our experience.

The third domain of experience, that of the relation to self, is perhaps the one in which transformation can be most effectively brought about by works of fiction. Novels such as Beckett's *Three Novels*, for example, are capable of provoking a change in the way we relate to ourselves as subjects of language. The tortuous and relentless self-questioning of the protagonists, combined with their elaborate and torturous experimentations, may be enough to bring about a shift in the way readers think about and relate to themselves. By exploring the limits of what it is to be human, we could say that Beckett constructs a line of flight from the human that also becomes, at least temporarily, available to the reader. Any undermining of the self-assurance of our sense of 'I', and any probing of our sense of ourselves as embodied beings, is likely to make it more difficult for us to persist with our everyday sense of ourselves. It is this sense that contributes to our ability to make moral judgements about others and to treat ourselves as centres of moral choice-making, and to the extent that it is disturbed, our activities as a subject of ethics are also disturbed. It is the possibility of this kind of wandering from ourselves that, at least in the case of Beckett, constitutes one of the core potentials of fiction.

Even if one agrees that there are books, for example works of philosophy, that deserve to be called experience books, and one agrees further that some works of literature might also deserve this epithet, a major question about the transformative experiences they might effect still remains to be addressed. That is, what is their value? If I want to maintain that literature has a part to play in ethics, then one might expect an account of the moral value of the changes that it is capable of effecting. But, is the approach I adopt here able to offer such an account? Before trying to answer this question, I would like to address one preliminary concern. To a large extent, the way I have been discussing literature and its possible effects has seemed to suggest that those effects are so varied, not to mention uncertain, that it would be very difficult to characterize them in a global, totalizing way. One might, in fact, be tempted to think that literature just happens to bring about a range of more or less random changes in people's experience  of the world, and that these changes are not susceptible to being organized in a particular ethical direction. In one sense, this is undoubtedly true; much of what literature does has no relevance to ethics, and that which is relevant may pull simultaneously in conflicting directions. Similarly, when we consider a range of works we will most likely find that their combined effects on any individual reader could only ever be partial, splintered and contradictory. One way of responding to this recognition would be, following Plato, to try to ensure that only the right kind of literature is consumed in one's community. In that case, we might for example promote, especially for young readers, a range of works that are thought to have the kinds of moral effects of which we approve. In the approach adopted here, however, the only possible response to this problem is to accept the fact of the chaotic and hazardous nature of the effects of literature, and to insist that part of the value of literature lies in its unpredictable nature. Whatever transformations are possible, therefore, there is no need to organize them in a pre-given, morally defined direction.

Now that I have answered this preliminary question in a way that rules out assigning any consistency to the changes that works of literature may effect, it might seem to be more difficult for me to answer the other question: that is, the question about the value of the transformations that fiction provokes. Am I now prevented from arguing that these transformations do have an assignable value? What I want to suggest is that if we view these chaotic and disorderly transformations through the prism of a Foucauldian conception of ethics, then we can argue for their value as promoters of a transformative, experimental attitude on the part of readers. Summarizing briefly once again, we can say that Foucault's conception of ethics is built on two key ideas. First, that the present, with all its modes of thought and action and all its possible experiences, is a contingent product of complex historical processes that are in a continuous state of change and fragility. Second, that through a range of intellectual and practical endeavours we can intervene in our present to change both it and ourselves. A Foucauldian ethics involves valorizing and promoting those changes that would allow us to loosen the bonds that tie us to particular forms of action and self-understanding (or 'thought', in Foucault's special sense); and, segueing into the arena of politics, Foucauldian ethics involves finding ways to change social structures and institutions so that they allow a continuous renewal of the work of transformation. If this style of ethics has a *leitmotif,* it is the idea of experiment; in general, our way of experiencing the world is experimental in form, and not only is the work of freeing ourselves from the forms of thought that are imposed on us an experimental undertaking, but any new forms that we may devise are themselves also experiments. If we accept that reading works of literature is one of the important modes of experimental experience that are available to us, then it follows that such works can be seen as making a contribution to this kind of ethics. Works of fiction allow us to experiment by giving us the opportunity to experience different worlds, by giving us different ways of experiencing this world, and by offering us different ways of experiencing our own subjectivity. We can say, therefore, that their value and their importance to ethics consists in their potential to modify our experience, in the sense that we would no longer experience the world in the same way as before.

At the beginning of this chapter I raised a question that, in a sense, is the reverse of the one we have been addressing up until now: that is, could a particular ethics make a contribution to our reception, or understanding, of fiction? In other words, if we adopted the approach I am suggesting here, would this have any effect on the way that we read, or discuss, works of literature? I think we can now say that the framework I am developing here calls for a critical approach to literature that would not confine itself to helping us to understand works of literature (their meaning, value, and so on), but would have the added aim of generating or facilitating a certain effect; an effect that would be analogous to the effect of the works themselves. This would be a mode of criticism, therefore, which combines the analysis and explanation of works with the promotion and amplification of their effects. In an interview from 1980, Foucault expresses his frustration with the type of criticism that confines itself to passing judgement on the text. He would prefer, he says, a criticism that proceeds by imaginative leaps; one that is not dressed in the red robes of the judge, but in the 'light of possible storms' (1980b: 323[107]). This form of criticism would bring something new into existence; it would 'multiply, not judgements, but signs of existence; it would call them forth, drag them from their sleep' (ibid.). Adopting this approach, let us say that the framework I am developing here would call for a form of criticism that brings to light and promotes the transformative potential of a range of fictional works. Its aim, in effect, would be to act as a catalyst in the experiment that the works make possible.

The idea that the effects of works of literature may be in need of amplification relates to the fact that, as I have emphasized at many points throughout this book, an individual work of fiction, or an individual poem, will usually only make a minuscule difference to our experience. There are very few works of literature that, for any given reader, would be massively transformative in a profound way. This is a fact of which Beckett, to take one example, seems to have been well aware. His friend and publisher, John Calder, reports that Beckett once said to him: 'All I ever wanted to do was put my forehead against the cliff-rock and move it a fraction of a millimetre' (Calder 2001: 41). But a millimetre may not satisfy everybody, and one way of compensating for this relative weakness would be to argue that it is not so much a single work (or author) that transforms our experience, but a wide range of works; perhaps a lifetime's reading, or the reading of our formative years. It is not, for instance, by chance that Foucault's own experience books (by Beckett and Nietzsche, in particular) were

works that he read or saw relatively early in life. For our purposes here, however, it is hardly necessary to approach the territory of the Sorites paradox by
trying to define exactly how many works could make a difference. Instead, we
can think of the effect of reading literature as operating in two ways. On the
one hand it is of course possible that, due to one's choice of reading, there will
be a cumulative effect that has a certain coherence and direction; this would be
the kind of effect that Plato, for example, hoped to achieve by restricting young
people's access to most poetry and drama. But it could also be the effect of
reading only works that tend to promote certain values and attitudes, such as
inclusiveness, tolerance, respect for difference, and so on. On the other hand,
and perhaps more fruitfully, we can think of the effect of reading works of fiction as one that is much less predictable and much more hazardous. On this
account, there would be two types of effect of which literature is capable, one
specific and the other more general. The first type of effect would be a particular product of the kind of shocking or arresting experience that characterizes
the experience book. This is an experience which, through the intensity of its
strangeness, would make a disruptive intervention in our everyday experience,
and would prevent that experience from reverting to its habitual pattern. This
is the kind of experience, we can assume, that Foucault refers to when he speaks
of the importance of Beckett's *Waiting for Godot*. The second type of effect would
be the cumulative product of a slower and more general transformation. This
would be the result of the cultivation, across an extended period of time, of a
particular kind of habit: the habit of opening oneself up to an experimental
engagement with both the world and oneself. It may seem paradoxical to speak
of cultivating the habit of going beyond one's habits, but that, after all, is a central feature of a certain critical attitude. This is the idea of an ethics that pursues
the practice of liberty by cultivating multiple forms of flight, wandering, and
self-abandonment; those techniques that allow us to detach ourselves from ourselves, and to think and act otherwise.

My suggestion is that works of fiction can play a significant role in the elaboration of this kind of ethics. From this point of view, the great value of fiction
would be its capacity to draw us into an experience of 'that which is not' in such
a way that it has an effect on 'that which is'. These works, by virtue of the intensity of their language and the pleasure they produce, are on occasion capable
of jolting us out of our habitual forms of experience and provoking us to cultivate new forms. And they also make possible a longer-term cultivation of a habit
of openness and experimentation that facilitates a continuous critical and
transformative intervention in the modes of experience that our time and our
inclinations sanction. This suggestion is clearly not to be taken as a general
characterization of all literature; nor is it to be taken as a general summary of
all the possible relations between literature and ethics. It is simply a way of
understanding *one* of the things that fiction can do, especially when seen
through the prism of *one* understanding of ethics and critical philosophy.

Understood in this way, literature is one of the forces in our world that makes possible, to borrow Joyce's words again, a resistance to the branding and fettering of time that ousts a myriad possibilities. This doesn't mean that literature is utopic, or that it offers a vision of a better world; but simply that it opens up new spaces for experimentation through which the limits of our present can be surpassed. And that would give us grounds for insisting that these 'minuscule events', these 'grains of sand', these fragile experience books, are not without their multiple, strange effects.

# Notes

## Chapter 1

[1] See Foucault 1984a: 9[15]. Throughout this book, references to Foucault's works usually include details of both English and French versions. The number in square brackets is always the page number of the French edition. Full details of these various editions are in the Bibliography. I also frequently modify the English translations, but if changes are substantial I indicate so in the reference. In this case, I would suggest that 'think otherwise' is a more satisfactory translation of '*penser autrement*' than the standard English 'think differently'.

[2] See the excellent discussion of these issues in Jay 2006: 9–11.

[3] Given the time in which he lived, Swift would not generally have identified himself as Irish (as opposed to English). And Beckett, of course, wrote much of his work in French.

[4] 'Yeats as an Example?', in Heaney 1980.

[5] For an excellent account of the early stages of Field Day's development see Richtarik 1994.

[6] Seamus Deane, 'Introduction', in Friel 1996: 22. Emphasis added.

[7] See Foucault 1984a: 25–8; and 1983a: 266–8.

[8] See my discussion of these issues in O'Leary 2002, Chapter 2.

[9] Deleuze discusses Francis Bacon's attempts to overcome the content that already appeared on any ostensibly blank canvas. See Deleuze 2004: Chapter 11, 'The painting before painting . . .'.

[10] Especially in the early 1970s, Foucault used the category of the 'intolerable' to understand, for example, unrest in the French prisons. See, for example, Foucault 1971a, 1971b.

[11] For a fuller treatment of this attempt to apply Foucault's categories to his own philosophical practice, see O'Leary 2002, Part Two.

## Chapter 2

[1] From 'Flight Path', in Heaney 1996a. According to the poem, the encounter occurred 'One bright May morning, nineteen-seventy-nine'.

[2] This shift in IRA strategy led, for example, to the election of Bobby Sands as an MP in 1981. The man's demand for (presumably) a poem makes sense in light of

the continuous use of poems (and ballads) as a feature of political action on both sides of the conflict in Ireland, since at least the seventeenth century.

[3] 'Did that play of mine send out/Certain men the English shot?', from W. B. Yeats, 'Man and the Echo', in Yeats 1990.

[4] A classic Irish example would be Patrick Pearse, but Yeats and the Field Day group (including Heaney himself) could also be mentioned.

[5] Translation modified. Foucault's essay is a review of Gilles Deleuze, *Difference and Repetition and The Logic of Sense*, two books which set themselves the task of overturning Platonism.

[6] Final lecture series, 'Le courage de la vérité', Collège de France 1984. Unpublished; recordings available at Fonds Michel Foucault, l'IMEC, Caen.

[7] This is Heaney's gloss.

[8] We can note that this quote is also used by Yeats as an epigraph to his strangely quietist poem 'Politics'.

[9] I have used the translation by Desmond Lee (Plato 1983).

[10] The title of this collection refers to a builder's or carpenter's tool that 'reveals whether a surface is perfectly level' (COD) – which may be known to some readers simply as a 'level'.

[11] By Carolyn Mulholland, a Northern Ireland sculptor.

[12] See for example 'Sailing to Byzantium', in which Yeats uses the phrase 'once out of nature'; these poems also echo 'Ode on a Grecian Urn' by John Keats.

[13] In 'Poet's Chair' the word shoulder-blades is hyphenated, while in 'The Swing' it is not. I shall assume that this has no significance.

[14] Heaney is drawing on Plato's account of Socrates' last days. See, especially, the *Phaedo*.

[15] In the days before his execution, Socrates has been composing poetry in his cell (verses in praise of Apollo, and versions of Aesop's fables). No doubt this is the kind of poetry of which Plato could approve. See, Plato, *Phaedo*, 60d–61b.

[16] The cultural and political relevance of excavation becomes central, especially in the collection *North* (Heaney 1975).

[17] See, Heaney 1980, 1989, 1996b, and his Nobel acceptance speech in 2006.

[18] Heaney is here quoting from Robert Lowell.

[19] A damson is a soft red fruit, a kind of plum.

[20] The heraldic description of the badge of Ulster: 'Argent, a sinister hand erect couped gules'.

# Chapter 3

[1] There has been surprisingly little sustained engagement with Foucault's work on literature. One major exception, which aims to give 'an interpretation of Foucault's analysis of modern society and culture for students of literature', is During 1992 (see p. 2). Other approaches to literature which are influenced by Foucault's work in general include Ian Hunter 1988; and the many writings grouped together under the 'New Historicism' rubric. But for a different perspective see also the recent collection, Artières 2004; and Rayner 2003.

² Foucault also wrote extensively on painters including Goya, Velasquez, Manet, Magritte, and on the French composer Pierre Boulez, but these writings are beyond the scope of my discussion here.

³ See, for example, Foucault 1964a. As the title suggests ('Pourquoi réédite-t-on l'oeuvre de Raymond Roussel? Un précurseur de notre littérature moderne'), Foucault here considers Roussel as a writer whose significance, for 'us', comes from his connection with later writers including Leiris and Robbe-Grillet.

⁴ This interview (Foucault 1988) was conducted in 1976 but is not included in either *Essential Works or Dits et écrits*.

⁵ For a more recent account of the turn see Revel 2004.

⁶ Rajchman speaks for instance in terms of 'the passing of a modernist sensibility', and of Foucault's attempt to discover where 'we' 'went wrong' (1985: 10, 12).

⁷ Note that the English translation gives: 'Bataille's exemplary enterprise: his desperate and relentless attack on the preeminence of the philosophical subject'. This seems to me to be a rather misleading translation of: '*Bataille qui n'a cessé de rompre en lui, avec acharnement, la souveraineté du sujet philosophant*' (1963a: 79[243]).

⁸ This discussion (Foucault 1964b) was published as 'Débat sur la poésie', along with its companion piece, 'Débat sur le roman'. Neither has been translated into English.

⁹ Note that for Foucault, and French historians in general, 'the classical age' refers to the period from the early seventeenth to the late eighteenth century.

¹⁰ Especially in *Locus Solus*, 2003.

¹¹ For a more extensive discussion of this book, see O'Leary 2008.

¹² The account given in 1963b gives precedence to Sade and the late eighteenth century, while the account in 1966b, in particular, privileges Mallarmé and the late nineteenth century.

¹³ For an excellent discussion of Foucault's relation to Heidegger, see Rayner 2007.

¹⁴ See Blanchot's later formulation of this experience: '"What is troubling you?" – "The fact of being implicated in a speech that is exterior to me"' (Blanchot, 1983: xix).

¹⁵ Translation modified – and note that the English 'content' is presumably a misprint for 'contest'.

¹⁶ This echoes Foucault's suggestion that man may just be 'a simple fold in our knowledge' (1966a: xxv[15]). Unfortunately this echo is lost in the English translation of The Order of Things.

¹⁷ Foucault 1963c and 1966d.

¹⁸ For a reading of this essay that gives it a great deal more importance, see Rayner 2003.

¹⁹ In the French, Foucault tells us that this experience was 'silently maintained' ['s'est maintenue sourdement'] from Diderot up to Roussel and Artaud; the English rather flatly and misleadingly tells us that the experience 'changes little'.

²⁰ In this regard, Foucault also singles out the engravings of Goya as significant.

²¹ Foucault 1981. I provide my own translations, but also refer to the relevant passages of the English publication.

[22] Foucault quotes, without reference, from the final lines of Beckett's novel, The Unnamable. See Beckett 1991: 414.

[23] It is important not to confuse this shift to 'external' conditions with Foucault's interest in the 'outside' of thought.

[24] Indeed, in the discussion after the lecture Foucault points out that if this lecture had been on the theme of the subject it would have analysed, in the same way, the 'subject-function' (1969: [818]). These comments are not reproduced in the English translation.

[25] Foucault 2004a, 1978.

[26] See also 1978: 199, where Foucault discusses the 'singular strangeness' and 'beauty' of the memoir.

[27] This appeal is famous in English, but in fact the French doesn't mention 'police' or 'bureaucrats' specifically. It speaks of the morality of the 'état-civil' (administrative status) that governs our papers ('régit nos papiers').

# Chapter 4

[1] See also the epigraph of Deleuze 1998 (a quote from Proust's *Contre Saint-Beuve*): 'Great books are written in a kind of foreign language'.

[2] Brian Friel, *Translations*, in Friel 1996: 446. Henceforth T, with page numbers given in the text.

[3] Auden praises Yeats' poetry, but seems to deny its political efficacy (1979: 82). It is, however, debatable whether the poem as a whole is committed to such a blanket denial of the efficacy of poetry.

[4] James Cousins, cited in Lee 1995: 165.

[5] Cited in Lloyd 1993: 45.

[6] Frank Fay, cited in Lee 1995: 170.

[7] Longley 1986 is a good example.

[8] Cited in Kearney 1988: 126.

[9] See, in particular, Deane 1998.

[10] Steiner 1975: 31, 415. The second quote is actually phrased as a rhetorical question (presumably to be answered in the affirmative).

# Chapter 5

[1] Two notable exceptions are Rayner 2003 and Gutting 2002. But see also Chapter 9 (on Bataille, Blanchot and Foucault) in Jay 2006.

[2] Lecture of 28 March 1984; unpublished, but recordings available at Fonds Michel Foucault, l'IMEC, Caen.

[3] See 2006b: xxxvi[167]. For Foucault's source, see Char 1967: 71.

[4] It is no surprise to find that the group of poems from which the Char quotation comes is called Partage Formel (Formal Division).

[5] It is worth noting that Foucault is not necessarily looking for access to madness in some sort of pure state. Indeed, he explicitly states later in the same Preface that

its 'wild state' and 'primitive purity' will always remain inaccessible (2006b: xxxiii[164]). Nevertheless, one might object that he does seem to assume that there is such a state, although we cannot access it.

6  Note that for Foucault, and French historians in general, 'the classical age' refers to the period from the early seventeenth to the late eighteenth century.

7  The English version, inexplicably, translates Foucault's '*toutes*' as 'many'.

8  Note, however, that '*expérience*' is mistakenly translated as 'experiment'. This is a good illustration of the point I made earlier that in French it is often difficult to tell in which sense the word *expérience* is being used.

9  The dictionary entry titled 'Foucault' which Foucault published under the name Maurice Florence is based on an early version of this Preface. See the introductory note in the French edition (the English translation of the note is incomplete) (1984e: [631]).

10  When Foucault systematized his 1960s methodological approach under the term 'archaeology', he described these forms as constituting an 'historical *a priori*'. See Foucault 2002: 142–8[166–73]. This concept is closely related to the concept of the *episteme* in *The Order of Things*. In both cases, Foucault is indicating a set of rules and formations that determine which statements will be accepted as falling within a particular field of scientificity; in other words, as being potentially true or false.

11  This may offer a way of differentiating Foucault's account of experience from that of phenomenology. This is not the place to address that issue, but see Gutting 2002.

12  For a similar categorization of Foucault's approach to the 'outside', see Revel 2004.

13  This translation also commits the error of translating the first 'faire moi-même' as 'construct myself'.

14  This novel is in Beckett 1991. The Unnamable is henceforth U, with page numbers given in the text.


# Chapter 6

1  Joyce 1992a. Henceforth P, with page numbers given in the text.

2  See, for example, Joyce 1991: 209, on the 'modern spirit' being 'vivisective'.

3  See, especially, Kenner 1976.

4  In fact, Agamben goes so far as to claim that today we are incapable of either having or communicating experience (1993: 13).

5  Even though taste doesn't appear in this short passage, it features in the immediately preceding passage (where some boys were said to have drunk the altar wine in the sacristy) and in the immediately following paragraph (where Stephen recalls being knocked over on the sports track and 'some of the grit of the cinders' getting into his mouth). See, P, 40, 41.

6  I recognize, of course, that 'a portrait of *the* artist' can also be read as 'a portrait of the artist who is making the portrait' (in this case, Joyce).

7 We can note, for example, that in the last pages of the book he walks through St Stephen's Green in central Dublin and for the first time claims it as his own green – on the basis of a shared name (P, 271).

8 Apart from the example discussed here, see 'belt' (P, 5), 'suck' (P, 8), and 'pock' (P, 45).

9 See, P, 312, fn. 67.

10 Foucault 1983b: 450[449].

11 In Chapter 1, I discussed the later Stephen's reflections on time and its 'ousted' possibilities (Joyce 1973: 31).

12 The phrase ('I will not serve') first appears in Latin in Father Arnall's sermon in Chapter 3 (P, 126); it is then adopted by Stephen in a conversation with Cranly towards the end of Chapter 5 (P, 260, 268).

13 Hugh Kenner is one of many critics who make this kind of judgment on Stephen's character. In an early paper, for example, Kenner (1962: 59) says that at the end we can only laugh at Stephen's idealistic perfectionism.

14 A prayer confessing sins and asking God's forgiveness.

15 See also: 'He had never once disobeyed or allowed turbulent companions to seduce him from his habit of quiet obedience' (P, 169).

16 As an image of this formation we can think of the young Stephen listening to the 'pock' of cricket bats in the grounds of a private Jesuit college, circa 1890 (P, 45, 61).

17 One could say that this pattern continues even beyond the novel, since the final high-point of Stephen's planned departure for Paris is followed by the opening chapter of Ulysses in which Stephen is stuck back in Dublin, impoverished and unhappy – and largely unpublished.

18 This theme is present, for example, in Heidegger, Benjamin, and Adorno.

19 Gadamer points out that one of the first appearances of the noun erlebnis is in Dilthey's biography of Schleiermacher (2003: 64).

20 In fact, Gadamer speaks of 'insight' rather than wisdom (2003: 356).

21 See, for example, the formulation offered in the translator's Introduction (2003: xiii): *erfahrung* is 'an ongoing integrative process in which what we encounter widens our horizon, but only by overturning an existing perspective, which we can then perceive was erroneous or at least narrow'.

22 This is one of the ways that Gadamer differentiates his dialectic of experience from a Hegelian dialectics.

23 It is interesting that Stephen, apparently, tries to do the opposite of this; that is, he tries to create himself by rejecting everything, even his memory of his own childhood self.

24 See, especially, 2003: 341–79.

25 Cf. Foucault's comments about his reading of Nietzsche: 'what is the maximum of philosophical intensity, and what are the current philosophical effects to be found in these texts?' (1983b: 447[446]).

26 It's important to remember that this is a *self-imposed* exile, a point which Stephen's friend Cranly makes when he says 'you need not look upon yourself as driven away if you do not wish to go' (P, 267).

27 Joyce 1992. Henceforth D, with page numbers given in the text.

28 Joyce 1991. Henceforth SH, with page numbers given in the text.

[29] Joyce uses this different spelling for the family name in SH.

[30] There are other stories (for example, 'The Dead' and 'A Painful Case') in which one could argue that the epiphany is shared, at least in part, by the protagonist. But even here, the full extent is really only available to the reader.

[31] Andrew Gibson (2006: 96–7) discusses the novel in relation to Thomas Mann's idea of entbildung.

# Chapter 7

[1] Swift 2003; Beckett 1991.

[2] In Beckett (1991), *Three Novels: Molloy, Malone Dies, The Unnamable*, Grove Press, New York. Henceforth *Molloy*, M; *Malone Dies*, MD; *The Unnamable*, U; all with page numbers to this edition given in the text.

[3] Beckett was undoubtedly an admirer of Swift, and of many other eighteenth-century novelists and philosophers. For a detailed investigation of these influences, see Smith 2002. Similarly, I have no intention of presenting a conspectus of Foucault's direct references to Beckett's work, many of which I have already discussed in earlier chapters. However, an article which does give such an overview, and which suggests that Foucault, under the influence of Blanchot, has misunderstood Beckett, is Hunkeler 2002.

[4] Part of Swift's epitaph, written by himself in Latin, and engraved on a marble plaque in St Patrick's Cathedral, Dublin, can be translated as: 'there savage indignation can no longer lacerate his heart'.

[5] Swift 2003. Henceforth G, with page numbers given in the text.

[6] Although Vladimir and Estragon, in *Waiting for Godot* (Beckett 2000), do toy with the idea of hanging themselves on the tree, it is never a real possibility, either for them or the audience.

[7] Paul Rabinow (1997: xxxviii) suggests 'disassemble the self' as a translation of the French phrase. It is certainly better than the published English version which gives 'to get free of oneself', but I would say that 'detach oneself from oneself' is closer to Foucault's idea.

[8] Quoted in a 1956 interview with Israel Shenker in the *New York Times*. See Graver 1979: 148.

[9] Notebook 35 [35], May–July 1885, in Nietzsche 2003: 20–21.

[10] Nietzsche's italics, throughout.

[11] Malone offers this version of the principle: 'It is better to adopt the simplest explanation, even if it is not simple, even if it does not explain very much. A bright light is not necessary, a taper is all one needs to live in strangeness, if it faithfully burns' (MD, 182).

[12] Georges Bataille, *review of Molloy*; see Graver 1979: 55.

[13] Beckett 1957. Henceforth Mu, with page numbers to this edition given in the text.

[14] Deleuze and Guattari 2004; especially Chapter 6.

[15] It is interesting that Deleuze and Guattari identify the three strata that most define and capture us as the organism, significance and subjectification (2004: 176). These three could be mapped on to the three lines of experimentation that

I identified in Beckett's novels: body, meaning (knowledge), and subjectivity (the 'I'). Unfortunately, however, I don't have space to pursue these parallels here.

[16] Nietzsche 2000, especially Sections 1 to 3.

[17] Deleuze and Guattari also warn that the construction of a body without organs can lead to one's own permanent annihilation (Deleuze and Guattari 2004: 178–9).

[18] Shortly before this, Malone had described a Mrs Lambert quietly sorting lentils into two heaps, but then impatiently, 'with a furious gesture', sweeping the two piles together and into the saucepan (MD, 214).

# Chapter 8

[1] See 'On the superiority of Anglo-American literature', in Deleuze 2002. Deleuze singles out, for example, Lawrence, Scott Fitzgerald, Miller, and Kerouac.

[2] See, especially, Foucault 1984b. The English title of this volume (*The Care of the Self*) is in fact misleading; a more accurate rendering would be *The Care of Self*. If the definite article were required, the French would read *Le souci du soi*, not *Le souci de soi*.

[3] See also the invocation of curiosity in 1984a: 8[14]).

[4] These considerations are more explicitly explored in Friel's later play, *Making History* (Friel 1999).

# Bibliography

## Works by Michel Foucault

(1954) 'Introduction', in L. Binswanger, *Le Rêve et l'Existence*. Untranslated. [Foucault, Michel (1994), *Dits et écrits 1954–1988: I 1954–1969*. Daniel Defert and Francois Ewald (eds). Paris: Gallimard.]

(1961) 'La folie n'existe que dans une soicété'. Untranslated. [Foucault, Michel (1994), *Dits et écrits 1954–1988: I 1954–1969*. Daniel Defert and Francois Ewald (eds). Paris: Gallimard.]

(1963a) 'A preface to transgression', in Foucault, Michel (2000), *Essential Works of Foucault, volume 2: Aesthetics, Method and Epistemology*, ed. James Faubion. London: Penguin Books. [Foucault, Michel (1994), 'Préface à la transgression (en hommage à Georges Bataille)'. *Dits et écrits 1954–1988: I 1954–1969*. Daniel Defert and Francois Ewald (eds). Paris: Gallimard.]

(1963b) 'Language to infinity', in Foucault, Michel (2000), *Essential Works of Foucault, volume 2: Aesthetics, Method and Epistemology*, ed. James Faubion. London: Penguin Books. [Foucault, Michel (1994), 'Le langage à l'infini'. *Dits et écrits 1954–1988: I 1954–1969*. Daniel Defert and Francois Ewald (eds). Paris: Gallimard.]

(1963c) 'Distance, aspect, origine'. Untranslated. [Foucault, Michel (1994), *Dits et écrits 1954–1988: I 1954–1969*. Daniel Defert and Francois Ewald (eds). Paris: Gallimard.]

(1964a) 'Pourquoi réédite-t-on l'oeuvre de Raymond Roussel? Un précurseur de notre littérature moderne'. Untranslated. [Foucault, Michel (1994), *Dits et écrits 1954–1988: I 1954–1969*. Daniel Defert and Francois Ewald (eds). Paris: Gallimard.]

(1964b) 'Débat sur la poésie'. Untranslated. [Foucault, Michel (1994), *Dits et écrits 1954–1988: I 1954–1969*. Daniel Defert and Francois Ewald (eds). Paris: Gallimard.]

(1966a) *The Order of Things: An Archeology of the Human Sciences*. (No translator given). London: Routledge (2001). [*Les mots et les choses: une archéologie des sciences humaines*. Paris: Gallimard (1966).]

(1966b) 'The thought of the outside', in Foucault, Michel (2000), *Essential Works of Foucault, volume 2: Aesthetics, Method and Epistemology*, ed. James Faubion. London: Penguin Books. ['La pensée du dehors', in Foucault, Michel (1994), *Dits et écrits 1954–1988: I 1954–1969*. Daniel Defert and Francois Ewald (eds). Paris: Gallimard.]

(1966c) 'A swimmer between two words', in Foucault, Michel (2000), *Essential Works of Foucault, volume 2: Aesthetics, Method and Epistemology*, ed. James Faubion. London: Penguin Books. ['C'était un nageur entre deux mots', in Foucault, Michel (1994), *Dits et écrits 1954–1988: I 1954–1969*. Daniel Defert and Francois Ewald (eds). Paris: Gallimard.]

(1966d) 'Behind the fable', in Foucault, Michel (2000), *Essential Works of Foucault, volume 2: Aesthetics, Method and Epistemology*, ed. James Faubion. London: Penguin Books. ['L'arrière-fable', in Foucault, Michel (1994), *Dits et écrits 1954–1988: I 1954–1969*. Daniel Defert and Francois Ewald (eds). Paris: Gallimard.]

(1968) 'Politics and the study of discourse', in G. Burchell, C. Gordon and P. Miller (eds) (1991), *The Foucault Effect: Studies in Governmentality*. Hemel Hempstead: Harvester Wheatsheaf. ['Réponse à une question', in Foucault, Michel (1994), *Dits et écrits 1954–1988: I 1954–1969*. Daniel Defert and Francois Ewald (eds). Paris: Gallimard.]

(1969) 'What is an Author?', in Foucault, Michel (2000), *Essential Works of Foucault, volume 2: Aesthetics, Method and Epistemology*, ed. James Faubion. London: Penguin Books. ['Qu'est-ce qu'un auteur?', in Foucault, Michel (1994), *Dits et écrits 1954–1988: I 1954–1969*. Daniel Defert and Francois Ewald (eds). Paris: Gallimard.]

(1970) 'Theatrum Philosophicum', in Foucault, Michel (2000), *Essential Works of Foucault, volume 2: Aesthetics, Method and Epistemology*, ed. James Faubion. London: Penguin Books. ['Theatrum Philosophicum', in Foucault, Michel (1994), *Dits et écrits 1954–1988: II 1970–1975*. Daniel Defert and Francois Ewald (eds). Paris: Gallimard.]

(1971a) 'Je perçois l'intolérable'. Untranslated. [In Foucault, Michel (1994), *Dits et écrits 1954–1988: II 1970–1975*. Daniel Defert and Francois Ewald (eds). Paris: Gallimard.]

(1971b) 'Préface à *Enquête dans vingt prisons*'. Untranslated. [In Foucault, Michel (1994), *Dits et écrits 1954–1988: II 1970–1975*. Daniel Defert and Francois Ewald (eds). Paris: Gallimard.]

(1972) 'Intellectuals and Power', in D. F. Bouchard (ed.) (1977), *Language, Counter-Memory, Practice*. New York: Cornell University Press, New York. ['Les intellectuels et le pouvoir', in Foucault, Michel (1994), *Dits et écrits 1954–1988: II 1970–1975*. Daniel Defert and Francois Ewald (eds). Paris: Gallimard.]

(1977a) 'The History of Sexuality', in Colin Gordon (ed.) (1980), *Power/Knowledge: Selected Interviews and Other Writings, 1972–1977*. New York: Pantheon Books. [Michel Foucault (1994), *Dits et écrits 1954–1988: III 1976–1979*. Daniel Defert and Francois Ewald (eds). Paris: Gallimard.]

(1977b) 'Truth and Power', in Foucault, Michel (2000), *Essential Works of Foucault 1954–1984, volume 3: Power* (ed. James Faubion). New York: The New Press. ['Entretien avec Michel Foucault', in Michel Foucault (1994), *Dits et écrits 1954–1988: III 1976–1979*. Daniel Defert and Francois Ewald (eds). Paris: Gallimard.]

(1978) *I, Pierre Rivière, Having Slaughtered my Mother, my Sister and my Brother*. Foucault, Michel (ed.). Harmondsworth: Peregrine Books.

(1980a) 'Interview with Michel Foucault', in Foucault, Michel (2000), *Essential Works of Foucault 1954–1984, volume 3: Power* (ed. James Faubion). New York: The New Press. ['Entretien avec Michel Foucault', in Michel Foucault (1994), *Dits et écrits 1954–1988: IV 1980–1988*. Daniel Defert and Francois Ewald (eds). Paris: Gallimard.]

(1980b) 'The masked philosopher', in Foucault, Michel (1997), *Essential Works of Foucault 1954–1984, volume 1: Ethics*. Paul Rabinow (ed.). London: Penguin. ['Le philosophe masqué', in Michel Foucault (1994), *Dits et écrits 1954–1988: IV 1980–1988*. Daniel Defert and Francois Ewald (eds). Paris: Gallimard.]

(1981) 'The Order of Discourse', in *Untying the Text: a Post-Structuralist Reader.* Robert Young (ed.). Boston: Routledge. [Foucault, Michel (1971), *L'ordre du discours*. Paris: Gallimard.]

(1982) 'The subject and power', in Foucault, Michel (2000), *Essential Works of Foucault 1954–1984, volume 3: Power* (ed. James Faubion). New York: The New Press. ['Entretien avec Michel Foucault', in Michel Foucault (1994). Originally published in English.]

(1983a) 'On the genealogy of ethics: an overview of work in progress', in Foucault, Michel (1997), *Essential Works of Foucault 1954–1984, volume 1: Ethics* (ed. Paul Rabinow). London: Penguin. [This interview was originally conducted and published in English, and the French translation was significantly revised by Foucault. See Foucault, Michel (1994), *Dits et écrits 1954–1988: IV 1980–1988*. Daniel Defert and Francois Ewald (eds). Paris: Gallimard.]

(1983b) 'Structuralism and post-structuralism', in Foucault, Michel (2000), *Essential Works of Foucault, volume 2: Aesthetics, Method and Epistemology*, ed. James Faubion. London: Penguin Books. ['Structuralisme et post-structuralisme', in Foucault, Michel (1994), *Dits et écrits 1954–1988: IV 1980–1988*. Daniel Defert and Francois Ewald (eds). Paris: Gallimard.]

(1984a) *The History of Sexuality, volume II, The Use of Pleasure*, trans. Robert Hurley. Harmondsworth: Penguin Books, 1990. [*Histoire de la sexualité, 2, L'usage des plaisirs*. Paris: Gallimard, 1984.]

(1984b) *The History of Sexuality, volume III, The Care of the Self*, trans. Robert Hurley. Harmondsworth: Penguin Books, 1990. [*Histoire de la sexualité, 3, Le souci de soi*. Paris: Gallimard, 1984.]

(1984c) 'What is enlightenment?', in Foucault, Michel (1997), *Essential Works of Foucault 1954–1984, volume 1: Ethics* (ed. Paul Rabinow). London: Penguin. [Originally published in English.]

(1984d) 'An Aesthetics of Existence', in Lawrence Kritzman (ed.) (1990), *Michel Foucault: Politics, Philosophy, Culture: Interviews and other writings 1977–1984*, trans. Alan Sheridan. New York: Routledge. ['Une esthétique de l'existence', in Foucault, Michel (1994), *Dits et écrits 1954–1988: IV 1980–1988*. Daniel Defert and Francois Ewald (eds). Paris: Gallimard.]

(1984e) 'Foucault', in Foucault, Michel (2000), *Essential Works of Foucault, volume 2: Aesthetics, Method and Epistemology*, ed. James Faubion. London: Penguin Books. ['Foucault', in Foucault, Michel (1994), *Dits et écrits 1954–1988: IV 1980–1988*. Daniel Defert and Francois Ewald (eds). Paris: Gallimard.]

(1984f) 'Preface to *The History of Sexuality*', in Paul Rabinow (ed.) (1991), *The Foucault Reader*. London: Penguin Books ['*Préface à l'histoire de la sexualité*', in Foucault, Michel (1994), *Dits et écrits 1954–1988: IV 1980–1988*. Daniel Defert and Francois Ewald (eds). Paris: Gallimard].

(1984g) 'The return of morality', in Kritzman, Lawrence (ed.) (1990), *Michel Foucault: Politics, Philosophy, Culture: Interviews and Other Writings 1977–1984*, trans. Alan Sheridan. New York: Routledge. ['Le retour de la morale', in Foucault,

Michel (1994), *Dits et écrits 1954–1988: IV 1980–1988.* Daniel Defert and Francois Ewald (eds). Paris: Gallimard.]

(1988) 'The functions of literature', in Laurence Kritzman (ed.), *Politics, Philosophy, Culture.* London: Routledge.

(1990) 'What is Critique?', in *What is Enlightenment?* (ed. James Schmidt, trans. K. P. Geiman) (1996). Berkeley, CA: University of California Press. ['Qu'est-ce que la critique?', *Bulletin de la Société française de Philosophie*, vol. 84, no. 2, 1990].

(1995) *Discipline and Punish: The Birth of the Prison*, trans. Alan Sheridan. New York: Vintage Books. [Foucault, Michel (1975), *Surveiller et punir: naissance de la prison.* Paris: Gallimard.]

(2002) *The Archaeology of Knowledge*, trans. Alan Sheridan. London: Routledge. [Foucault, Michel (1969), *L'archéologie du savoir.* Paris: Gallimard.]

(2004a) *Death and the Labyrinth*, trans. Charles Ruas. London: Continuum.

(2006a) *History of Madness*, trans. J. Murphy and J. Khalfa. London: Routledge. [Foucault, Michel (1972), *Histoire de la folie a l'âge classique.* 2nd edition. Paris: Gallimard. (References here are to the Gallimard edition of 2001)].

(2006b) 'Preface to the 1961 edition', in *History of Madness*, trans. J. Murphy and J. Khalfa. London: Routledge. ['Préface', in Foucault, Michel (1994), *Dits et écrits 1954–1988: I 1954–1969.* Daniel Defert and Francois Ewald (eds). Paris: Gallimard.]

## Works by Other Authors

Agamben, Giorgio (1993) *Infancy and History: Essays on the Destruction of Experience*, trans. Liz Heron. London: Verso.

Artières, Philippe (ed.) (2004) *Michel Foucault, la littérature et les arts.* Paris: Editions Kimé.

Auden, W. H. (1979) 'In Memory of W. B. Yeats', in E. Mendelson (ed.), *W. H. Auden: Selected Poems.* London: Faber and Faber.

Beckett, Samuel (1957) *Murphy.* New York: Grove Press.

—— (1987) *Proust and Three Dialogues with Georges Duthuit.* London: John Calder.

—— (1991) *Three Novels: Molloy, Malone Dies, The Unnamable.* New York: Grove Press.

—— (2000) *Waiting for Godot.* London: Faber and Faber.

Benjamin, Walter (1999) 'On some motifs in Baudelaire', in *Illuminations*, trans. H. Zorn. London: Pimlico.

Blanchot, Maurice (1982) *The Space of Literature*, trans. Anne Smock. Lincoln, NB: University of Nebraska Press.

—— (1983) *The Infinite Conversation*, trans. Susan Hanson. Minneapolis, MN: University of Minnesota Press.

Calder, John (2001) *The Philosophy of Samuel Beckett.* London: Calder Publications.

Calvino, Italo (1987) *The Uses of Literature.* New York: Harcourt Brace.

Carroll, Noël (1998) 'Art, narrative and moral understanding', in Jerrold Levinson (ed.), *Aesthetics and Ethics.* Cambridge: Cambridge University Press, 126–60.

Char, René (1967) *Fureur et mystère.* Paris: Gallimard.

Danto, Arthur (1986) *The Philosophical Disenfranchisement of Art.* New York: Columbia University Press.

Deane, Seamus (1982) 'Joyce and nationalism', in Colin MacCabe (ed.), *James Joyce: New Perspectives*. Sussex: Harvester Press.

—— (1990) 'Introduction', in Terry Eagleton, Frederick Jameson and Edward Said, *Nationalism, Colonialism and Literature*. Minneapolis, MN: University of Minnesota Press.

—— (1992) 'Introduction', in James Joyce, *A Portrait of the Artist as a Young Man*. London: Penguin Books.

—— (1998) 'Irish theatre: a secular space', in *Irish University Review* 28:1, 163–74.

Deleuze, Gilles (1995) *Negotiations: 1972–1990*, trans. Martin Joughin. New York: Columbia University Press.

—— (1998) *Essays Critical and Clinical*, trans. Daniel W. Smith and Michael A. Greco. London: Verso.

—— (2004) *Francis Bacon: The Logic of Sensation*, trans. Daniel W. Smith. London: Continuum.

Deleuze, Gilles and Felix Guattari (1986) *Kafka: Toward a Minor Literature*, trans. Dana Polan. Minneapolis, MN: University of Minnesota Press.

—— (2004) *A Thousand Plateaus*. London: Continuum.

Deleuze, Gilles and Claire Parnet (2002) *Dialogues II*, trans. Hugh Tomlinson and Barbara Habberjam. London: Contiuum.

Dewey, John (1980) *Art as Experience*. New York: Perigree Books.

During, Simon (1992) *Foucault and Literature: Towards a Genealogy of Writing*. London: Routledge.

Friel, Brian (1996) *Plays One*. London: Faber and Faber.

—— (1999) *Plays Two*. London: Faber and Faber.

Gadamer, Hans-Georg (2003) *Truth and Method*, 2nd edition, trans. J. Weinsheimer and D. G. Marshall. New York: Continuum.

Gibson, Andrew (2006) *James Joyce*. London: Reaktion Books.

Graver, Lawrence and Raymond Federman (eds) (1979) *Samuel Beckett: The Critical Heritage*. London: Routledge and Kegan Paul.

Gros, Fréderic (2004) 'De Borges à Magritte', in Philippe Artières (ed.) (2004), *Michel Foucault, la littérature et les arts*. Paris: Editions Kimé.

Gutting, Gary (2002) 'Foucault's philosophy of experience', in *boundary 2*, vol.29, no. 2, 69–85.

Heaney, Seamus (1975) *North*. London: Faber and Faber.

—— (1980) *Preoccupations: Selected Prose 1968–1978*. London: Faber and Faber.

—— (1989) *The Government of the Tongue*. London: Faber and Faber.

—— (1991) *Death of a Naturalist*. London: Faber and Faber [orig. 1966].

—— (1996a) *The Spirit Level*. London: Faber and Faber.

—— (1996b) *The Redress of Poetry*. London: Faber and Faber.

—— (2004) *Anything Can Happen*. Dublin: Townhouse.

—— (2006) 'Crediting poetry', in *Nobel Lectures*. (No editor given). Melbourne: Melbourne University Press.

Hunkeler, Thomas (2002) 'The role of the dead man in the game of writing: Beckett and Foucault', in Richard Lane (ed.), *Beckett and Philosophy*. Hampshire: Palgrave, 68–79.

Hunter, Ian (1988) *Culture and Government: The Emergence of Literary Education*. London: Macmillan.

Jay, Martin (2006) *Songs of Experience: Modern American and European Variations on a Universal Theme.* Berkeley, CA: University of California Press.

Joyce, James (1973) *Ulysses.* Harmondsworth: Penguin Books.

—— (1991) *Stephen Hero.* London: Paladin.

—— (1992a) *A Portrait of the Artist as a Young Man.* London: Penguin Books.

—— (1992b) *Dubliners.* London: Penguin Books.

—— (2000) *Finnegans Wake.* London: Penguin Books.

Kearney, Richard (1988) *Transitions: Narratives in Modern Irish Culture.* Dublin: Wolfhound Press, Dublin.

Kenner, Hugh (1962) 'The *Portrait* in Perspective', in Thomas Connolly (ed.), *Joyce's Portrait: Criticisms and Critiques.* New York: Meredith Publishing.

—— (1976) 'The Cubist *Portrait*', in T. F. Staley and B. Benstock (eds), *Approaches to Joyce's Portrait: Ten Essays.* Pittsburgh, PA: University of Pittsburgh Press.

Kundera, Milan (1988) *The Art of the Novel.* London: Faber and Faber.

Lee , Josephine (1995) 'Linguistic imperialism, the early Abbey Theatre, and the translations of Brian Friel', in J. Ellen Gainor (ed.), *Imperialism and Theatre: Essays on World Theatre, Drama and Performance.* London: Routledge.

Lloyd, David (1993) *Anomalous States: Irish Writing and the Post-Colonial Moment.* Dublin: Lilliput Press.

Longley, Edna (1986) *Poetry in the Wars.* Newcastle upon Tyne: Bloodaxe Books.

Macherey, Pierre (1995) *The Object of Literature*, trans. David Macey. Cambridge: Cambridge University Press.

McMillan, Dougald and Martha Fehsenfeld (eds) (1988) *Beckett in the Theatre.* New York: Riverrun Press.

Nietzsche, Friedrich (1979) 'On truth and lies in a nonmoral sense', in D. Breazeale (ed.), *Philosophy and Truth: Selections from Nietzsche's Notebooks of the Early 1870s.* New Jersey: Humanities Press.

—— (1989) *On the Genealogy of Morals*, trans. Walter Kaufmann. New York: Vintage Books.

—— (2000) *The Birth of Tragedy*, ed. Raymond Geuss and Ronald Speirs, trans. Ronald Speirs. Cambridge: Cambridge University Press.

—— (2003) *Writings from the Late Notebooks*, ed. Bittner Rudiger, trans. Kate Sturge. Cambridge: Cambridge University Press.

Nussbaum, Martha (1992) *Love's Knowledge: Essays on Philosophy and Literature.* Oxford: Oxford University Press.

O'Leary, Timothy (2002) *Foucault and the Art of Ethics.* London: Continuum (re-published 2006).

—— (2008) 'Paying attention to Foucault's Roussel', in *Foucault Studies* no. 6, February 2009, 141–8.

Plato (1983) *The Republic*, trans. Desmond Lee. Harmondsworth: Penguin Books.

—— (2003) *Phaedo*, in *The Last days of Socrates*, trans. Hugh Tredennick and Harold Tarrant. London: Penguin Books.

Rabinow, Paul (1997) 'Introduction', in Michel Foucault (1997), *Essential Works of Foucault 1954–1984, volume 1: Ethics.* (ed. Paul Rabinow). London: Penguin.

Rajchman, John (1985) *Michel Foucault: The Freedom of Philosophy.* New York: Columbia University Press.

Rayner, Timothy (2003) 'Between fiction and reflection: Foucault and the experience book', *Continental Philosophy Review* 36(1), 27–43.

—— (2007) *Foucault's Heidegger: Philosophy and Transformative Experience.* London: Continuum.

Revel, Judith (2004) 'La naissance littéraire du biopolitique', in Philippe Artières (ed.) (2004), *Michel Foucault, la littérature et les arts.* Paris: Editions Kimé.

Richtarik, Marilynn (1994) *Acting Between the Lines: The Field Day Theatre Company and Irish Cultural Politics, 1980–1984.* Oxford: Oxford University Press.

Roussel, Raymond (2003) *Locus Solus,* trans. R. C. Cuningham. London: John Calder.

Sartre, Jean-Paul (2001) *What is Literature?* London: Routledge.

Smith, Frederik (2002) *Beckett's Eighteenth Century.* Hampshire: Palgrave.

Steiner, George (1975) *After Babel: Aspects of Language and Translation.* New York and London: Oxford University Press.

Swift, Jonathan (2003) *Gulliver's Travels.* London: Penguin Books.

Williams, Raymond (1976) *Keywords: A Vocabulary of Culture and Society.* London: Fontana.

Yeats, William Butler (1955) *Autobiographies.* London: Macmillan.

—— (1976) *Selected Criticism.* London: Pan Books.

—— (1990) *The Poems,* ed. D. Albright. London: J. M. Dent and Sons.

# Index

Lightning Source UK Ltd.
Milton Keynes UK
UKOW042224140612

194444UK00002B/3/P